The Panama Canal in American Politics

*Domestic Advocacy and
the Evolution of Policy*

J. MICHAEL HOGAN

Southern Illinois University Press

Carbondale and Edwardsville

To my mother

Chapter 8 of the present work appeared in a slightly different version in *Quarterly Journal of Speech (QJS)* 71 (1985): 302–17. Copyright 1985 by Speech Communication Association.

National Review has generously given permission to use extended quotation from the copyrighted work "On Voting Yes or No on the Panama Treaties," by William F. Buckley, Jr., and Ronald Reagan, *National Review*, February 1978, 210–17. Copyright 1978 by *National Review*.

Library of Congress Cataloging-in-Publication Data
Hogan, J. Michael, 1953–
   The Panama Canal in American politics.
   Bibliography: p.
   Includes index.
   1. United States—Foreign relations—Panama.
2. Panama—Foreign relations—United States.
3. Panama Canal (Panama) I. Title.
E183.8.P2I I64   1986   327.7307287'5   85-30347
ISBN 0-8093-1277-8

CONTENTS

ACKNOWLEDGMENTS

Many people assisted in the preparation of this book, principally my teachers, colleagues, and friends at the University of Wisconsin and at the University of Virginia. Lloyd Bitzer, Edwin Black, Donald K. Smith, and James Baughman offered valuable advice as members of my graduate committee at Wisconsin. I owe special debts to Stephen E. Lucas, who directed my dissertation and suggested that I write this book, and to Michael C. McGee, now at the University of Iowa, who offered encouragement and sound advice. At Virginia, John Sullivan and Ted J. Smith, III, have been especially insightful critics of the final manuscript, and James Aune, Frederick J. Antczak, William Lee Miller, John Graham, Michael Prosser, John Rodden, Joanne Stevens, and Margaret Sugarman have been valued advisors. I also would like to thank Joli Jensen of the University of Texas and Cindy Bisset of the Media Institute in Washington for carefully reading portions of the manuscript. Ray McKerrow of the University of Maine and John Lucaites of the University of Alabama are among the many people who provided valuable comments on portions of the manuscript presented at professional conferences. David Zarefsky of North-

Acknowledgments

western University deserves special thanks for his encouraging comments about an earlier version of the study.

For help with the research, I am indebted to the staffs of the Congressional Research Service, the Library of Congress, the Democratic Congressional Campaign Committee, the State Historical Society of Wisconsin, the University of Wisconsin's Memorial Library, and the University of Virginia's Alderman Library. K. Larry Storrs of the Congressional Research Service was particularly helpful with unpublished materials for the study, and Bernard Roshco of the Department of State helped with information about public opinion polls. Greg and Susan Bryant contributed immeasurably to the success of my research in Washington, D.C.

Finally, I would like to thank the staff of Southern Illinois University Press and their director, Mr. Kenney Withers, for their professionalism and hard work. I am especially grateful to my editor, Curtis Clark, for his enthusiasm and for his friendly and tactful approach to shortening the manuscript.

The Panama Canal in American Politics

*Domestic Advocacy and
the Evolution of Policy*

INTRODUCTION

Jimmy Carter had no special interest in the Panama Canal before he became president. Like generations of politicians before him, he became embroiled in controversy over the canal because it was a convenient symbol of American adventurism in the international arena. For Carter the Panama Canal represented a philosophy of international relations that had eroded America's prestige and produced the tragedy of Vietnam. He viewed the canal as a monument to national chauvinism, misguided interventionism, and the perversion of American ideals.

With the euphoria of his successful presidential campaign not yet muted by the frustrations of governing, Carter sought to fulfill promises of a new era in American foreign policy by negotiating a new treaty with Panama. Like all new presidents, he expected cooperation, even deference, during his "honeymoon" period. But instead he found himself fighting a bitter political battle over the Panama Canal throughout most of his first year in office. Carter did not seem to realize the depth of domestic political opposition to the idea of a new treaty with Panama. He did not seem to realize that in calling for a new treaty with Panama, he rekindled one of the most persistent, intractable controversies over American foreign policy in the twentieth century.

Four previous administrations—both Democratic and Republican—had endorsed the idea of a new Panama Canal treaty. But Presidents Kennedy, Johnson, Nixon, and Ford were quick to learn that the Panama Canal was no ordinary issue of American foreign policy. Other foreign policy issues (particularly wars) have been contested more vigorously in the twentieth century, and other issues undoubtedly have been more important to America's interests abroad. But few controversies of twentieth-century American foreign policy have been as persistent and as seemingly irresolvable as the question of America's stewardship over the Panama Canal.

The issue of America's presence in Panama historically has been one of the great battlefields in a never-ending ideological war over this nation's proper role in world affairs. Throughout the twentieth century this presence has been an important locus of conflict between advocates with fundamentally differing philosophies of American international relations. The Panama Canal has been more than a tangible asset debated in terms of its commercial or strategic utility. It has always been an issue with larger symbolic import, representing to some people all that is right, to others all that is wrong with America's attitude toward the rest of the world.

For some Americans, the Panama Canal represents the promise of American globalism; it has demonstrated the political, economic, and even spiritual benefits to be realized from aggressive leadership, demonstrations of power, and risk-taking in the international arena. From the expansionists at the turn of the century to the contemporary New Right, American conservative leaders have cited an inspirational story of America's construction of the canal in Panama as a tutorial in the proper role of America in world affairs. For modern American conservatives, the Panama Canal remains the preeminent symbol of the "good old days" in American policy.

For other Americans, the Panama Canal is a different sort of symbol. To critics of American international interventionism, the canal has been the classic, enduring symbol of American

4

"imperialism" and "colonialism" in the underdeveloped world. For these advocates, the story of American involvement in Panama is a shameful tale of international belligerence and exploitation of the powerless. For modern critics of American globalism, the canal has symbolized the brand of militaristic foreign relations championed by Theodore Roosevelt—an approach to international relations that they consider both morally abominable and practically anachronistic.

Public opinion historically has tipped the domestic political scales in favor of those celebrating the Panama Canal as a symbol of the benefits of aggressive globalism. Whatever the objective state of public opinion—however it may have evolved over the years or however unimportant most Americans actually considered the issue—generations of American policymakers have *perceived* the canal as a cherished national monument. The perception that the Panama Canal occupied a special place in the hearts and minds of the American people took root even before construction of the canal; the Senate decided to build the canal largely because of the belief that "the people" demanded it. Subsequently, Theodore Roosevelt presided over a national celebration of the canal-building project that reinforced the belief that "the people" embraced the canal with a special affection. Over the decades that followed American policymakers refused time and time again to approve any significant relaxation of America's control over the waterway, citing "the people's" unwillingness to accept such changes. By the 1950s virtually the entire foreign policy establishment agreed that maintaining the status quo in Panama damaged America's international image. But few of America's elected policymakers thought it politically feasible to pursue a significantly new course.

Then, in 1974, Secretary of State Henry Kissinger publicly agreed in principle to transfer control over the canal to Panama. Instantly the canal's long history of transcendent symbolic significance, along with its presumed special status in the American popular mind, were reflected in vigorous opposition to Kissinger's initiative. Thirty-eight U.S. senators immediately announced their opposition to any new treaty that altered American powers, and New Right political organizations, hoping to exploit the issue to build their political base, launched major campaigns. Not surprisingly, Kissinger's initiative stagnated for lack of political leaders willing to carry the banner. In the domestic political arena, there simply seemed too much to lose— and little to gain—in associating oneself with "giving away" the canal.

Perhaps Jimmy Carter failed to comprehend the symbolic heritage of the Panama Canal. Or perhaps he thought he could mollify domestic opposition to surrendering the canal with the same skills of public persuasion that had won him the presidency. Whatever his thinking, President Carter became the first American president to confront head on the political forces that for so long had prevented any fundamental revision of American canal policy. And thus began what some observers dubbed the "Great Debate Over Panama"—a contest for congressional and public opinion between the Carter administration and antitreaty forces led by the New Right.

By the time the Carter administration finished negotiating two new treaties with Panama in 1977, the campaign of the opposition forces was already in full swing. The Carter administration had refrained from promoting the treaties publicly until they were ready to be signed on September 6, 1977. But hoping to overcome the late start, President Carter launched his protreaty campaign in spectacular fashion with "the biggest diplomatic extravaganza Washington had seen in years." Presidents, prime ministers, and ambassadors from every nation in the Western Hemisphere except Cuba attended a ceremony to mark the signing of the treaties, along with a related series of ceremonies, meetings, and parties. For a week, Washington became the scene of an elaborate production designed to build support for the treaties. Carter's "Week of Panama," confessed a White House aide, was "right out of Cecil B. DeMille."[1]

During January of 1978 the campaigns on both sides escalated further. *Time* reported that "suddenly everyone was headed somewhere to talk about the Panama Canal treaties."[2] A Panama Canal "Truth Squad," composed of several members of Congress and a former chairman of the Joint Chiefs of Staff, was dispatched with the support of several New Right groups on a tour of U.S. cities in specially targeted states. Meanwhile, the same groups sent out millions of letters and raised millions of dollars for additional campaigning. The Carter administration countered with its own "January offensive," featuring a road show of senior cabinet officials and dozens of speeches and interviews by Carter himself, including his second "fireside chat." By late February 1978, Carter administration officials had given more than eight hundred speeches and interviews in a blitzkrieg of public appearances. The administration was aided by the Committee of Americans for the Canal Treaties— technically an independent group, it raised hundreds of thousands of dollars for protreaty activities—and by virtually the entire business and religious establishment in America. Still, the treaties became a consuming political cause for President Carter. As one aide commented in March 1978, there had been "no other single foreign policy issue that, politically, consumed more of his time."[3]

The efforts on both sides culminated with the debate on the floor of the Senate in February, March, and April 1978. The Senate first took up the neutrality treaty, which outlined U.S. rights after the year 2000, when the Panamanians were to assume control over the canal. After six weeks of debate, this treaty was approved by a vote of sixty-eight to thirty-two—one vote more than the required two-thirds majority. After an additional month of debate, the second treaty, providing for the gradual transfer of authority over the canal to Panama, was ratified by exactly the same vote. When it was over, protreaty forces claimed a great victory. Senate leaders supporting the treaties had managed to ward off seventy-seven amendments, most of which were apparently designed to cripple or kill the pacts.[4] President Carter, although criticized for some of his tactics, enjoyed one of the few great victories in his otherwise beleaguered presidency.

The Senate debate over the Panama Canal treaties was historic for several reasons. First, it lasted thirty-eight legislative days, making it the second longest treaty debate in the history of the Senate. Only the debate over the Treaty of Versailles con-

7

sumed more time.[5] Second, it was the first Senate debate broadcast live over national radio, with some fourteen million Americans listening to at least some portion of the deliberations.[6] Third, the Senate utilized the Committee of the Whole procedure (considering the treaties article by article on the floor) for the first time in fifty years. Finally, the Senate demonstrated its new assertiveness in foreign affairs by amending the treaties—again an event not witnessed in half a century.[7]

Political commentators have written often about the larger significance of the debate over Panama in American domestic politics. On the Democratic side, the debate was seen as a major test of President Carter's leadership. If Carter could not push the treaties through the Democratic Senate, some observers reasoned, then his stature as a leader would be damaged and a series of similar setbacks would likely follow.[8] The debate was to determine whether Carter and like-minded Democrats would continue to lead their party into the eighties. On the other side, the Republicans also considered the debate a test of leadership for the future. The most conservative wing of the party, the so-called New Right, billed the Panama treaties as a political "litmus test." The conservatives reportedly hoped to exploit the issue to capture control of the Republican party and to become a dominant force in American national politics.[9]

In historical perspective, however, the debate's greatest significance stemmed from the fact that it came at a critical juncture in the history of American foreign policy. As the first major foreign policy debate to follow the war in Vietnam, it came at a time when Americans sought explanations for past failures and guidance toward new directions; it promised to help define America's role in world affairs in the coming generation. The significance of the debate over Panama went well beyond questions of party politics. The controversy initiated a national dialogue over what basic philosophy should guide American foreign policy in the post-Vietnam era.

From its beginning, America's presence in Panama has demonstrated the impact of domestic politics on American foreign policy. A broad historical perspective—a consideration of the issue's political heritage and the evolution of American canal policy—provides an illuminating case study in how foreign policy may be constrained primarily by domestic rather than by international exigencies. American policy in Panama has never been the product of diplomatic calculation insulated from the passions and vagaries of domestic political thought. On the contrary, it provides perhaps the clearest, most persistent example of a policy shaped by the character of the national self-image. As a lasting monument to Theodore Roosevelt's brand of internationalism, the canal has symbolized an internationalist vision of America's destiny. And since the turn of the century, debate over that vision, more than any other factor, has shaped American policy in the Panama Canal Zone.

Perhaps at some other moment in history the debate over Panama would have gone relatively unnoticed. Perhaps if disillusionment over Vietnam had not hung so heavily in the air, advocates might not have worried so much about the debate's "larger significance." But in the late 1970s, the stage was set for a major debate, not just over the details of American policy in Panama, but over very different conceptions of America's proper role in the world.

THE PANAMA CANAL AND THE NATIONAL POLITICAL DIALOGUE

Unlike the state of the economy, the prevalence of crime, or the condition of highways or other public works, foreign affairs are not experienced directly by the average American. For most citizens, knowledge of foreign affairs must be received at second or third hand, and the information typically is colored by partisan advocacy. Especially in matters of foreign affairs, the rhetoric of political elites shapes popular attitudes with minimal competition from direct, first-hand experience; personal experience is not likely to contradict what one is persuaded to believe by speeches, news reports, editorials, and the like. With Americans increasingly dependent upon the media of mass communications for their political information, those political elites with the greatest access to the media exercise more and more influence over public opinion on matters of American foreign policy.

The debate over the Panama Canal illustrates the power of the president to set the agenda and to define the terms of debate over American foreign policy. It displays how the communicative resources of the presidency may be used to catapult a previously ignored issue into national headlines. Issues that touch the lives of few Americans may come to dominate our national political life because the president chooses to address them. A sitting administration can recruit elite special interest groups to contribute special "expertise" to a national policy debate or to speak more directly to the concerns of special constituencies. Ultimately, the debate over Panama demonstrates how an administration and its allies have the power, not only to decide the issues to be debated, but also to define the terms of disagreement and the range of "responsible opinion."

Yet the debate also reveals the limits of presidential persuasion on matters of foreign policy. It shows that the president does not exercise total control over the national dialogue on foreign affairs. The president may enjoy greater access to the means of mass communication than other political advocates in America and his word may carry more weight than the opinions of others. But a variety of individuals and groups cultivate the means of mass political persuasion in today's publicity-wise society, and they often become formidable opponents of the administration in national political debate.

Presidents seldom welcome the opposition of other elected officials, academicians, business and professional people, or representatives of special interests in a debate over foreign policy. But the speeches, articles, reports, and letters-to-the-editor of such opposing political elites bring more balance to national debates over controversial issues and thereby serve the interests of the broader polity. Similarly, hostile questioning by journalists or unfavorable news reports or editorials may annoy presidents and impair their ability to build public support for foreign policy initiatives. But the skepticism and criticism of the American news media may serve the interests of the polity by forcing an administration to consider alternative points of view and to make a better case for its foreign policy decisions.

Over the years since the Panama Canal first became a political issue in America, the technology of political campaigning has changed considerably. Theodore Roosevelt's editorials and marathon speaking tours have been supplanted by computerized direct mail and satellite television. But one factor in mass political persuasion has not changed substantially: the importance of the message. Today, as in Roosevelt's day, *what* is said—the intellectual and emotional substance of political rhetoric—probably determines more than anything the effectiveness of political campaigns. Mass media may have enabled political advocates to broaden or target their audiences. But in order to be persuasive they still must craft messages that ring true, that tap shared emotions, and that provide rationales for political commitments and actions.

Considerations of "objective reality" often overshadow considerations of political rhetoric in modern discussions of domestic support for American foreign policy. Among the "hard-headed realists" who plan foreign policy, as Franck and Weisband have observed, it is "fashionable" to discount the role of words, principles, and doctrines in relations among nations, and this "scorn for verbal conceptualization" within government sometimes infects the scholars who study domestic political support for America's policies abroad.[10] In searching for the unspoken significance or the deeper meaning of public debate over foreign affairs, political analysts often distinguish between words and deeds—between the symbolic and the concrete, between the rhetorical and the real—and dismiss the former as mere ornamentation for the latter. But when one is concerned with how issues of foreign policy become news, how debate is conducted, how public opinion is shaped, or how foreign policy is shaped, one must take into account the powerful role of language as a mediator of objective reality.

As Murray Edelman has written, "it is language that evokes most of the political 'realities' people experience." Language does not merely reflect political reality, but rather "creates it by organizing meaningful perceptions abstracted from a complex, bewildering world." In the political world there can "only rarely . . . be direct observation of events, and even then language forms shape the meaning of what the general public and government officials see." Moreover, "the verbal symbols we use to make sense of the world," as Stephen Lucas has written, "coerce our perceptions in ways which invite some types of behavioral responses and deter others."[11] Ultimately, political behavior stems from how we perceive conditions and events, regardless of how those perceptions may distort objective reality.

Advances in the technology of mass communication have changed the means by which advocates relay political messages to their audiences. To emphasize the importance of substance in political rhetoric is not to denigrate the impact of new technologies. Advocates now may disseminate sophisticated, even laboratory-tested messages to millions of citizens through computerized direct mail, vast telecommunications networks, and other media beyond imagination only a few decades ago. If political influence in the modern world is to be understood fully, one must examine the technological means used by advocates to make their ideas prominent in the crowded, complex communicative environment.

But in the final analysis, one must return to the substantive content of political rhetoric to account for specific structures of belief and opinion in political audiences. With the new technologies widely available and increasingly affordable, few political victories are attributable to monopolies over media or superior hardware. Most Americans continue to hear more than one side during major political controversies, and they choose to believe some advocates while rejecting the arguments of others. In short, persuasiveness still counts in political communications.

This study does not seek to "cut through the rhetoric" in search of the "reality" of controversy over the Panama Canal. Instead, it looks to the rhetoric itself—to the *perceived* realities reflected in, and promoted by, debate over the issue. Both citizens and policymakers formed opinions about America's presence in Panama on the basis of what they were *persuaded* to believe, regardless of how political messages may have distorted objective reality. By studying what Americans were persuaded to believe—and how they were persuaded—we gain insight, not only into the debate over American policy in Panama, but also into the processes by which foreign policy issues generally are created, debated, and resolved in America.

THE PAST AND THE PRESENT

Reporters, political commentators, and scholars have written extensively on the "Great Debate Over Panama." Yet most existing accounts lack balanced historical perspective, or they unabashedly advocate particular policies. It remains to assess the debate over Panama in the 1970s comprehensively and dispassionately—to chart its course, to describe the activities of participants on both sides, to analyze its themes, and to account for its resolution. It remains to analyze the debate from the inception of the various controversies dividing the advocates through ratification of new Panama Canal treaties by the U.S. Senate in 1978.

The debate over the Panama Canal treaties must be understood in the context of some seventy-five years of domestic political controversy over America's role in Panama. The issue's heritage is one of domestic political divisions dating back to well before the first treaty with Panama was signed in 1903. The participants in the most recent debate, along with their governing premises, their assumptions, and their passions, can be understood only by recognizing the history of the issue as a long-term ideological battleground. Furthermore, the most recent debate over Panama resurrected historical controversies left unsettled by preceding generations of political advocates. Advocates in the seventies often cited "lessons" from America's history in Panama or raised legal and ethical issues left over from the past. Without firm grounding in the historical record, one cannot make sense of such arguments. Without attention to the origins of long-term controversies, one can not judge which versions of history deserve to be believed.

This study thus begins by reconstructing the heritage of

domestic political controversy over the Panama Canal in the twentieth century. Part 1 examines the origins and evolution of two very different perspectives on America's history in Panama. Chapter 1 charts the emergence of an internationalist vision near the turn of the century—a vision which dictated that the canal be built and which shaped American canal policy for decades. Chapter 2 examines the legitimation of this internationalist vision during a massive national celebration of the canal-building project—a celebration that silenced early critics of the project, created a new generation of American heroes, and transformed the canal into a popular symbol of America's international leadership. Chapter 3 examines the emergence of a revisionist critique of America's history in Panama and its growing popularity within the foreign policy establishment in the Cold War era. It charts the early political battles between these revisionists and the defenders of Theodore Roosevelt's internationalist legacy in Panama, thereby setting the stage for examination of the "Great Debate Over Panama" in the late 1970s.

Part 2 begins the description and analysis of the debate of the seventies by analyzing the coalitions on each side of the issue, the resources committed to their campaigns, and their basic strategies for shaping public and congressional opinion. Chapter 4 examines the protreaty campaign of the Carter administration and its political, business, and religious allies. It reveals how the Carter administration marshalled the vast resources of the American presidency to sell the Panama Canal treaties to a skeptical Congress and a hostile public. Chapter 5 reveals the special place of the debate over Panama in the growth and success of the so-called New Right in the late seventies. It examines how a number of New Right organizations united for the first time in the crusade against the Panama treaties and began to realize the potential of new communicative strategies and technologies.

Part 3 examines the argumentative substance of the debate over the new Panama Canal treaties, both in the contest for public opinion, and in the deliberations of the U.S. Senate. Chapter 6 examines the competing versions of America's historical presence in Panama promoted by pro- and antitreaty advocates in popular mass media. Chapter 7 assesses the other broad category of issues debated in mass media: issues concerning the likely impact of the proposed treaties on America's economic and military interests in the future. Chapter 8 explores the deliberations of the U.S. Senate and seeks to account for the decision to ratify the treaties. It explains the important role that arguments about public opinion played in the outcome of the debate.

When the Carter administration finally initiated the long-awaited national debate over America's presence in Panama, both the administration and its allies underestimated the opposition and failed to significantly reshape public opinion. The campaign to win public support for the treaties apparently did little to supplant the powerful historical myths surrounding the Panama Canal. Opponents of the 1977 treaties campaigned vigorously to remind Americans of the glorious heritage of America's presence in Panama, while the administration and its allies recalled less familiar and less appealing aspects of America's history in Panama. Similarly, the administration and its allies failed to argue convincingly that the United States no longer really needed the canal economically and militarily. Opponents of the treaties offered elaborate arguments about the canal's continued importance, while treaty supporters offered only perfunctory responses to critical questions about the canal's future utility. Most important, the protreaty cause was hurt by revelations that Panamanian and American officials had differing interpretations of crucial treaty provisions, particularly those governing America's rights to use and defend the canal after Panama assumed control over the waterway in the year 2000. In the war for public opinion on the treaties, this only added to the problems of protreaty campaigners already fighting an uphill battle.

When the treaties reached the Senate, debate focused on these provisions governing America's defense and use of the canal. With the outcome in doubt, the Senate added two amendments to the treaties—amendments which supposedly assured America's right to defend and use the canal after the Panamanians took over. These amendments proved crucial to the Senate's vote in favor of ratification. They allayed the major objection to the treaties voiced by a number of senators. But more important, protreaty senators successfully argued that the amendments produced a turnabout in public opinion. In the end, many previously reluctant senators voted for ratification, thinking that the amended treaties would serve both the national interest and the national will.

In retrospect, however, the Senate appeared neither to clarify the agreement nor to defer to an accurate conception of the will of the people. The amendments adopted by the Senate did little to address the problems of conflicting interpretations of the original documents; indeed, one could argue that they just muddied the waters further. And poll after poll following the Senate's action revealed that public opinion remained at the same high level of opposition to the treaties as had been evident in polls taken before the debate. Over the next few years the New Right would exploit the Panama Canal issue to expand its power and to "punish" liberal senators, giving credence to the notion that the Senate misread public opinion. Whether the Senate also ratified an agreement which was dangerously ambiguous, however, will not be known until the treaties are put to the test in the international arena.

Part 1
The Heritage

1

The Internationalist Vision and the Panama Canal

Americans associate the Panama Canal with Theodore Roosevelt. But American interest in an isthmian canal actually dates back to 1825, and throughout the nineteenth century the American government negotiated canal treaties, proclaimed canal-related doctrine, and conducted studies of canal routes.[1] In 1889 an American company actually commenced digging a route in Nicaragua,[2] and the United States even threatened war when the famed builder of the Suez Canal, Ferdinand de Lesseps, led a French canal project in Panama in the 1880s. Eventually, bad planning and tropical diseases did more to remove the French from Panama than did American warships.[3] But the threats served as yet another sign of America's longstanding commitment to building a canal.

America would have built an interoceanic canal eventually even if Roosevelt had not championed the project. But as the most visible member of a group of "internationalists" with a distinctive rationale for immediately building a canal, Roosevelt helped shape the attitudes that expedited the project in the early 1900s. While economic rationales animated most canal advocates before the turn of the century, the internationalists promoted an ideology of strategic superiority and national spiritual health. The internationalists viewed an American canal not as a tool of international trade but as a prerequisite to American naval power and as a symbol of the American spirit.

The internationalist perspective on the Panama Canal and its role in America's destiny did not die with Theodore Roosevelt. Instead, it guided American canal policy for nearly three decades, and it provides many of the governing premises in public discussions of the canal to this day. Much of the public sentiment and myth evoked by those opposed to relinquishing control over the canal in the 1970s—including the belief that the American public would not stand for "giving away" the canal— can be traced to the campaign of Roosevelt and the internationalists. Their contribution to the intellectual and emotional heritage of the Panama Canal proves crucial to an understanding of the canal as a persistent political issue.

THE EMERGENCE OF THE INTERNATIONALIST VISION

In the 1890s the long dream of an American interoceanic canal assumed unprecedented urgency, mostly because of economic concerns. From 1893 to 1897 "concise and conscious economic analyses by the Cleveland administration, the business community, and leading congressional figures led these three groups to conclude that foreign markets were necessary for the prosperity and tranquillity of the United States."[4] An interoceanic canal seemed essential for economic expansion because South American and Oriental markets offered the greatest untapped potential. By the mid-1890s there remained little controversy over the commercial necessity of an isthmian canal. William L. Merry summarized this economic impulse in 1895:

> On the Pacific Coast of the United States the commercial necessity for the prompt construction of the Nicaragua Canal is so obvious that it finds no opponents worthy of consideration. The Southern States are almost equally interested, and two great Canal conventions have been held there to promote it. The Eastern seaboard States are also ardent advocates of the Canal, and what indifference to the beneficent enterprise exists today, is found in the Middle West, where its immediate benefits are not so evident to the casual observer, although easily demonstrated upon examination.[5]

20

But not all Americans promoted an interoceanic canal on economic grounds in the 1890s. A group including Theodore Roosevelt, Alfred T. Mahan, Brooks Adams, and Henry Cabot Lodge—a group I shall call the internationalists—espoused expansion and the need for a canal in strategic and spiritual terms. Throughout the 1890s these men corresponded extensively and held meetings in Washington, where they "concerned themselves deeply with schemes for expansion and for impressing the world with [U.S.] power."[6] They also publicized their ideas with considerable success, and by the end of the decade internationalist ideas had assumed a prominent place in public dialogue over American foreign policy.

For the internationalists, expansionism became part of a comprehensive ideology that reached well beyond economic concerns and even beyond the realm of foreign policy. Like most expansionists in the 1890s, the internationalists attributed the economic and social chaos of the period to the closing of the frontier—to the end of unrestrained expansion and development in the American West. Virtually all expansionists were motivated by the desire to find new frontiers outside American borders. But the internationalists had a sweeping philosophical and historical perspective that reduced the frontier thesis and its economic implications to relatively minor status.

Characteristic of the broad thinking of the internationalists was the thesis of Brooks Adams' *The Law of Civilization and Decay*.[7] Adams postulated a "law" of history by which societies oscillate between domination by the military and religious classes and domination by an economic class. When dominated by the military and religious classes, society generates a store of surplus "energy." But as the surplus accumulates, society succumbs to greed and the dominance of the economic class, which expends more energy than it produces. With the ascendance of the economic class, the religious and martial spirit disappears and the surplus of energy declines. Thus, according to Adams, society declines until it is again infused with the martial spirit.

Although Adams' theory blamed economic factors for the decline of societies, it clearly suggested noneconomic remedies. When applied to the United States in the 1890s, it advised against expansion which aimed merely at exploiting foreign

21

markets. The infusions of new energy from economic exploitation would treat only symptoms, not causes, and thus might postpone the decline of the nation. But according to the internationalists, America could reverse the decline evident in America during the 1890s only by restoring the martial spirit.[8]

The internationalists formulated a strategy for instilling the martial spirit in the "advanced" American culture without evoking the "barbarism" associated historically with martial societies. Their plan included an informal military and spiritual alliance with England and a scheme for American expansion and dominance in the West. The plan specifically required an isthmian canal, an expanded Monroe Doctrine, a battleship navy, and possession of strategic bases in approaches to the canal. But at bottom, the vision called for a martial spirit, and the internationalists symbolically paraded this ideal before the American public throughout the 1890s.

The vision of a new national character manifested itself most strikingly in the glorification of militarism by Roosevelt and other internationalists. As LaFeber has argued, Alfred T. Mahan probably contributed most to this celebration of the martial spirit, but "when Brooks Adams concluded that only through the valor of the soldier could the American people escape the fiat of [his] 'law,' he differed only in slight degree from Mahan's extreme view."[9] For his part, Roosevelt popularized the theme, both in numerous public speeches and writings, and in several historical works.

Roosevelt promoted the theory of martial spirit in popular forums with simple rhetorical motifs. He presented the abstruse colloquially, translated theory into everyday applications, and actively exploited a variety of media. He sought public support for his views, not by reference to theories, but by evoking deeply embedded beliefs and values—the common sense of Americans. In promoting the martial spirit, Roosevelt called upon the everyday experiences and ethical norms of the American people by creating conceptions of world affairs that paralleled everyday life.

Roosevelt often evoked the everyday concept of character to promote martial spirit in the nation. In his most famous pre-

presidential address, "The Strenuous Life," he asked his audience to think of the attributes of virtuous personal character as equally applicable to the "character of nations." He began by praising "clean, vigorous, healthy lives" that result

> when the children are so trained that they shall endeavor, not to shirk difficulties, but to overcome them; not to seek ease, but to know how to wrest triumph from toil and risk. The man must be glad to do a man's work, to dare and endure and to labor; to keep himself, and to keep those dependent upon him. The woman must be the housewife, the helpmeet of the homemaker, the wise and fearless mother of many healthy children. . . . When men fear work or fear righteous war, when women fear motherhood, they tremble on the brink of doom; . . . they are fit subjects for the scorn of all men and women who are themselves strong and brave and high-minded.

TR then applied the same lessons to the matter of "character" in nations:

> As it is with the individual, so it is with the nation. . . . Far better it is to dare mighty things, to win glorious triumphs, even though checkered by failure, than to take rank with those poor spirits who neither enjoy much nor suffer much, because they live in the gray twilight that knows not victory nor defeat.

By proclaiming "so it is with nations," TR stressed how the legacy left by "great work" allowed both men and nations to "live forevermore."[10]

In a short but productive career, Roosevelt the historian also promoted the martial spirit. He did not specialize in any particular historical period, but he did specialize in glorifying militarism. His first major book was a military history, *The Naval War of 1812.*[11] His most popular work, the four-volume *Winning of the West*, pictured westward expansion primarily as a glorious militaristic struggle: "Our frontiers were pushed westward by the warlike skill and adventurous personal prowess of the individual settlers. . . . Every man was accustomed to the use of arm from his childhood; when a boy was twelve years old he was given a rifle and made a fort-soldier. . . . The war was never-ending for even the times of so-called peace were

23

broken by forays and murders." Henry Cabot Lodge and Roosevelt together wrote *Hero Tales From American History*, which glorified militarism with accounts of the battlefield death of Stonewall Jackson ("one of the ablest of soldiers and one of the most upright of men") and a romantic rendition of the fall of the Alamo. Similarly, Roosevelt's *Life of Oliver Cromwell* expressed unrestrained admiration for Cromwell's military genius and for the stern, religious warriors whom he commanded.[12]

Roosevelt did not share the primarily economic motivations of many expansionists. He often contrasted the martial spirit directly with the spirit of his business-oriented contemporaries. He told the Naval War College in 1897 that the "fight well fought, the life honorably lived, the death bravely met . . . count for more in building a high and fine temper in a nation than any possible success in the stock market." TR made the same contrast in "The Strenuous Life." Bemoaning the worship of men "wedded to that base spirit of gain and greed which recognizes in commercialism the be-all and end-all of national life," he insisted that America could survive only if the economic spirit were supplanted by the martial spirit and the strenuous life:

> We of this generation . . . have our tasks, and woe to us if we fail to perform them! We cannot, if we would, . . . be content to rot by inches in ignoble ease within our borders, taking no interest in what goes on beyond them, sunk in a scrambling commercialism; heedless of a higher life, the life of aspiration, of toil and risk, busying ourselves only with the wants of our bodies for the day, until suddenly we should find, . . . that in this world the nation that has trained itself to a career of unwarlike and isolated ease is bound, in the end, to go down before other nations which have not lost the manly and adventurous qualities.[13]

The stress on a new national character grounded in the martial spirit complemented a belief among Roosevelt and the internationalists in the necessity for Anglo-American alliance. This further distinguished the internationalists from economic expansionists, most of whom were anti-British.[14] It also distinguished the internationalists from advocates like the immensely popular lecturer John Fiske who championed economic alliance with Great Britain.[15] While Fiske longed for the "victory of the industrial over the military type of civilization,"[16] the internationalists envisioned a decidedly militaristic Anglo-Americanism. They envisioned a future in which the "English-speaking peoples," infused with the martial spirit and unchallengeable in their combined naval might, would protect "civilization" from the "barbarians" of the world. The British and the Americans would be, in effect, the police of the world.

Mahan wrote prolifically on this subject. In March 1893 he emphasized that Great Britain and the United States were alike in "inherited traditions, habits of thought, and views of right" and that "our political traditions and racial characteristics still continue English." In another article on the subject published in 1894, Mahan called for a "natural" rather than a "purely conventional" relationship—an informal "kinship" rather than a formal "alliance." Furthermore, given that the United States and Great Britain alone were "so severed geographically from all existing rivals as to be exempt from the burden of great land armies," it was natural that this kinship should manifest itself in control of the "general course of events at sea." No longer could the seas be controlled by a single nation, he argued, but such control was not beyond "the conjoined energies of the race."[17] In 1894, Mahan hoped only to "cast the seed of this thought into the ground" so that it later might "spring and grow up." But by 1900 he believed the "harvest" of political results had begun: "We have begun to know each other, in community of interest and of traditions, in ideals of equality and of law. As the realization of this spreads, the two states, in their various communities, will more and more closely draw together in the unity of spirit, and all the surer that they eschew the bondage of the letter of alliance."[18]

Roosevelt joined Mahan in speaking of "the interests of the English-speaking peoples." As a historian he deemed "the spread of the English-speaking peoples over the world's waste spaces" not only "the most striking feature in the world's history, but also the event of all others most far-reaching in its effects and its importance." TR hoped that "all the English-

speaking peoples" would "be able to unite in some kind of con-
federacy" in the future.[19] Rather than wishing for the decline of
England's military might, he saw much to emulate in the combination of advanced culture and martial spirit displayed by the
history of England:

> England's history is rich in splendid names and splendid deeds.
> Her literature is even greater than that of Greece. In commerce she
> has stood in the modern world as more than ever Carthage was
> when civilization clustered in a fringe around the Mediterranean.
> But she has risen far higher than ever Greece or Carthage rose, be-
> cause she possesses also the great, masterful qualities which were
> possessed by the Romans who overthrew them both. England has
> been fertile in soldiers and administrators; in men who triumphed
> by sea and by land; in adventurers and explorers who won for her
> the world's waste spaces; and it is because of this that the English-
> speaking race now shares with the Slav the fate of the coming
> years.[20]

The ruling principles of the new world envisioned by Roosevelt and the internationalists were order and stability. With
the Anglo-American combination and the martial spirit, the
British could police the East while the Americans policed the
West. Each could defend the interests of "civilization" against
the "barbarians" within their sphere, and the seas would be
kept peaceful by the world's two greatest navies. Roosevelt summarized the prospects in 1899: "Together, . . . the two branches
of the Anglo-Saxon race . . . can whip the world."[21]

Yet at the turn of the century the United States still needed
several things to fulfill its part in the internationalist scheme.
First and foremost, an American-controlled isthmian canal
would be required to establish American dominance of the Caribbean and the Pacific. Second, America would need to reinterpret the Monroe Doctrine to ground its dominance of the
West in principle. Third, America would require an offensive,
sea-going, battleship navy to protect the canal and to exploit its
potential. Finally, America would have to expand into strategic,
noncontiguous areas surrounding the canal in order to establish naval bases in the arena of dominance.

Both Roosevelt and Mahan became convinced early of the

need for an isthmian canal controlled by the United States. In *The Influence of Sea Power upon History,* Mahan began a decade-long campaign to convince Americans of this need by comparing the future of the Caribbean to the past and present of the Mediterranean Sea. With an isthmian canal, he predicted, "the Caribbean will be changed from a terminus, and place of local traffic, . . . into one of the great highways of the world." This would bring the "interests of the other great nations, the European nations, close along our shores, as they have never been before." Then it would not be so easy for the United States to "stand aloof from international complications." The United States would need to defend its special status in the region, which meant that controlling the canal was "the central strategic issue." Indeed, the "piercing of the Isthmus" would be "nothing but a disaster to the United States" without its military control of the canal, Mahan wrote elsewhere, for that would merely expose the defenseless West Coast to enemy attack.[22]

Roosevelt's belief in the vital need for a canal dated from his first interest in foreign affairs and was "greatly intensified by the hurried voyage of the U.S.S. *Oregon* around the Horn to join the fleet off Cuba in the Spanish War." Roosevelt, like Mahan, spoke of the canal "in terms of national defense, not economic importance,"[23] and in the 1890s he vigorously opposed any measure permitting foreigners a voice in the building, operation, or defense of a canal. Both in public and in private statements Roosevelt emphasized the threat to American naval power and to the integrity of the Monroe Doctrine posed by any sort of foreign involvement in the canal project. In a letter to Secretary of State John Hay in 1900, Roosevelt echoed Mahan's contention that a canal not fortified by the United States would be "a menace . . . in time of war"; it would be "an added burden, an additional strategic point to be guarded by our fleet." If a canal not under American control had existed in 1898, he argued, the Spanish fleet could have sailed through the canal "to attack Dewey or to menace our stripped Pacific Coast." Besides, he wrote, joint ownership or control of the canal would render the Monroe Doctrine meaningless: "To my mind, we should consistently refuse to all European powers the right to control,

27

in any shape, any territory in the Western Hemisphere which they do not already hold."[24]

Both Roosevelt and Mahan were concerned with more than the maintenance of the Monroe Doctrine. Both wanted the doctrine expanded beyond its traditional interpretation as a negative check on acquisition of new territory in the West by Europeans. In the bustling Caribbean of the future, Mahan wrote in the early 1890s, the United States could not depend on "the sanction of international law nor the justice of a cause" for the "fair settlement of differences." International law could not "prevent the interests of belligerents and neutrals from clashing"; nor could it "speak with perfect clearness in all cases where they do." Thus the United States would have to rely on its own policies and its ability to enforce them. Mahan hinted that "certain corollaries" to the Monroe Doctrine would make American policy "more applicable to present conditions," but he averred that it was "beyond the professional province of a naval officer to inquire how far the Monroe doctrine itself would logically carry us, or how far it may be developed . . . by the recognition and statement of further national interests."[25]

Roosevelt was not so humble, and he laid the intellectual groundwork for vast expansions of the Monroe Doctrine, including the later corollary that bears his name. He disdained those who treated the Monroe Doctrine legalistically. The doctrine, he wrote in 1896, should not be considered "a question of law" but a "question of policy": "Lawyers, as lawyers, have absolutely nothing whatever to say about it. To argue that it cannot be recognized as a principle of international law, is a mere waste of breath. Nobody cares whether it is or is not so recognized, any more than any one cares whether the Declaration of Independence and Washington's farewell address are so recognized." Roosevelt argued that the Monroe Doctrine could be expanded unilaterally as much as national self-interest dictated, as long as America had the ability to enforce it. Indeed, he considered any expansion of the doctrine "patriotic," and he envisioned the day when it would be used to force Europeans out of the West entirely: "Every true patriot, every man of statesmanlike habit, should look forward to the day when not a single European power will hold a foot of American soil."[26]

The internationalist vision had prerequisites in hardware as well as in principle. Neither control of the canal nor enforcement of an expanded Monroe Doctrine could be achieved with a navy designed merely for coastal defense. The isthmian canal, Mahan wrote in the early 1890s, would "belong wholly to the belligerent which controls the sea by its naval power," and the United States was "impotent, as against any of the great maritime powers, to control the Central American canal." Moreover, the Monroe Doctrine "formulated an idea to which in the last resort effect could be given only through the instrumentality of a navy." The United States needed a navy based on the "received military maxim" that "war, however defensive in moral character, must be waged aggressively if it is to hope for success."[27] An enemy "must not be fended off, but smitten down," Mahan wrote in 1897, and this involved "the offensive in naval war"—the battleships, and "the cruisers of various sizes and purposes, including sea-going torpedo-vessels capable of accompanying a fleet, without impeding its movements by their loss of speed or unseaworthiness."[28] With such a fleet, the dominance of the United States in the isthmian theater would follow "with mathematical certainty," and all threats to the United States could be met "outside her own territory—at sea."[29]

Roosevelt first popularized Mahan's ideas with a review of *The Influence of Sea Power upon History* in the *Atlantic Monthly* of October 1890. After praising the book as "the best and most important . . . on naval history . . . on either side of the water for many a long year," he editorialized on its "bearing on our present condition." He wrote that Mahan's book exposed the danger of America's lack of naval preparedness and the folly of coastal fortification. "Passive defense," he said, "is always a most dangerous expedient." America needed the offensive capabilities of "a large navy, composed not merely of cruisers, but containing also a full proportion of powerful battle-ships, able to meet those of any other nation."[30] Later, Roosevelt defended naval preparedness and offensive capabilities by comparing the existing navy to a prize fighter incapable of throwing a punch: "It is not enough to parry a blow. . . . No master of the prize ring ever fought his way to supremacy by mere dexterity in avoiding punishment." In typical Rooseveltian style, analogies to familiar situations led to a lesson for the nation as a whole: "We cannot rely upon coast protection alone. . . . In the last resort we most trust to the ships whose business it is to fight and not to run, and who can themselves go to sea and strike at the enemy when they choose, instead of waiting to peacefully receive his blow when and where he deems it best to deliver it." [31]

Naval preparedness was more than a military necessity. According to Roosevelt, a powerful navy could also inspire and sustain the martial spirit in the American people. As Roosevelt told the Naval War College in 1897: "It is very important that we should, as a race, keep the virile fighting qualities and should be ready to use them at need; . . . One of the surest ways to attain these qualities is to keep our Navy in first-class trim." Naval power would bring national self-respect and the ability to avenge those abridgments of national honor that mattered little to the economic man, "who cares only whether shares rise or fall in value." [32] The navy could serve an important inspirational function in addition to its mundane duties patrolling the West. With strategic bases and the isthmian canal, the navy could roam the Western world, inspiring the martial spirit at home while commanding "civility" abroad.

The need for strategic bases rendered expansionism a corollary of naval predominance in the West. In contrast to the common economic rationales for a canal and expansion into noncontiguous areas, Mahan urged America "to take possession, when it can be done righteously, of such maritime positions as contribute to secure command." There must be "no hesitation," he wrote in 1893, "about taking the positions—and they are many—upon the approaches to the Isthmus, whose interests incline them to seek us." [33] Mahan was not concerned with the markets that such possessions might provide. Rather, he sought to reduce the amount of time needed to respond to the "central strategic issue" and to provide coaling and repair stations for a sea-going navy.

Roosevelt pointed out additional international and domestic benefits of expansion. Internationally, expansion by the civilized powers was the only means of bringing peace to barbarian areas. Writing in December 1899, he noted that the world was still plagued by barbarians for whom peace was "the exceptional condition." Every expansion of a civilized power therefore brought a "victory for law, order, and righteousness." Domestically, the expanding nation could realize benefits more important than economic return. While Roosevelt insisted that the spread of "civility" had been "of benefit, not so much to the power nominally benefited, as the whole world," he also spoke often of how expansion could win glory and a historical legacy for the nation. In his essay "Expansion and Peace," he wrote that "nations that expand and nations that do not expand may both ultimately go down, but the one leaves heirs and a glorious memory, and the other leaves neither."[34]

Thus the internationalists envisioned a "civilized" new world order maintained by the naval power of the two advanced English-speaking peoples. Infused with the martial spirit, both might control vast spheres without jealousy, while recognizing their common spirituality and interests. In order to fulfill its part in the vision, the United States would need to expand the Monroe Doctrine, build a battleship navy, and take possession of certain strategic areas. At the center of the scheme was the isthmian canal. Without the canal, America would have little rationale for proclaiming itself "policeman" of the West, nor would it have the key tool of naval dominance in the West.

The internationalist vision remained only a dream in the 1890s—a dream about what America might become. Indeed, it may have seemed a grandiose scheme, even in an era of boundless confidence and limitless expectations. But the internationalists were not content to formulate only concepts and schemes. They sought to translate their ideas into policies of government and to shape America's role in the world for decades to come. Soon they would be promoting their vision from positions of power.

IMPLEMENTING THE VISION

When he became president after the assassination of William McKinley in 1901, Roosevelt brought a "dramatic shift in Presidential style and attitude" to the White House. TR wasted little time in exploiting the "bully pulpit" to promote the internationalist vision of a new world order. He knew the persuasive potential of his new office, and he pursued the role of symbolic leader with relish. Roosevelt always had enthusiasm for public speaking—witness his nearly seven hundred speeches during a twenty-one-thousand-mile tour as a candidate for vice president.[35] As president, he continued to popularize his ideas with public speaking tours of exhausting dimensions. During one tour in 1903 he covered fourteen thousand miles by rail and several hundred miles by stagecoach or carriage. During sixty-five days on the road, he made 265 speeches. Virtually everywhere he went the audiences were large and enthusiastic. The energetic new president proved a "dream come true" for American reporters and the reading public.[36]

As president, Roosevelt continued his critique of the economic spirit by attacking big business and monopolies.[37] He also promoted the martial spirit with speeches exalting the life of toil and risk and with his own rigorous work habits and expeditions for big game. The programmatic requirements of the internationalist vision now received top priority, however, as Roosevelt made the isthmian canal, an even stronger Monroe Doctrine, and the Mahanian navy the major features of his new foreign policy.

Roosevelt continued to speak of the isthmian canal in military terms after assuming the presidency. In a speech in Chicago, he emphasized the need to assure that a canal "could never be used to our detriment by any nation which was hostile to us." Increasingly, however, he also celebrated the canal as a great national challenge. In portraying the project as a lasting achievement, he began talking of the "great material work"—a project which would be "one of the greatest engineering feats of the twentieth century; a greater engineering feat than has yet been accomplished during the history of mankind." In his first annual message to Congress, he argued that a canal should not arouse sectional interests or be considered primarily in economic terms. Instead, it should inspire patriotic pride in all Americans: "It is emphatically a work which it is for the interest of the entire country to begin and complete as soon as possible;

it is one of those great works which only a great nation can undertake with prospects of success, and which when done are not only permanent assets in the nation's material interest, but standing monuments to its constructive ability."[38]

Roosevelt's call for a new national monument complemented his advocacy of a revised Monroe Doctrine. He announced the substance of the Roosevelt Corollary in his second annual message to Congress on December 2, 1902, when he suggested that building the canal would require America to police the region. He warned nations in the area of the proposed canal to maintain order within their own boundaries and to discharge their "just obligations to foreigners." If they did so, he promised, they could "rest assured that, be they strong or weak, they have nothing to dread from outside interference." But should they fail to fulfill their obligations, and thus threaten the canal, it would become "incumbent on all civilized and orderly powers to insist on the proper policing of the world."[39] Roosevelt later advocated an expanded Monroe Doctrine as a means of forbidding foreigners a part in building or operating the proposed canal. Involvement of foreigners, he claimed, would be in "effect . . . equal to territorial aggrandizement." Since America's "interests in this hemisphere are greater than those of any European power," only the United States would "police and protect" the canal "and guarantee its neutrality."[40]

Finally, Roosevelt made naval preparedness a top priority early in his presidency. He stressed that "an efficient navy of adequate size" was "the best guarantee of peace" as well as "the surest means for seeing that if war does come the result shall be honorable to our good name and favorable to our national interests." He also articulated a broader, spiritual rationale for a Mahanian navy. It was a matter of patriotism, he told an audience in Washington in 1903, to build and keep up "a navy suited to the part the United States must hereafter play in the world." In a speech in Chicago he linked his advocacy of naval build-up to the "homely old adage" that came to symbolize his presidency: "Speak softly and carry a big stick; you will go far." He left no doubt that seapower was the "stick" referred to in his famous maxim: "If the American nation will speak softly and yet build, and keep at a pitch of the highest training, a thoroughly efficient navy, the Monroe Doctrine will go far." [41]

Roosevelt enjoyed rousing success spinning his images of national greatness before audiences across the country. But the real test of the internationalist vision would come in the U.S. Senate, where battles over U.S. canal policy remained to be fought. Roosevelt did not rush into these battles. Instead, he took "to heart the advice from [Senator] Mark Hanna that it was best to go slow." [42] TR charted a moderate course in the early stages of his presidency, apparently intent on first building public support for the internationalist philosophy.

The situation changed radically following Senate passage of the Spooner Act—an authorization for the president to purchase French properties and concessions in Panama and to negotiate with Colombia for rights to build a canal on its Isthmus of Panama. The treaty that resulted, the Hay-Herran treaty, was ratified by the Senate in March 1903. [43] On August 12, however, the Colombian Senate unanimously rejected the treaty as economically inadequate and as a threat to Colombia's sovereignty over Panama. [44] Rather than mourn the lost opportunity, TR decided to teach the Colombians a lesson. Instead of resuming negotiations with Colombia or moving on to a Nicaraguan route, he supported Panamanian rebels unhappy with Colombia's rejection of the treaty. [45] After years of aiding Colombia in suppressing internal revolts, the United States sent warships to both coasts of the Panamanian isthmus and prevented Colombia from suppressing the secessionist movement. Coupled with behind-the-scenes diplomacy by French adventurer Philippe Bunau-Varilla, Roosevelt's military display secured from the revolutionaries a treaty granting liberal canal rights to the United States. The treaty granting the United States the right to build a canal across the new Panamanian nation was even more favorable to the United States than the Hay-Herran treaty had been. [46]

The Senate debate over the Hay-Bunau-Varilla treaty of 1903 became a test of Roosevelt's philosophy of foreign relations. The isthmian canal was most obviously at stake. But the incident also gave Americans a taste of how America might use an expanded navy to enforce "civility" under an expanded Monroe Doctrine. In his message to Congress in December 1903, Roosevelt claimed that the interests of "the whole civilized world" justified his actions in Panama. In a second message on January 4, he again articulated the essence of the Roosevelt Corollary as justification for his aggressive actions: "We, in effect, policed the Isthmus in the interest of its inhabitants and of our own national needs, and for the good of the entire civilized world."[47]

Most U.S. senators recognized that Roosevelt's defense transformed the vote on the 1903 treaty into a referendum on his philosophy of international behavior. Roosevelt's opponents in the Senate, led almost fanatically by Senator John Tyler Morgan of Alabama,[48] argued that the president had committed an act of war against Colombia, thereby usurping the war-making powers of Congress. They also argued that the president had violated the Spooner law, which directed the president to build the canal in Nicaragua if he failed to achieve a treaty with Colombia within a "reasonable time." Morgan seemed particularly concerned that ratification of the treaty would legitimize TR's philosophy of international behavior and make the president all-powerful by establishing precedent for skirting the "plain mandate" of laws with appeals to "higher law."[49] In response, Roosevelt talked less about the legal issues surrounding his actions and more about results. He simply pointed out that the long dream of building the canal was now within the Senate's grasp. In his message to Congress in December he said: "All that remains is for the American Congress to do its part and forthwith this Republic will enter upon the execution of a project . . . of well-nigh incalculable possibilities for the good of this country and the nations of mankind." In any case, he added in his later message, "failure to ratify the treaty will not undo what has been done." The question, and the only question, he concluded, "is whether or not we shall build an isthmian canal."[50]

In justifying the Senate's sixty-six-to-fourteen vote to ratify the treaty, some lawmakers tried to separate approval of the agreement from approval of Roosevelt's actions. Senator Furnifold Simmons of North Carolina called the president's actions "hasty, rash, improvident, and dangerous" but insisted that a vote for the treaty was not "tantamount to condoning the action of the Administration." Others, like Senator James Berry of Arkansas, simply agreed with the president that what had been done could not be undone by rejecting the treaty. "I do not approve of what the President did," said Berry. "But, . . . it is accomplished. It has been done." [51]

Perhaps the most common rationale for ratifying the treaty, however, was that "the people" demanded it. Senator Augustus Bacon of Georgia claimed there was "no doubt left upon our minds" that it was "the wish of a large majority of the people of Georgia that we should vote for this treaty." Similarly, Senator Berry proclaimed that "the most persuasive reason" for his pro-treaty vote was that "four-fifths of the people of the State from which I come want me to vote for it," and he added that "the people of the South want this canal." Finally, Senator Hernando Money of Mississippi and Senator Stephen Mallory of Florida spoke of the nation as a whole, suggesting that there was a national consensus that the treaty should be approved. "We know the people of the United States want an isthmian canal," proclaimed Money, while Mallory warned that rejection of the treaty would be an "overwhelming disappointment to many millions of our citizens." [52]

Thus began an important strain in political rhetoric on the Panama Canal: the myth of "the people's" special affection for the project. As a controlling motif in canal-related rhetoric throughout the twentieth century, the notion that the American people coveted the Panama Canal would serve proponents of internationalist policies time and time again in political battles against those favoring relaxed American control over the waterway. In Roosevelt's time the reluctance of the U.S. Senate to act in defiance of public opinion (as they perceived it) resulted in ratification of a treaty symbolizing the internationalist philosophy of foreign affairs; ratifying the treaty in a sense ratified the "Big Stick" that produced it. Legally, little justification existed for Roosevelt's actions. Even his own secretary of war, Elihu Root, reportedly told the president: "You have shown that you were accused of seduction and you have conclusively proved that you were guilty of rape."[53]

With the precedent established and legitimized by the Senate, Roosevelt was able to formally announce the Roosevelt Corollary and to continue his aggressive, interventionist approach to foreign affairs. Of course, much remained to be done if the seed planted by Roosevelt and the internationalists was to grow and bear fruit. Specifically, there remained the not-so-minor matter of building the canal. If the story of the canal-building project proved one of good news and glory, the canal could become the ultimate endorsement of the philosophy of internationalism. But if the story brought failure and national humiliation, it could serve as a strong rationale for isolationism and more modest aspirations. Already the French had suffered a humiliating defeat at the hands of the Panamanian jungle—a defeat which tarnished that nation's image as a great world power. The Americans too could be defeated by the wilderness of Panama. The fate of the internationalist vision hinged largely on the American people's perceptions of the canal-building project, and Theodore Roosevelt worked all the harder to shape those perceptions.

2

Theodore Roosevelt and the Heroes of Panama

Ratification of the Hay-Bunau-Varilla treaty in 1904 ended many years of dreaming and diplomatic wrangling, and it signaled the beginning of the canal-building era. "On to Panama" was the exuberant cry of the American press in 1904 as Americans turned their attention to the glorious project.[1] Later, as the canal neared completion, America's celebration of this "greatest feat in the history of mankind" made the canal a multi-faceted symbol; it came to represent all the national virtues behind America's rise to world power and international leadership during the first few decades of the twentieth century.

Americans eagerly consumed the story of Panama; they relished its grand human drama, embraced its heroes, and urged politicians to heed its lessons. As told in the United States, the story of the canal-building project was one of those great, heroic tales filled with timeless lessons about how a nation should conduct itself. The story of the Panama Canal demonstrated the benefits of great national challenges. It revealed the benefits of hard work, perseverance, and the "martial spirit" in a nation. More than half a century later the impact of this national celebration could still be seen in the emotional recollections of the canal's history by those opposed to the treaties of 1977.

President Roosevelt contributed significantly to the popular history that shaped attitudes about the Panama Canal within the United States and served generally as an endorsement of international adventurism. He campaigned energetically while in office in an effort to transform an initially scandalous story of the canal project into a great heroic epic. Subsequently, dozens of storytellers joined TR in celebrating the canal, and the result was nothing short of a new national monument. Roosevelt and the storytellers buried critical accounts of the project with a conscious celebration of the power, the ingenuity, and the perseverance demonstrated by America's success in building the canal. They created a new generation of American heroes— heroes with all the attributes of the traditional war hero—by romanticizing the lives of everyone working on the canal, from the chief engineer to the common laborer. In the process they obscured the history of diplomatic controversy over American involvement in Panama and rendered it unpatriotic to speak negatively of the project. Most important, they created a persistent public consciousness which constrained American policymakers throughout the twentieth century. When advocates of change in U.S. policy in Latin America called for relaxing American control over the canal to atone for alleged exploitation of Panama, Americans generally rejected their arguments because Roosevelt and the storytellers, in effect, had erased America's sins from the popular historical record.

THE SCANDAL OF PANAMA

For the first few years, the American canal project in Panama was plagued by controversy and seemed doomed to repeat the failure of the French project in the 1880s. Conditions on the isthmus appalled the first Americans on the scene, and early efforts to carry on the work of the French were plagued by health hazards, insufficient supplies, and a lack of experienced personnel. The newly appointed Isthmian Canal Commission, headed by John G. Walker, was partly to blame for the discouraging situation. "The well-meaning but intractable Walker and his commissioners had to pass with due formality on virtually every purchase voucher, irrespective of importance, with the inevitable result that delivery of equipment and material took months instead of weeks to reach Colon."[2] The failure of the nation's leaders to settle on a comprehensive plan for either a sea-level or a lock-type canal also hampered the project. Combined with an incessant public cry to "make the dirt fly," the lack of a plan resulted in seemingly random excavation in Panama and increasing criticism back home. On the isthmus, workers under Chief Engineer John F. Wallace became increasingly skeptical that the canal would ever be built.

Skepticism turned to panic in 1905 with an outbreak of yellow fever. Chief Engineer Wallace joined the mass exodus of workers back to the United States and shortly thereafter resigned his position. Railroad man John F. Stevens, Wallace's successor, reached Panama in July 1905 to face "about as discouraging a proposition as was ever presented to a construction engineer." There was still no final plan for the canal and much of the labor supply (including some five hundred technicians and skilled workers) had vanished from the scene. To make matters worse, those remaining were "scared out of their boots." As Stevens said upon arriving on the scene: "There are three diseases in Panama. They are yellow fever, malaria, and cold feet; and the greatest of these is cold feet."[3]

Ignoring the clamor to "make the dirt fly," Stevens immediately shifted the emphasis from digging to preparing to do the job right. He gave health and sanitation top priority, and he recruited skilled and unskilled labor. He also established adequate provisions for feeding and housing the labor force and developed recreational facilities to sustain morale. But most significant, Stevens built a railroad. The rail system salvaged the project by providing an efficient means of supply and the solution to the most troublesome problem of construction—the removal of spoil. The rail system alone should have secured for Stevens a prominent place among the heroes of Panama.[4]

But during the regimes of Wallace and Stevens, criticism of the project never let up. The initial exuberance over the project quickly faded as every problem in the early years, no matter how minor, became cause for an exposé. Letters from embittered canal workers began appearing in American papers during the Wallace regime. "Tell the boys at home to stay there," wrote one worker in a letter picked up by the papers. "Everyone is afflicted with running sores. We are compelled to sleep in an old shed, six to a room. . . . The meals would sicken a dog." Then came the worst of all possible headlines: Yellow Fever in Panama! Soon fleeing employees "filled the newspapers with panic-stricken interviews and doleful prophesies that the Canal would never be built."[5]

Despite great improvement in conditions during the Stevens regime, criticism back home intensified in 1906. So common and widespread were the attacks that canal officials perceived a conspiracy. Joseph Bucklin Bishop, the secretary of the Isthmian Canal Commission, recalled that the "great flood of newspaper and magazine literature" criticizing the project was "so systematic as to suggest that powerful influences of some sort were instigating it." According to W. Leon Pepperman, former chief of the Office of Administration for the commission, "there existed a mysterious and, seemingly, organized opposition to the construction of the Panama Canal." So detrimental to the project, so "morbid and malignant" was this conspiracy to "infect public opinion," that Pepperman labeled the critics "human mosquitoes."[6]

Yet the most influential criticism in 1906 came from a seemingly disinterested and reputable source. With an article in January 1906, Poultney Bigelow, a journalist respected for his studies of "colored races" around the world, "created a national sensation" with a dramatic, sweeping indictment of the canal project.[7] Writing in *The Independent*, a periodical reputed to be impartial and fair, Bigelow criticized the living conditions of workers in Panama in vivid, lurid language:

The street was a pool of water in front of her—the water lay green and slimy under the house. . . . The word house is misleading . . . . They would disgrace the most unworthy sections of shanty town. . . . At the back of the house is a swamp whose bottom we know not. Out in this swamp is . . . green slime, from out of which protrudes now and then some coarse weed or piece of broken furniture. . . .

41

My experience of life in the slums of Chicago, of Canton, of San Francisco—nothing prepared me for the smell of Colon. . . . Madame Therese told me that . . . when the breeze blew across the poisoned waters it made her head ache and she could not sleep well. . . . Little children were crawling around the crazy board walks or gangplanks in imminent danger of falling into the poisonous water.[8]

Bigelow also criticized political jobbery by American officials in the Zone, the brutality of the Canal Zone police, the quality of the equipment, and the "red tape" which inhibited work and held up the pay of black workers. He even alleged that "the United States authorities had imported at considerable expense hundreds of colored ladies" and scolded: "Prostitutes are not needed on the Isthmus—and if they were there is no call to send them at the expense of the taxpayer." Bigelow vigorously assured his readers that he was an objective, thorough observer, unlike the officials who gave "a very pleasing picture of conditions down here." He charged that the American public had been misled by politicians who visited the scene, refused to inspect the works closely "for fear of catching some disease germ," and then returned home with glowing reports which "read like the circulars of doubtful land companies."[9]

Bigelow refused to identify his sources before the Senate Committee on Interoceanic Canals on January 18, 1906, and much was made of the fact that he had spent only twenty-eight hours on the isthmus conducting his investigation.[10] Yet a return visit of six weeks, sponsored by *Cosmopolitan*, did little to change his tone. He still characterized the Americans on the job as incompetent or corrupt and portrayed Colon as "one smelling cesspool." He now singled out Dr. William Gorgas, head of the health and sanitation effort. Gorgas' war on mosquitoes, he charged, succeeded only in frightening the public and the press. Gorgas was doing nothing "for the people who are dying of real disease" because he was "playing with diseases of the fancy." Again Bigelow called upon American officials to visit Panama without the planned tours reserved for high officialdom. He even challenged President Roosevelt to "learn the truth" by visiting the scene "disguised as a plain man."[11]

Roosevelt Strikes Back

President Roosevelt responded to Bigelow's challenge with a determined counteroffensive beginning in 1906. First, he sent a special message to Congress on January 8, criticizing the "sensation-mongers," and claiming that all accusations (including Bigelow's specific charges) had "proved to be without foundation in any shape or form."[12] Then, in November, he sailed to Panama onboard the battleship *Louisiana*.[13] The trip was perhaps the most effective of Roosevelt's many public relations maneuvers as president, and the result was nothing short of a rebirth for the project. By exploiting the power of the president to dominate national attention, Roosevelt in effect wrote the first chapter in a whole new story of the Panama Canal.

Never before had a president left American soil while in office, and perhaps never again would one do so with such impact. The nation's attention was riveted on TR's three-day tour, and the trip immediately allayed most Americans' worries about the project. In obvious response to Bigelow's challenge, Roosevelt "appeared determined not to be led around but rather . . . to break through the barriers that always surround high officials."[14] He journeyed to Panama during the worst of the rainy season, frequently left his official escorts for surprise inspections, and randomly interviewed workers on the line. As Roosevelt splashed through the mud in constant, driving rain, photographers preserved the spectacle for the folks back home. Out of the trip came some of the most famous photographs of Roosevelt—portraits which would forever define his presidential image.[15]

Roosevelt cultivated the image of a commander visiting his troops at the front, and military metaphors dominated his speaking on the isthmus. The workers—much to their delight—were made out to be military heroes, as in TR's speech of

43

November 16: "I have had more and more a feeling towards you, gentlemen, and further toward all . . . who are going along and doing their duty, that they are earning a right to the gratitude of the country such as can ordinarily be earned only by soldiers who have served in the few great wars of history. I have just the feeling about you men down here, that I have in meeting the men who have done well in a big war, necessary for the honor and interest of the country." In bidding the workers farewell the following day, Roosevelt again proclaimed that they were putting the country "under an obligation . . . just as a soldier who does his work well in a great war," and again he claimed to feel like he had met "the picked men of my country engaged in some great war." Roosevelt promised the workers that they would "stand exactly as the soldiers of a few, and only a few, of the most famous armies of all the nations stand in history." And to assure such recognition, he promised them "some little memorial, some mark, some badge, which will always distinguish the man who . . . has done his work well on the Isthmus, just as the button of the Grand Army distinguishes the man who did his work well in the Civil War." [16]

Roosevelt campaigned vigorously upon his return from Panama to solidify the image of the canal project as a glorious venture. The centerpiece of his campaign was one of the most unusual special messages to Congress in the history of the republic. [17] It was the first special message to Congress with a photographic supplement, and the first and only to employ Roosevelt's infamous simplified style. The appearance of the odd message in the Senate, according to Joseph Bucklin Bishop, "caused a feeling approaching consternation in that august body, whose members looked upon it as that abhorrent thing called 'an innovation,' a breach of tradition amounting almost to treason." The House, on the other hand, reportedly "hailed it . . . as a public document of high interest and value for circulation among the people," and ultimately the message was widely circulated both in the United States and in Europe. [18]

Roosevelt's illustrated special message responded comprehensively to Bigelow's charges about the work in Panama. It labeled the critics "slanderers and libelers" and accused them

44

of "trying to interfere with, and hamper the execution of, the greatest work of the kind ever attempted." He accused them of "seeking to bring to naught the efforts of their countrymen to put to the credit of America one of the giant feats of the ages," and again he portrayed the work at Panama as a glorious, military-like venture. This "conquest of peace," he said, would "stand as among the very greatest conquests, whether of peace or of war, which have ever been won by any of the peoples of mankind." He repeated his call for a "badge" to honor the workers and reemphasized in conclusion that they were "entitled to the same credit that we would give to the picked men of a victorious army": "Our fellow-countrymen on the Isthmus are working . . . in the same spirit and with the same efficiency that men of the Army and Navy work in time of war. It behooves us . . . to do all we can to hold up their hands and to aid them in every way to bring their great work to a triumphant conclusion."[19]

THE NEW STORY OF PANAMA

Roosevelt's special messages and his trip to Panama produced a stunning result. They immediately "stopped the barrage of critical writings and placed detractors on the defensive."[20] They began to transform the project from a symbol of corruption and failure into a symbol of national greatness. A large number of writers and speakers began to tell a new story of Panama filled with praise for everyone involved, with military imagery, and with patriotic musings about the wonder of it all. As the canal neared completion, workers returned home proudly wearing their "Roosevelt medals" and brimming with "patriotic pride" in their work.[21] As lecturers, as authors, or as chief sources for other speakers and writers, those connected with the enterprise joined Roosevelt in completing a tale filled with "good news" and glory.

By 1913 American publishing houses and magazines were scrambling to quench the national thirst for the good news from Panama. More than twenty-five full-length books and innumer-

45

able articles were published between the Panamanian revolution and the completion of the canal in 1915, and the vast majority of these were published between 1913 and 1915.[22] As it became obvious that the canal would be completed, publishers could not keep up with the demand for the story of Panama. Many of the books went through several editions or reprints in only a year or two. Joseph Pennell's *Pictures of the Panama Canal* went through six editions in but a single year.[23] Some publishers even pulled hoaxes to keep up with the demand. More than one book reappeared with the name of a new author and perhaps a new format, while scant revisions could be found in the text.[24]

Now it was as if Roosevelt himself had written the story of Panama. Almost all the storytellers condemned the earlier critics of the project,[25] and almost all portrayed the workers as military-like heroes. Even books and articles not written by former workers relied heavily upon their viewpoints and all sought the stamp of official approval. The title page of Willis J. Abbot's *Panama and the Canal in Picture and Prose* boasted that the book was "approved by leading officials connected with the great enterprise," while Frederic Haskin's *The Panama Canal* bore the following statement by Chief Engineer George W. Goethals: "I have read the chapters in 'The Panama Canal' dealing with the engineering features of the Canal and have found them an accurate and dependable account of the undertaking." Others dedicated their books to the workers—those men of "brains and brawn" whose "matchless skill and inspiring courage made the dream of ages a reality."[26] The scathing exposés of 1905–1906 were nowhere to be found. Now everything on the Isthmus received unbridled acclaim.

The health and sanitation campaign which Bigelow had ridiculed now became the latest wonder of the world. To "old Charles Francis Adams—brother of Henry Adams, railroad expert, historian"[27]—it was the most impressive aspect of the project. "Face to face with it, . . . seeing the American at his very best," Adams felt "as never before—a pardonable pride of race." Other storytellers promoted national pride by contrasting the French failure in health and sanitation with the success of the Americans. The French "actually made things easier for their tiny but most deadly foe," wrote William Showalter in telling a common tale in the new story of Panama. "They set the posts of their hospital beds in little pans of water to keep the ants away—and the yellow-fever mosquito reveled in it."[28] The Americans, on the other hand, "learned the secret that the mosquito had kept hidden from humanity for all the generations before."[29] The storytellers deemed the "sanitary control of the jungle" a "distinctively . . . American triumph"—a triumph that would "eventually make the Caribbean Sea an American Mediterranean."[30] In the military imagery which came to dominate the new story of Panama, they told of how a "small army" of sanitation workers had protected the "large army of canal diggers against a flank attack of the enemy most dreaded in Panama—the mosquito." And they made the leader of that army, Colonel William Gorgas, "the health wizard of the isthmus," the first among many national heroes in the new story of Panama.[31]

While the wondrous victory in sanitation became evident as early as 1906, the actual construction of the canal did not warrant celebration until 1912 or 1913. By then it had become obvious that the job would be completed. Some obstacles remained, but they were not cause for disillusionment. Indeed, they just added excitement to the story; they were challenges to overcome and to add to the glory. Not all the details of the complicated project attracted the attention of the storytellers, however. Some aspects of the project made for better drama than others.

The story of the Gatun Dam, for instance, had all the ingredients of great legend. Although the dam blended into the surrounding hills and was even hard to notice, the storytellers marveled at how it tamed the "death-dealing Chagres" River and restrained all the water needed to operate the canal.[32] Earlier the Gatun Dam had been the most criticized part of the project with the early critics telling sensational stories of its impending collapse.[33] But now the storytellers celebrated the permanence and sheer size of the dam, and they inundated their readers with statistics testifying to its greatness. The dam contained "21 million cubic yards of material," reported William Showalter—"enough to make a wall of earth three feet high and three feet thick and reaching nearly half way around the world."[34] John Barrett contemplated an even more amazing statistic—the 206 billion cubic feet of water restrained by the dam. By creating such a massive lake, the dam conquered the "matted, tangled, impenetrable jungle" which for centuries had ruled the area. In typically dramatic fashion, Fraser wrote: "As the water creeps into the dips and climbs the hills all vegetation seems to give up the struggle. It just rots and dies. The thick-leaved trees go bare; they stand grim in the water like skeletons of themselves." Farnham Bishop reported that the natives could comprehend the awesome magnitude of the dam only in biblical terms: "It was not easy to make the natives believe that these places that had been inhabited for hundreds of years would soon be under forty feet of water. Some thought the Americans were prophesying a second deluge. 'Ah, no, Senores,' protested one old Spaniard, 'the good God destroyed the world that way once, but He will never do so again.'"[35]

The storytellers celebrated the system of locks in the canal in similar fashion. "These will be the largest, most wonderful, and most interesting locks in the world," gushed John Barrett. Joseph Bishop preferred to call them "stupendous, prodigious, overwhelming," and insisted that "even these adjectives are inadequate." They were, of course, the largest locks in the world—"too big to fully grasp at a glance."[36] The concrete in the locks could build a wall "half way around the State of Delaware," or a pyramid larger than any in Egypt, or "a row of six-room houses, reaching from New York to Norfolk."[37] But the locks were distinguished by more than sheer magnitude. They were also ingenious, moving "as if by magic," with their "unseen power" overcoming the "dogged resistence of water" with "absolute safety."[38] Of all the engineering aspects of the canal project, the locks stood most clearly as the work of man and testified to his genius. Not only did their "ponderous walls" dwarf locomotives and make workmen look "like flies," but they also were "fool proof" and "as solid and eternal as the hills of Panama."[39]

The most celebrated aspect of construction at Panama was, of course, the excavation, or "making the dirt fly." In mind-boggling comparisons, the storytellers marveled at how the dirt removed would build sixty-three pyramids the size of Cheops, a tunnel fourteen feet in diameter "through the very heart of the earth," and a longer version of the Great Wall of China— "from San Francisco to New York."[40] The soil excavated for the canal would fill a train long enough to encircle the earth nearly four times—a train that could be pulled only by "a string of Panama Railroad engines reaching almost from New York to Honolulu."[41] But beyond sheer magnitude, the excavation, in particular at the Culebra Cut, offered drama, sublimity, mystery, and suspense. There was "something dramatic, majestic, and occasionally terrible" about the scene at Culebra, wrote John Fraser. A concerned, yet fascinated public read of great landslides, "with terrifying details of such incidents as whole forests moving, vast cracks opening in the earth, large buildings in imminent danger of being swept into the Cut, the bottom of the Canal mysteriously rising ten to fifteen feet in the air, while smoke oozed from the pores of the adjacent earth." It was as if an "irresistible force" with "apparently human malice" were fighting the Americans.[42] But, of course, the Americans were winning. In battlefield imagery, the storytellers reported that the "canal army," with "the same discipline and organization as an army in the field" and their "mighty engines of war," had defeated that "remorseless foe" Mother Nature. As Frederic Haskin summarized the engagement, "the barrier of the continental divide resisted to the utmost the attacks of the canal army," but "the attackers fought on" and "the mountain was defeated."[43]

THE NEW AMERICAN HEROES

The assault on Culebra, like all "wars," produced new American heroes. So eager were the storytellers to bestow honors upon those responsible for the canal that even steamshovels acquired life-like, heroic personalities. To "see them all puffing

49

and rooting together, more like a herd of living monsters than a collection of machinery," wrote Farnham Bishop, was "one of the most wonderful spectacles in the world." Others preferred to personify the steamshovels as indispensable feminine companions, as in Arthur Bullard's *The Panama Canal:* "A steamshovel, on intimate acquaintance, develops a remarkable charm. You use the feminine pronoun in referring to them even more instinctively than to a ship. . . . No one could question the gender of a steam-shovel. 'Why,' one of the men said, 'she'll do anything for a man who treats her decent.' She is not exactly good-looking, but mighty amiable. She grumbles considerably, and sometimes grunts and snorts in an unlady-like way. But the steam-shovel man, knowing her whims, pets her a bit and says 'Please,' and up she comes with a load that fills a quarter of a flat car!" [44]

Among the literally alive heroes of Panama, one stood supreme. As the embodiment of the "martial spirit" and "Americanism" of the Rooseveltian variety, Colonel George W. Goethals was an epic-writer's dream. On first glance, Goethals seemed unsuited for national heroism. A "solitary and enigmatic figure," he lacked the color and excitement of most American heroes, and he engaged in little self-promotion. Nonetheless, "praise . . . for Goethals was boundless" back home. Even John Collins, in his comparatively dispassionate *The Panama Guide,* waxed exuberant on the topic of "The Master Builder":

Everywhere one goes on the Isthmus he will hear: "The Colonel said," and "the Colonel did," and many other references to "The Colonel." "The Colonel" is Geo. W. Goethals. . . . He shows every day the decision, resourcefulness, and the tact that mark a great executive. Some of his coworkers disagree with him in questions of policy, but they all pay tribute to his ability. With the mass of the workers he commands the respect that only able and honest men can win, and such sympathy as is accorded only to very human men.

He is six feet tall, every inch bone and muscle. No one on the force works harder than he. . . . His record of wise, honest service is quite unique.

Now that his fame is secure, many men are flattering him, great universities have conferred degrees upon him, and many who have

50

watched his work in Panama hope that his country may one day have his services as its President. But no tribute that may fall to him will be counted so great as this—The men who have worked with and under him believe him Able, Wise, and Just.[45]

According to the storytellers, Goethals was everything and everywhere on the isthmus. He was the "absolute autocrat" there, and his personal court was the system of justice.[46] Yet his exercise of power was always fair and honest; his decisions were invariably right. Goethals was also the foreman *par excellence*. Always pictured near the blasting and shoveling in his bright yellow private car dubbed "the Yellow Peril" by the workers, he directed the project as "an Omnipotent, Omniscient, Omnipresent ruler." But above all, Goethals possessed the martial virtues. Although he wore no military garb and had "never heard the shrapnel scream by overhead," he received the acclaim of a great battlefield hero. Goethals himself promoted the image upon taking command: "I am no longer a commander in the United States Army. I now consider that I am commanding the Army of Panama, and that the enemy we are going to combat is the Culebra Cut and the locks and dams at both ends of the canal." Roosevelt also contributed to the image in his *Autobiography:* "Colonel Goethals has succeeded in instilling into the men under him a spirit which elsewhere has been found only in a few victorious armies."[47]

The martial spirit, along with a host of other qualities inculcated by Goethals, also made heroes of the average workers in Panama. The "typical" American in the Canal Zone became a model of the Rooseveltian ideal—hard-working, law-abiding, sober, honest, humble, patriotic, and totally devoted to the job. The life of the worker was not glamorous; it consisted of "eat, sleep, and work."[48] In contrast to the Frenchman who proceeded him, the typical American lived simply, contributed to charity, sent earnings back home, and ended a "strenuous week's work" with "the same recreation on Sunday that engages thousands of his countrymen at home."[49] The Americans were men "in flannel shirts and khaki, mud up to their knees, grime on their hands, sweat on their brow—men who were working like galley slaves in a poisonous climate, digging the biggest ditch on earth, and proud of it." Charles Francis Adams observed that the workers were "conspicuously law-abiding," contrary to what one might expect under such conditions: "The region, and those living and laboring there, impress one . . . as singularly sober, orderly, well conducted, and policed. There is a noticeable absence of that roughness, drunkenness and immorality—that carelessness of life and defiance of its decencies traditionally associated with our American improvised communities pushing to rapid completion some great enterprise."[50]

Above all, the storytellers praised the American worker in Panama for his martial and patriotic spirit. The storytellers observed that a "strong national sentiment" characterized the Americans in Panama; "nowhere in the world" was "July Fourth celebrated with more enthusiasm" than on the isthmus.[51] This patriotism manifested itself in the zeal of the workers. This "army of peace," these "soldiers in the field," approached their work as "Grant approached Vicksburg." As a result, the American, unlike the Frenchman, never became discouraged—his spirit was never broken—by the disappointments and frustrations inevitably encountered. Harry Franck drew the contrast in *Zone Policeman 88:* "As to catastrophies, a great 'slide' or a premature dynamite explosion are serious disaster to Americans on the job just as they would be to Europeans. But whereas the continental European would sit down before the misfortune and weep, the American swears a round oath, spits on his hands, and pitches in to shovel the 'slide' out again. He isn't belittling the disasters; it is merely that he knows the canal has got to be dug and goes ahead and digs it. That is the greatest thing on the Zone."[52]

In the end, every American became a hero of Panama, for the storytellers stressed that "the people of the United States . . . are doing this canal job." The "Spirit of Americanism" built the canal; the "zeal and enthusiasm of the men" on the line merely reflected "the spirit of the nation itself." As Henry L. Stimson expressed the feeling: "We are engaged in completing the greatest engineering work of the ages. Our national pride is keenly centered around it. We love to dwell on the spectacular triumphs which have already been achieved."[53] Because "the nation as a whole" was digging the canal, "a pilgrimage" to the scene became "not only worth while but patriotic." Those witnessing the canal "emerged invariably in a glow of patriotic enthusiasm, with an irrepressible desire to remove their hats and cheer for the American flag—to let the 'eagle scream.'" Americans boasted, as Roosevelt had hoped they would, that this "most wonderful thing in the world . . . is American—the work of my countrymen."[54]

The new story of Panama was a glorious tale of the martial spirit, along with Yankee ingenuity, skill, and power, in "the greatest engineering project of all history."[55] The rhetoric of Theodore Roosevelt played a major part in initiating this new story, but dozens of other storytellers helped TR reshape public consciousness of the canal. As the canal neared completion, the possessive, nationalistic attitude promoted by the storytellers seemed universal. Virtually all Americans eagerly anticipated the elaborate, patriotic celebration planned for its opening. Goethals and the workers with their "Roosevelt medals" would all be there as a great fleet of warships passed through the canal led by the president onboard the *Mayflower*.[56] Imagining the prospect, Fraser predicted that "you will scarcely be able to see the canal for star-spangled banners." Then the ships would proceed to San Francisco for the opening of the Panama-Pacific International Exposition—a mammoth world's fair "celebrating the great triumph of American genius at Panama."[57] The fair was to announce to the world that America's success in Panama marked its assumption of a dominant position of leadership in the international arena.

As it turned out, the celebration was cut back and upstaged because of the growing war in Europe. Nonetheless, the spirit remained. Even without a massive party to cap off the national celebration, Americans took great pride in their canal and all they believed it represented. That pride in turn had important political repercussions, both in Roosevelt's day, and decades later when Americans debated relinquishing control over the Panama Canal. As a symbol of the material and spiritual

benefits of international adventurism, the Panama Canal persuasively countered rationales for isolationism throughout
much of the twentieth century.

THE LOST STORY OF PANAMA

A less flattering story of American involvement in Panama
became lost amidst the rhetoric celebrating the canal-building
project. Virtually nobody acknowledged that there was a grain
of truth in Poultney Bigelow's charges concerning the exploitation of non-American workers or the problems of political favoritism. The project became instead "an object lesson in honest,
intelligent and efficient management." Nor did the storytellers
report the fact that America had established a "rigid caste society" and even "a sort of socialism" in the Canal Zone.[58] In the
storytellers' judgment, controversy over Roosevelt's use of gun-
boat diplomacy to secure the 1903 treaty barely warranted mention.[59] And none of the storytellers even began to convey the
depth of Panamanian dissatisfaction with the terms of that
agreement.

Panama continued to protest for decades that the treaty of
1903 did not "imply cession of territory and absolute transfer
of sovereignty" over the Canal Zone to the United States.[60] But
the United States continued to behave as if it did; indeed, the
United States behaved as if it controlled not only the Canal
Zone but Panama as a whole.[61] Meanwhile, the storytellers, if
they paused to address the diplomatic friction at all, deemed
the Panamanian complaints of no real consequence. Frederic
Haskin, for instance, credited American power and diplomatic
finesse for the absence of any serious conflict between the two
states:

> On the whole, . . . the relations entered into between the two Re-
> publics in 1904 have been such as to leave no serious ground for
> complaint. They have permitted the satisfactory construction of the
> canal, and they will permit its satisfactory operation. With the
> United States as the ultimate judge of every question vital to Ameri-

can interests, little is left to be desired. The fact is that the canal has been built with less friction and fewer difficulties with the Republic of Panama than could reasonably have been hoped for at the outset. This has been due principally to the fact that the Americans responsible for the success of the work have approached the Panaman situation with tact where tact was needed and with firmness where firmness was essential.[62]

In Roosevelt's day the popular history of the Panama Canal proved of great political value in silencing critics of international adventurism. Superficially the story was not political. With its patriotic form it seemed to transcend partisan differences by celebrating the great achievements of the nation as a whole. But in fact it promoted Roosevelt's hard line against concessions to Panama, and more generally it supported his program of naval expansion and international involvement. The story seemed made-to-order as a rationale for "the strenuous life" and the "martial spirit" in international affairs and it testified to the necessity of a Mahanian battleship navy to protect the canal and to exploit its potential.

Mention of the "beneficent result" also silenced criticism of Roosevelt's use of American warships in securing the treaty. When asked to respond to legal or ethical issues raised by his critics, Roosevelt responded with remarks wholly avoiding the issues but "greatly pleasing to the country"—as when he reacted to criticism from a group of Yale professors with "Tell them that I am going to make the dirt fly!"[63] In 1911 he even boasted that he "took the Canal Zone" and "let Congress debate." When critics deemed the remarks an admission of wrongdoing, he again emphasized results. His critics, he charged, were "really criticizing . . . having the canal dug at all."[64]

Yet the critiques of Roosevelt's actions in 1903, along with Panamanian complaints about the terms of the 1903 treaty, left a political legacy of considerable importance. Although the dissenting voices were muted in Roosevelt's day, the moral, legal, and political indictments of U.S. policy developed early in the century evolved into the rationale for America's retreat from Panama in the 1970s. The early critics would be remembered by later "revisionists"—historians, politicians, and reporters who recalled the darker side of America's history in Panama while developing the rationale for American withdrawal from the Canal Zone. Roosevelt's critics at least planted the seeds of a revisionist history of the Panama Canal, and those seeds eventually grew into the rationale for American withdrawal.

3

The "New Look" in U.S. Canal Policy

Prior to World War II, there were few challenges to the patriotic, Rooseveltian story of the Panama Canal. Few Americans paid much attention to Panamanian claims that America had "stolen" the canal in 1903 or had infringed upon Panama's sovereignty over its national territory. For many years the United States continued to control the site of its great national triumph and to exercise its self-appointed role as "policeman" of the West.

As Panamanian accusations of "colonialism" and "imperialism" began to damage America's image during the Cold War, America's foreign policy establishment came to view the status quo in Panama as harmful to America's larger foreign policy interests. In the postwar struggle for the hearts and minds of the nonaligned nations, the architects of American foreign policy increasingly became willing to sacrifice holdings like the Panama Canal Zone for the somewhat less tangible blessings of favorable "world opinion." This, at bottom, characterized what has been called the "new look" in American diplomacy during the Cold War era.[1]

But American policymakers also had to take into account the special place of the Panama Canal in America's political folk-

57

lore and popular history. For domestic political reasons, they had to think of the Panama Canal as more than just a waterway; they could not treat it simply as a tangible asset to be figured into diplomatic cost-benefit ratios. Concessions designed to silence Panama's agitation inevitably outraged the guardians of Theodore Roosevelt's legacy, and the American people seemed to rally behind defenders of the status quo. Diplomats had to balance carefully Panama's demands for change against domestic political pressures so as to jeopardize neither America's standing in world opinion nor their domestic political legitimacy.

Relations with Panama during the Cold War era thus became "a three-cornered matter," with successive Republican and Democratic administrations negotiating with Congress as well as with the Panamanians.[2] Most of these negotiations involved disputes over sovereignty, especially questions about whether Theodore Roosevelt, in effect, "stole" the Canal Zone in 1903 and about the locus of sovereignty in the Canal Zone under the Hay-Bunau-Varilla treaty of 1903.

Although every president since FDR seemed convinced of the need for fundamental change in the basic relationship between the United States and Panama, few considered it worth the political cost. For years American policy consisted of incremental, piecemeal changes in Panama which seemingly satisfied no one. While minor revisions of U.S. policy inevitably failed to satisfy the Panamanians, they prompted vociferous opposition within the United States.

By the mid-1960s, the architects of American foreign policy had concluded that the United States would inevitably have to relinquish its claim to sovereignty in the Canal Zone. This "new look" in thinking about American canal policy evolved into negotiations over a new treaty arrangement and set the stage for the "Great Debate" over Panama in the 1970s.

"Taking" the Canal Zone

The suggestion that Theodore Roosevelt "stole" the Panama Canal Zone did not originate with Panamanian critics of American foreign policy. The Colombians first complained about how Roosevelt obtained the rights to build the Panama Canal. After Colombia rejected a treaty granting the United States the right to build a canal across that portion of its territory known as the Isthmus of Panama, Roosevelt helped give birth to a new nation of Panama by protecting a secessionist movement with American warships. The revolutionaries favored the treaty rejected by Colombia, and they eagerly signed a canal treaty with the United States while under its protection. Thus, Colombia, not Panama, first complained that America had "stolen" the Panama Canal Zone. And Roosevelt's political opponents within the United States saw the complaints as useful weapons against the president.

John Tyler Morgan, the chairman of the Senate Committee on Interoceanic Canals, led Roosevelt's critics within the United States during the debate over the Hay-Bunau-Varilla treaty in 1903. Refering to Roosevelt's protection of the Panamanian rebels, Morgan argued on the floor of the Senate that the president had exceeded his authority under the Spooner law (the congressional authorization to negotiate a canal treaty) and under the constitution by performing a "caesarean operation by which a republic of Panama [was] taken alive from the womb of Colombia." He accused Roosevelt of waging "war, but not declared war" on Colombia when "nothing could be more remote from the purposes . . . of Congress . . . than a war upon Colombia . . . if her Congress should refuse to ratify the treaty."[3]

At the time, Roosevelt claimed that the Spooner Act authorized him to negotiate with whomever happened to control the needed land at the moment. According to Roosevelt, "the purpose of the law was to authorize the President to make a treaty with the power in actual control of the Isthmus of Panama," and he observed that "this purpose has been fulfilled." He defended his military support for the Panamanian rebels with reference to an 1846 treaty with Colombia and to precedents for intervention in the area, declaring that "only the active interference of the United States has enabled [Colombia] to preserve so much as a semblance of sovereignty."[4] In fact, the Spooner Act specifically named the government TR was empowered to negotiate with—the Colombian government[5]—and the treaty and precedents authorized, if anything, American suppression of the Panamanian revolt. The treaty of 1846 explicitly guaranteed that the United States would preserve, not undermine, the sovereignty of Colombia over its territory, and every prior case of American intervention had been for that purpose.

Roosevelt's legal case was at best shaky. But with the American people eager to realize the long dream of an American canal between the Atlantic and Pacific, he was able to transcend the legal issues with appeals to national self-interest. After even some of his harshest critics in the Senate cited popular demand for a canal and voted for the treaty with Panama, Roosevelt recognized that the popularity of a canal treaty outweighed most reservations about how it was obtained. Facing reelection in 1904, TR instructed his campaigners to emphasize "Panama in all its details" and challenged the Democrats to make it an issue.[6] In a public letter accepting the presidential nomination, he made his controversial actions a selling point; he cited the canal treaty as the best example of his presidential leadership:

> The decisive action which brought about this beneficent result was the exercise by the President of the powers vested in him, and in him alone, by the Constitution; . . . The Constitution must be observed positively as well as negatively. The President's duty is to serve the country in accordance with the Constitution; and I should be derelict in my duty if I used a false construction of the Constitution as a shield for weakness and timidity, or as an excuse for governmental impotence.[7]

After his sweep of Alton B. Parker by the greatest popular majority in American history, Roosevelt continued to sidestep most of the legal issues surrounding his actions in 1903. Those who continued to call his actions illegal were now met with the response: "Tell them I am going to make the dirt fly."[8] At a banquet in Denver in May 1905, TR also brushed aside the question of whether his actions were unethical, citing the "higher law" of national self-interest and advancing "civilization." He simply dismissed the matter of fairness for Colombia: "It is perhaps unnecessary for me to say that I am perfectly aware that many most admirable gentlemen disagreed with me in my action toward the Panama Canal. But I am in a wholly unrepentant frame of mind in reference thereto. The ethical conception upon which I acted was that I did not intend that Uncle Sam should be held up while he was doing a great work for himself and all mankind."[9]

The beginning of serious inquiry into Roosevelt's actions came after he left office. Roosevelt prompted the reexamination himself with his infamous boast of 1911: "I took the Canal Zone and let the Congress debate." Appearing in academic gown at the Greek Theatre at the University of California on March 23, TR reportedly told the eight thousand people present: "I am interested in the Panama Canal because I started it. If I had followed traditional conservative methods I would have submitted a dignified state paper of probably 200 pages to the Congress, and the debate would have been going on yet. But I took the Canal Zone and let the Congress debate, and while the debate goes on, the canal does also."[10] Although "I took the Canal Zone" was the kind of exaggeration that came naturally to Roosevelt,[11] the statement provoked a strong protest from Colombia. According to the Colombian envoy, the speech constituted a "public, deliberate, and spontaneous . . . confession of a man who . . . boasts of having committed an act of the most far-reaching gravity against the country I have the honor to represent." Roosevelt's braggadocio also "aroused much comment" at home, as Joseph Bucklin Bishop observed, "and was construed by his critics as an admission that he had used arbitrary and unjustifiable methods" in obtaining the canal treaty.[12]

Foremost among the domestic critics was Congressman Henry T. Rainey. On April 16, 1911, Rainey introduced a resolution directing the House Committee on Foreign Affairs to investigate Roosevelt's actions in 1903.[13] Roosevelt sought to upstage the hearings on the Rainey resolution with a major editorial in *Outlook* on October 7, 1911. The former president again defended an active presidency and he insisted that "every ethical consideration, national and international," demanded that he act as he did. He argued that the United States had "no more honorable chapter [in its history] than that which tells of the way in which our right to dig the Panama Canal was secured," and again he emphasized the result of his actions: "If I had observed a judicial inactivity about what was going on at the Isthmus, had let things take their course, and had then submitted an elaborate report thereon to Congress, I would have furnished the opportunity for much masterly debate in Congress, which would now be going on—and the canal would still be 50 years in the future."[14] Still, hearings on the Rainey resolution commenced on January 6, 1912. Nearly a decade after the events in question, Roosevelt's actions in securing the canal treaty were to be investigated fully for the very first time.

The hearings on the Rainey resolution proved a one-man show, with testimony dominated by Henry N. Hall, a staff correspondent for *The New York World*. Hall's testimony in turn relied almost exclusively on a voluminous statement by New York lawyer William Nelson Cromwell—a statement originally submitted to arbitrators in support of Cromwell's demand for eight hundred thousand dollars in legal fees for striking a deal between the liquidators of the failed French canal company and the American government. Cromwell insisted in his statement that he had been privy to plans within the Roosevelt administration to foment revolution in Panama. He maintained that he had produced American support for the conspirators well before the revolution, and that such support made possible the successful revolution and hence the sale of French concessions and equipment to the American government.[15] Cromwell's story was suspect because of his financial motivations, of course, and it was convincingly challenged by Philippe Bunau-Varilla—the Frenchman who negotiated the 1903 treaty on behalf of the Panamanians.[16] Nonetheless, Hall's testimony was published as *The Story of Panama*, and Roosevelt stood convicted in the minds of some Americans of impropriety, if not of a crime.

The Wilson administration embraced the cause of "justice" for Colombia. In 1914 the administration offered to atone for Roosevelt's sins with a treaty expressing "sincere regret" and paying $25 million.[17] Negotiated by Secretary of State William Jennings Bryan, the treaty enraged Roosevelt and generated his intense hatred of Wilson—"the consuming passion" of his "closing years."[18] That hatred was thinly veiled in Roosevelt's effort to prevent ratification of what he called "The Panama Blackmail Treaty."

"If there is warrant for [the treaty]," Roosevelt wrote of the Thomson-Urrutia treaty in February 1915, "then we have no business to be on the Isthmus at all." The treaty labeled the United States "a thief" and "a receiver of stolen goods," he argued, and if that were the case then the United States had "no right to take any pride in anything that has been done on the Isthmus." TR contrasted a story which he said would "smirch the name of America" with the heroic story of the ca-nal-building project. And the Senate, refusing to put a damper on America's celebration of the newly completed canal, de-clined to consider the Thomson-Urrutia treaty.[19]

Seven years later, however, on April 20, 1921, the U.S. Sen-ate ratified the Thomson-Urrutia treaty. No longer did it express "sincere regret," but the United States did pay Colombia the $25 million.[20] The treaty went into effect on March 1, 1922, almost two years after the formal opening of the Panama Canal and over three years after Roosevelt's death. With Roosevelt no longer around to defend his actions, the United States admitted to impropriety warranting monetary compensation. In effect, ratification of the treaty endorsed the view that Roosevelt had "stolen" the canal from Colombia in 1903.

Perhaps some supporters of the Thomson-Urrutia treaty wanted to lay to rest a seemingly endless controversy, while others may have sought to embarrass the Republican party. But decades later, when the propriety of Roosevelt's actions in 1903 would again be contested, the fact that the U.S. government ad-mitted wrongdoing in 1921 gave credibility to those revising the Rooseveltian history of Panama.

When the matter was later resurrected, it would be Pan-ama, not Colombia, claiming injury from the actions of Theo-dore Roosevelt. The Panamanians would reinterpret Roosevelt's protection of their revolution as an attempt to create a depen-dency and to force approval of the Hay-Bunau-Varilla treaty. The Panamanians would be able to appropriate America's ap-parent admission that the Canal Zone was "stolen" for their own political purposes. The United States had admitted impropriety in the obtainment of its rights to build the Panama Canal, and it seemed to matter little that Panama had once considered itself the beneficiary rather than the victim of those events. At bottom, America's self-indictment for the "crimes" of 1903 cast a shadow over anything gained by methods later deemed too aggressive or "imperialistic," and Americans would feel compelled to consider sympathetically demands for economic and political restitution.

THE PROBLEM OF SOVEREIGNTY

For many years the story of American involvement in Panama told north of the Rio Grande was a story of liberation. In justifying America's intervention against Colombia, Theodore Roosevelt and his supporters portrayed the Panamanians as an oppressed, deservedly liberated people.[21] However, the tiny, newborn nation began to complain almost immediately about new oppression by its liberators from the north. Panamanians began to think that they had traded a weak, inefficient oppressor for a large and effective one. But most Americans turned a deaf ear to Panama's complaints during the canal-building years. The story of Panama told in the United States suggested that Panamanians were grateful, not only for their independence, but also for the riches the canal would bring to their nation. Panama's complaints against the United States were duly recorded in the historical record. But it would be many years before Panamanian complaints were publicized widely by revisionist historians and American policymakers.

The first Panamanian complaints about sovereignty under the 1903 treaty came in protests against the establishment of U.S. ports, customhouses, tariffs, and post offices in the Canal Zone in June 1904. In a series of notes in July and August, Panamanian officials protested that the actions violated the Hay-Bunau-Varilla treaty of 1903. According to the protest lodged by Panama's ambassador to the United States, the "interpretation given to . . . the Bunau-Varilla-Hay treaty" threatened to bring upon Panama "ruin and dishonor as an autonomous entity."

Then, in a theme that Americans would hear for many years to come, Ambassador de Obaldia argued that the treaty did "not imply cession of territory and absolute transfer of sovereignty," but rather constituted a "legal relation" like that "which exists between a lessor and a lessee."[22]

Theodore Roosevelt reassured the Panamanians by responding: "We have not the slightest intention of establishing an independent colony in . . . Panama, or of exercising any greater governmental functions than are necessary to enable us conveniently and safely to construct, maintain, and operate the canal." But the official response to the protests, penned by Secretary of State John Hay, was far less conciliatory. Hay stated flatly that "the United States acquired the right to exercise sovereign powers and jurisdiction over the canal zone" and was willing only to acknowledge Panama's "titular sovereignty"—a concept he called a "barren scepter."[23]

Hay's note might have escalated the controversy, but a visit to the isthmus by Secretary of War Taft calmed the Panamanians. Taft admitted that "the people of Panama . . . have not been done justice" and he echoed Roosevelt's contention that the United States had "no desire to exercise any power except that . . . necessary . . . to insure the building, maintenance, and protection of the canal."[24] To correct the "injustice," Taft negotiated an agreement that settled the conflict over ports, customhouses, tariffs, and postal service, and he left the appreciative Panamanians with the cry, "Viva la Republica de Panama."[25] But upon returning to the United States, Taft claimed that little had been conceded. The acknowledgment of Panama's "titular sovereignty," he reported to the president, was "dear to them but . . . of no real moment whatever" to the United States. In testimony before the Senate Committee on Interoceanic Canals, Taft called "titular sovereignty" a "barren ideality" with appeal only to "poetic and sentimental" Latin minds—minds that dwelled "much on names and forms."[26]

Taft's insult did little to dampen the good cheer when Roosevelt visited Panama in 1906. The presidents of both countries spoke of their happy partnership in the "great work," while Roosevelt promised to "never interfere" in Panama "save to give her our aid in the attainment of her future." Yet Roosevelt also lectured the Panamanians on civilized behavior. He warned: "Progress and prosperity . . . can come only through the pre-servation of both order and liberty; through the observance by those in power of all their rights, obligations and duties to their fellow-citizens, and through the realization of those out of power that the insurrectionary habit, the habit of civil war, ulti-mately means destruction to the republic."[27]

The United States repeatedly demonstrated over the fol-lowing years that Roosevelt's warning was not empty. Even before Roosevelt's visit, the United States disbanded the Pana-manian army when the political aspirations of its leader threat-ened disorder. The United States subsequently intervened in Panama on numerous occasions to preserve order during elec-tions or to quell rioting that often stemmed from friction be-tween Panamanians and American military personnel.[28] Yet American intrusions upon Panamanian sovereignty were not limited to preserving order. Throughout the canal-building era and beyond the United States also controlled radio communica-tions in Panama, dictated the nation's foreign policy, dominated its economy, and repeatedly expropriated additional lands out-side the Canal Zone.[29]

Panamanian protests did little to alter the opinion in the United States that relations with Panama remained good in the canal-building era. When the American storytellers paused to address diplomatic issues, they told of only minor and tempo-rary conflicts. William Scott, for instance, acknowledged the disputes over sovereignty but claimed that the "issue passed off in talk" after Taft's visit.[30]

By the 1920s, however, Americans found it increasingly difficult to pretend all was well in U.S.-Panamanian relations. In 1921, and again in 1923, Panama called for negotiations to re-move the "unilateral and oppressive character" of the 1903 treaty.[31] In response, Secretary of State Charles Evans Hughes firmly reasserted American rights under the Hay-Bunau-Varilla treaty, and later the United States even abrogated the Taft agree-ment.[32] Still, the United States finally agreed to negotiations, and in 1926 negotiators reached agreement on a new treaty. The new agreement "did little more than perpetuate the existing situation and alleviated almost none of Panama's long-standing grievances."[33] The legislature of Panama "indignantly rejected the treaty, and negotiations dragged on for another decade." Meanwhile, Americans continued to think of Panama as something less than an independent nation. In 1928, President Coolidge even referred to Panama as "an outlying possession" of the United States.[34]

The election of Franklin D. Roosevelt gave new hope to Panamanians demanding recognition of their sovereignty. On September 21, 1933, the Panamanian legation requested a meeting between Roosevelt and President Arias of Panama to discuss questions deemed "a matter of life or death for the Republic of Panama." Roosevelt agreed to the meeting, and the two presidents eventually announced a meeting of minds on "certain general principles." According to their statements, the two presidents reaffirmed the validity of the treaty of 1903, but the United States pledged to help protect "the prosperity of the Republic of Panama" and to "sympathetically consider . . . arbitration of any important question" which divided the countries.[35]

Negotiations to fulfill the promises of the meeting between Roosevelt and Arias proved difficult. Under intense domestic political pressures on both sides, 110 diplomatic conferences were convened. Finally, the United States agreed to significant concessions in the context of FDR's "Good Neighbor Policy" and the rising Axis threat, and on March 2, 1936, the two nations signed the Hull-Alfaro treaty.[36]

The new treaty seemingly settled all outstanding disputes. As Gerstle Mack wrote in 1944, the pact conceded to Panama "practically every point in dispute since 1903."[37] The treaty abrogated the protectorate status of Panama, renounced the right of the United States to intervene in Panama to maintain order, declared that the United States could not seize any additional lands without Panamanian consent, granted a number of economic concessions, and increased the annuity paid to Panama to $430,000. Perhaps the greatest concession, however, was symbolic; the treaty acknowledged Panama's sovereignty over the entire isthmus by referring to the Canal Zone as "territory of the Republic of Panama under the jurisdiction of the United States." [38]

Yet it eventually became clear that the United States had conceded little of practical import in the treaty of 1936. When the Senate Foreign Relations Committee considered the treaty, it deemed the provision for joint defense of the canal unacceptable and premised its approval of the pact on the understanding that the United States could "act individually" to defend the canal in an emergency. [39] A three-year delay ensued as the two nations debated the issue. Panama ultimately agreed to the interpretation in an exchange of notes. Many Panamanians would realize some time after the U.S. Senate finally ratified the treaty in August 1939 that the interpretation of defense rights rendered their victory hollow. While the treaty and some other concessions in the early 1940s seemingly "eliminated practically all remaining sources of friction" between the two nations, [40] the pressures of a world at war would soon lead the United States to claim that its security interests took precedence over Panamanian claims to sovereignty. And as a result, an era of more serious conflict with Panama would soon begin.

THE PIECEMEAL RETREAT

The good cheer surrounding ratification of the Hull-Alfaro treaty of 1936 dissipated rapidly with the approach of World War II. In 1940 the United States requested additional lands to bolster the defense of the canal, and when the Panamanians responded with economic demands, the U.S. Army simply occupied the lands, evoking the defense provisions of the 1936 treaty. Only then did the United States agree to negotiate the terms of the occupation. After the war, the United States did not vacate the lands as agreed, and the two nations negotiated another agreement to extend the occupation. Before the agreement was finalized, however, Panamanian protesters asserted themselves. With the Panamanian Assembly threatened by "ten thousand boys with knives," [41] the legislators unanimously rejected the agreement. The United States evacuated the lands three months later. [42]

The controversy over defense sites marked a watershed in U.S.-Panamanian relations. For the first time "a massive nationalist movement successfully thwarted United States policies in Panama."[43] Students of the National University took the lead in the revolt, but U.S. officials perceived communist agitators behind the challenge to U.S. policy.[44] Within the American foreign policy establishment, these changes prompted new ways of thinking about America's approach to Panama. As Edwin Hoyt observed, American officials "found it increasingly inexpedient simply to stand pat on its legal rights" under the treaty of 1903. Because they perceived a "deadlock among the Great Powers" following World War II, they began to perceive the need "to compete for allies among the smaller nations" like Panama.[45] U.S. policymakers "became increasingly sensitive to world opinion as expressed in the United Nations and by foreign governments."[46] While they believed that the United States stood on firm legal ground for maintaining the status quo in Panama, they began to consider how Panama's complaints about U.S. "imperialism" and "colonialism" hurt America's image around the world and strengthened the hand of communists in the region.

Dwight Eisenhower was among those convinced that competition for the hearts and minds of Latin America demanded a new American approach in Panama. With the Panamanian clamor for revision of the 1903 treaty, and with instability within the Panamanian government increasing, Eisenhower decided the time was right for a major concession. Eisenhower agreed to "sympathetic consideration" of Panama's complaints in 1953, and the two nations signed a new treaty on January 25, 1955. The pact promised a number of economic benefits for Panama in exchange for American use of Panamanian lands.[47] But the United States again refused to repudiate any of its rights of sovereignty under the treaty of 1903.

The guardians of Teddy Roosevelt's legacy smelled a "sellout." They portrayed the treaty as an entering wedge that ultimately would split the United States from its sovereign rights in the Canal Zone. The Zonians led the protest against any diminuation of U.S. control over the canal. "With each replacement of a United States citizen with an alien employee," a Zonian repre-

69

sentative told the Senate Foreign Relations Committee, "Panama's wedge to obtain sovereignty is enlarged." If the treaty passed, he argued, the Panamanians would start "asking that the entire Panama Canal be turned over to them, and if such is not granted all her workers will be withdrawn from their work in the zone."[48] On the floor of the Senate Richard Russell of Georgia sounded a similar theme, calling the treaty only "a temporary settlement" which would inspire the Panamanians to make "demands upon us for greater concessions." Senator Warren Magnuson of Washington called the treaty "only the beginning" of Panama's effort to "take over the canal," and he argued that it at least "had the implication" of forfeiting American sovereignty in the Canal Zone: "The treaty . . . has the effect . . . of taking away from or decreasing what we have considered the sovereignty of the United States in the Panama Canal Zone. . . . It seems to me that the effect or the implication of the treaty is that . . . the sovereignty of the United States will be encroached upon, or at least some inroads will be made upon it."[49]

Administration spokesmen responded by suggesting that the treaty actually reaffirmed American sovereignty in the Canal Zone. Assistant Secretary of State Henry F. Holland noted that American negotiators had refused "several small requests," including a request that Panama's flag be flown in the Zone, because they "did not want to leave 1 grain of evidence that could a hundred years hence be interpreted as implying any admission by the United States that we possess and exercise anything less than 100 percent of the rights of sovereignty in this area."[50] The Senate Foreign Relations Committee endorsed this interpretation of the treaty, claiming that the agreement would "protect the broad jurisdictional powers of the United States in the Canal Zone." In recommending ratification, the committee argued that it would recognize Panama's "legitimate interests" while preserving "every necessary right and power in the zone." Senator William Fulbright defended the treaty on the floor of the Senate against charges that it would just lead to greater demands—perhaps ultimately to a surrender of sovereignty. The negotiators had "emphasized to the Panamanians that there was no right of reopening the agreement and no expectation that it would be reopened," he said, but he acknowledged that the United States could not prevent Panama from making more demands "unless we wish to assert the power of the 'big stick.'"[51]

Debate over the treaty of 1955 showed that virtually nobody within the United States was yet willing to suggest that America relinquish sovereignty over the Panama Canal Zone. At the same time, however, more and more Americans were suggesting a new approach to U.S.-Panamanian relations—a more conciliatory approach repudiating the tradition of the "big stick" in Panama. Ratification of the 1955 treaty by a vote of seventy-two to fourteen revealed that few hard-liners on Panama remained in the Senate. But continuing agitation by the Panamanians following ratification of the treaty drove many back into the hard-line camp. The signatures had barely dried on the 1955 treaty when Panamanian leaders "voiced their dissatisfaction . . . that the sovereignty demands had not been honored and announced that they considered them still to be pending."[52] Thus began another new era in U.S.-Panamanian relations—an era characterized by America's first real retreat on the issue of sovereignty in the Canal Zone.

THE TRIUMPH OF THE "NEW LOOK"

Nasser's takeover of the Suez Canal in 1956 inspired a new round of conflict in U.S.-Panamanian relations. Panamanian protestors and government officials again demanded recognition of their sovereignty in the Canal Zone, while the Eisenhower administration tried to explain the legal differences between the two situations. "The conditions aren't the same," President Eisenhower explained. "You see from the convention of 1888 . . . that the Suez Canal will always be an international waterway, free for use to all nations of the world," while the Panama Canal was "a national undertaking carried out under bilateral treaty." Secretary of State John Foster Dulles provided a fuller explanation of the legal issues and firmly as-

71

serted American rights in the Canal Zone in his news conference of August 28, 1956:

I'm not aware of any misunderstanding, at least at the official level. There has been a good deal of speculation as to possible similarities between the Suez Canal and the Panama Canal. Actually, the situation is totally dissimilar. . . . The Suez Canal by the treaty of 1888 is internationalized. The Panama Canal is a waterway in a zone where, by treaty, the United States has all the rights which it would possess if it were the sovereign "to the entire exclusion of the exercise by the Republic of Panama of any such sovereign rights, power or authority." And there is no international treaty giving other countries any rights at all in the Panama Canal except for a treaty with the United Kingdom which provides that it has the right to have the same tolls for its vessels as for ours.[53]

The administration's legalistic rhetoric did little to stem the tide of Panamanian agitation over the next few years. Even as Eisenhower announced that "one more link in the long chain of friendship" had been forged by passage of legislation to implement the 1955 treaty,[54] an anti-American protest campaign dubbed "Operation Sovereignty" was culminating in a march into the Canal Zone to plant Panamanian flags. The students leading the march became instant national heroes. And while American officials in Panama were "inclined to laugh off the incident as a student prank,"[55] the demonstrations were taken so seriously in Washington that the president sent his brother, Dr. Milton Eisenhower, on a fact-finding mission to the area.

Milton Eisenhower reported upon his return from Panama that "far and away the hottest issue . . . involved a question of national sovereignty, hence of national pride." He reported that "Panama wanted its flag flown in the Zone as an acknowledgment of its sovereignty," and he launched a personal crusade to influence "anybody who could act" on the matter: "I pounded desks and raised my voice . . . because I was convinced that there would be the devil to pay in Panama, probably on the next Independence Day, unless we made a good showing before then." Eisenhower found support in the State Department for raising the Panamanian flag. But "when Congress got wind of this there were violent protests, as there were from the Secretary of the Army and the Governor of the Zone."[56]

Representative Daniel Flood led the congressional uprising. Flood, an "unreconstructed Rooseveltian Rough Rider" who traced his political lineage directly to TR,[57] virtually made a career of documenting America's legal claim to "exclusive sovereignty" in the Canal Zone. He became particularly incensed over talk of Panama's "titular sovereignty," for such talk was "purely academic" and had "no purpose except that of agitation and aggravation." He bristled at suggestions that the Panamanian flag should be flown in Canal Zone, arguing that it "would constitute a symbol of sovereignty that does not in fact exist." Flood's strongest suit, however, was anticommunism: his claim that relaxing American control over the canal would play into the hands of the global Communist conspiracy. In the context of concern over Castro's actions in Cuba, Flood's descriptions of rioting and "mountain guerrilla operations" by Panamanian radicals or of Panama's "worldwide propaganda derogatory of the United States" became persuasive arguments against retreat in Panama. At the time it did not seem all that bizarre to suggest that "radical efforts in the Caribbean and isthmian areas" resulted from "the hidden hand of cunning and malignant Sovietism manipulating their local puppet figures to destroy the just rights of the United States and to jeopardize the peace of the world."[58]

The Panamanian government did more than anyone else to bestow credibility upon Flood. By designating Flood Panama's "Public Enemy Number One," the Panamanian National Assembly made it obvious that the congressman had struck a nerve. The Panamanians further incensed Americans by launching a new international campaign to discredit America's claim to sovereignty in the Zone.[59] Finally, as if on cue, Panamanian protestors took to the streets and provoked an international incident that gave urgency to the cause. The trouble began on Panamanian Independence Day in 1959 when students again tried to display their country's flag in the Canal Zone. Rioting broke out and U.S. troops were called in to quell the disturbance, giving credence to Flood's charges of radicalism and anti-Americanism in Panama.[60]

The Eisenhower administration responded to the violence in 1959 by finally addressing the issue of sovereignty. Although

73

the administration initially delayed some planned economic benefits so they would not appear a response to the violence,[61] the president eventually rewarded the protestors with an unprecedented interpretation of "titular sovereignty." Suddenly the administration supported flying Panama's flag within the Canal Zone. On December 2, 1959, Eisenhower said: "This is one of the points that's been talked about for many years, since for 50 years the United States has recognized the titular sovereignty of Panama. . . . The one question of the flag has never been specifically placed before me, no decision has ever been made about it; but I do in some form or other believe we should have visual evidence that Panama does have titular sovereignty over the region." On December 10, Secretary of State Christian Herter went further, confirming that the administration was "considering with considerable sympathy the question of whether or how to raise the flag in the Canal Zone." Finally, the administration decided to fly the Panamanian flag in the area of the Canal Zone known as Shaler Triangle, although the administration insisted that the decision would not be interpreted as "modifying in any way the Treaties and Agreements in force."[62]

In typically frenzied rhetoric, Congressman Flood called the decision to fly the flag "a further appalling example of American diplomatic appeasement, loss of leadership, and weakened integrity in the eyes of the world."[63] Despite administration claims that the decision did not affect existing treaties, many members of Congress also viewed the action as a direct violation of a House concurrent resolution stating that "any variation in the traditional interpretation of the treaties of 1903, 1936, and 1955 . . . shall only be made pursuant to treaty."[64] With the initial count of White House mail running 180 to 3 against the decision to raise the Panamanian flag, it also seemed that the move was not very popular among the American people.[65]

Opponents of Eisenhower's decision to raise the Panamanian flag may have overreacted. The decision was merely symbolic, with the substantive rights of sovereignty retained by the United States. But the incident reveals just how powerful symbolism can be in international relations, for the decision to raise the flag altered U.S.-Panamanian relations perhaps more fundamentally than the 1955 treaty and the various economic benefits bestowed upon Panama over the years. As subsequent U.S. presidents would learn, the first American concession on sovereignty did not satisfy the Panamanians; instead, it only raised expectations that Panama could "reclaim" complete sovereignty in the Canal Zone. John F. Kennedy would be the first president to learn this lesson while dealing with an escalation of tensions and violence in the area.

THE FINAL CONCESSION

John F. Kennedy's presidency brought little change in thinking about relations with Panama. For some time the United States kept trying to "buy" calm in Panama. The Kennedy administration showered the Panamanians with new loans and grants totaling tens of millions of dollars and promised more in the context of the Alliance for Progress.[66] For a time it seemed to work; relations between the two nations remained stable. But this lull in hostilities in U.S.-Panamanian relations probably stemmed more from the popularity of Kennedy's ambassador to Panama, Joseph S. Farland, than from the economic concessions.[67] Before long the Panamanians again demanded recognition of their sovereignty in the Canal Zone and relations again began to deteriorate.

Kennedy followed in Eisenhower's footsteps by employing a conciliatory approach. In a letter to Panamanian president Chiari in November 1961, he wrote: "It seems clear . . . that when two friendly nations are bound by treaty provisions which are not fully satisfactory to one of the parties, arrangements should be made to permit qualified representatives of both nations to discuss these points of dissatisfaction with a view to their resolution."[68] Next, Kennedy invited Chiari to a meeting in Washington in the summer of 1962. The two presidents agreed to establish a commission to discuss further economic benefits for Panama and to arrange "for the flying of Panamanian flags in an appropriate way in the Canal Zone."[69] Obviously, the flag at Shaler Triangle no longer sufficed as far as the Panamanians were concerned. Indeed, the whole notion of "titular sovereignty" had become inadequate, as President Chiari subsequently interpreted Kennedy's friendliness as a willingness to renounce the 1903 treaty and to replace it with a new treaty acknowledging Panamanian sovereignty in the Canal Zone.[70]

A familiar scenario of deteriorating relations unfolded following the disagreement over renegotiating the 1903 treaty. Renewed official tensions brought new agitation in the streets of Panama, while the Zonians became agitated over the protests and the seemingly endless string of concessions. When the joint commission finally carried out its original mandate and ordered the flying of the Panamanian flags at additional sites in the Canal Zone, the protests of the Zonians became so vigorous that the commission disbanded and Ambassador Farland resigned in disgust.[71] Although at this point the United States had granted by executive fiat many of the demands "flatly rejected during the negotiations for the 1955 treaty,"[72] an atmosphere of crisis again prevailed. But now, because of the assassination of John F. Kennedy, Lyndon Baines Johnson would have to deal with the problem.

LBJ soon faced the most explosive situation ever in Panama. On January 7, 1964, Panamanian students again tried to raise their flag in the Canal Zone, and this time the situation escalated into four days of "virtual war." When it was over four U.S. soldiers and twenty-four Panamanians lay dead.[73] On January 10 Panama severed diplomatic relations with the United States and requested that the U.N. Security Council consider the "repeated threats and acts of aggression committed by the Government of the United States of America in the Republic of Panama."[74] On the other side, President Johnson also responded forcefully. An official White House statement issued on January 14 praised American forces for behaving "admirably under extreme provocation by mobs and snipers" and firmly warned Panama that U.S. defense interests would not be compromised: "The United States tries to live by the policy of the good neighbor and expect others to do the same. The United States cannot allow the security of the Panama Canal to be imperiled. We have a recognized obligation to operate the Canal efficiently and securely. And we intend to honor that obligation in the interests of all who depend on it."[75]

Despite the strong U.S. response, the rioting of 1964 accomplished precisely what the Panamanians hoped it would accomplish. It focused world attention on Panama's claim to sovereignty in the Canal Zone and provided new international forums for its complaints. First, the Organization of American States (OAS) became involved in the conflict. The Inter-American Peace Committee of the OAS convinced the two nations to reestablish diplomatic relations and to commence new talks, while the OAS Council heard Panama's portrayal of the rioting as an "inhuman attack" on defenseless young students by American troops with "war tanks and heavy arms."[76] Next, the National Bar Association of Panama persuaded the International Commission of Jurists to investigate their allegation that the United States had violated the Universal Declaration of Human Rights by attacking a "defenseless . . . civil population." Again, Panama gained an international forum for its emotional complaints against the United States, even though the Jurists exonerated the United States of all formal charges.[77]

Panama's campaign to embarrass the United States, along with its insistence that renewed negotiations focus on relinquishment of U.S. sovereignty in the Canal Zone, prevented any real progress toward settling the dispute. LBJ simply refused to renew negotiations with "preconditions of what they will produce" or under "any kind of pressure with respect to such discussions." Meanwhile, the Panamanians continued to insist that the two nations negotiate a replacement for the 1903 treaty. Eventually LBJ won this battle, as the United States and Panama finally agreed to talks "without limitations or preconditions of any kind." Johnson, in comments following the announcement of the new talks, stressed that it was "very clear, in our agreement, that we would discuss the problems that exist between the two nations, without any precommitments or . . . preconditions."[78]

Although President Johnson eventually won the battle over "preconditions," he surrendered in the long war over sovereignty by the end of the year. On December 18, 1964, Johnson announced on nationwide radio and television that "an entirely new treaty" would be negotiated with Panama—a treaty terminating the 1903 treaty, recognizing Panamanian sovereignty in the Canal Zone, and relinquishing complete control over the canal to the Panamanians on a designated date.[79] On June 26, 1967, the two governments announced agreement on the texts of three new canal treaties. Copies of the draft treaties were not released in the United States, but in July the *Chicago Tribune* published texts of the treaties obtained on the isthmus.[80]

The treaties of 1967 fundamentally reshaped domestic political debate over the Panama Canal. For the first time there was serious debate about relinquishing U.S. sovereignty in the Canal Zone, although the case for doing so remained underdeveloped. One notable American developing that case was the former ambassador to Panama, Joseph S. Farland. As chairman of a panel studying the issue under the auspices of Georgetown University's Center for Strategic Studies, Farland argued that "unsettled Canal issues could . . . lead to further deterioration of relations between the United States and Panama."[81] Joining Farland in developing a rationale for pulling out of Panama was Canal Zone Governor Robert Fleming. In articulating the basic premise behind the "new look," Fleming stressed that the 1903 treaty had become antiquated in the changing international realities of the Cold War era.[82]

Of course, the guardians of the Rooseveltian legacy did not remain silent; indeed, vociferous opposition prevented the 1967 treaties from ever making it to the floor of the Senate. In contrast to the small group beginning to develop a rationale for withdrawal from Panama, the opposition included such large and influential groups as the American Legion, the Daughters of the American Revolution, and the Military Order of the World Wars. The Zonians also developed "grass roots in every one of the fifty states" and pressured lawmakers to oppose the treaties.[83] Meanwhile, an ad hoc group called the American Emergency Committee on the Panama Canal (AECPC) established a Congressional Liaison Committee and circulated "tens of thousands" of petitions opposing the treaties. AECPC, under the leadership of Spruille Braden (former ambassador to Cuba and assistant secretary of state for Latin American affairs), sent out mailings and held conferences to "mobilize and articulate American public opinion."[84]

The rhetoric of treaty opponents, as usual, contained a heavy dose of anticommunism. With the battle cry "Remember what happened to Cuba," treaty opponents called preservation of American sovereignty in the Canal Zone "more vital to this nation than victory in Vietnam." They evoked the domino theory with predictions that "forfeiture of [sovereignty would] . . . trigger communist takeovers of governments in Latin America."[85] In Congress, Daniel Flood proclaimed that the treaties would send Panama "down the Communist drain," while Lenore K. Sullivan, chairman of the Subcommittee on the Panama Canal, observed that it was not "news to anyone that communists are active in Panama!"[86]

Treaty opponents further objected that Panama lacked the skill and political stability to run and defend the canal, and they raised questions about the fate of American military bases in Panama and about the prospect of large toll increases under a Panamanian regime.[87] But perhaps more important than any of these "logical" arguments, many shared Minority Leader Everett Dirksen's anger and frustration over finding the United States in "the amazing position of having a country with one-third the population of Chicago kick us around."[88]

The final blow to prospects for new treaties in the 1960s came with the military coup in Panama in 1968. The uprising deeply distressed Secretary of State Dean Rusk, who cited the removal of a "constitutionally elected chief of state" in breaking diplomatic relations with Panama. Rusk firmly reminded the new government of America's "stake in the stability of the isthmus in view of our presence there as stewards of the vital Panama Canal."[89] But the unspoken fear was that the new leader of Panama, General Omar Torrijos, would turn out to be another Fidel Castro. Not only did Torrijos' penchant for Army fatigues and Cuban cigars raise eyebrows, but his strident anti-American rhetoric offended even proponents of a new treaty. Torrijos praised student protestors and publicly expressed his preference for military dictatorships over constitutional orders. More substantively, he forced the United States to evacuate its giant military base at Rio Hato and summarily rejected the treaties of 1967.[90]

Torrijos fueled the anger of a congressional contingent already strong enough to block any new treaty. The House alone passed 105 resolutions opposing any relinquishment of American sovereignty in the Canal Zone, while in both houses critics of the "new look" were virtually unopposed.[91] Nonetheless, the "new look" did not die when the Johnson administration chose not to submit the 1967 treaties for congressional consideration. The new philosophy continued to animate the State Department, even in two subsequent Republican administrations. Neither Republican administration embraced the philosophy with sufficient dedication to risk a fight with their own conservative constituencies. Neither sought to demonstrate a commitment to the "new look" by making a new treaty with Panama a significant priority. But Jimmy Carter, fresh from his victorious campaign, embraced the "new look" fully and designated a new treaty with Panama a top priority.

Part 2

The "Great Debate"

4

Selling New Canal Treaties

During the presidential campaign of 1976, Jimmy Carter spoke of a humane foreign policy reflecting the values of the American people. Calling for a government as wise and as good as the people, Carter criticized the philosophy and practice of Republican foreign policy and promised a more open, democratic approach. During the second presidential debate he said: "We've lost in our foreign policy the character of the American people. We've ignored or excluded the American people and the Congress from participation in the shaping of our foreign policy."[1] Yet, as president, Carter changed his view. In his first major foreign policy initiative—the Panama Canal treaties—he not only embraced a policy overwhelmingly opposed by the American people but also reneged on his campaign promise to "never give up complete control or practical control of the Panama Canal Zone."[2]

Carter renewed negotiations with Panama almost immediately upon assuming office and made every effort to conclude the talks with an agreement. Next, he tried to "sell" the treaties to a skeptical Senate and a hostile public. Carter's lobbying tactics provoked considerable criticism, as the president resorted to old-time political horsetrading and presidential favors. But

83

even more incongruous with his campaign rhetoric was the massive, sophisticated campaign to sell the treaties to the American people—a campaign involving not only the White House but also dozens of public relations specialists from cabinet departments and from the political, business, and religious establishment.

In sharp contrast with Carter's campaign rhetoric, administration officials spoke of the "great ignorance" and "emotionalism" behind public attitudes on the Panama Canal treaties.[3] Suddenly, "the people" became an enemy to be defeated rather than an oracle to be obeyed. In its "war" against the public, the Carter administration utilized all the weapons of persuasion within the American presidency. The administration mobilized hundreds of advocates, exploited all available media, and executed sophisticated strategies for "selling" the treaties to special-interest constituencies. The Panama campaign involved meticulous planning, audience analyses, and preparation of speeches, questions-and-answers, interview responses, and advertising for use by hundreds of campaigners in local areas. The attempt to sell the Panama Canal treaties displayed the state-of-the-art in campaign strategy and technology. As such, it deserves close scrutiny, regardless of whether it succeeded. (The question of the campaign's success—of whether it significantly altered public opinion and relieved political pressures against ratifying the treaties—shall be reserved for treatment in chapter 8.)

THE NEW TREATIES

Despite the outcry against the Panama Canal treaties of 1967, the American foreign policy bureaucracy did not wait long before again promoting new treaties with Panama. During renewed negotiations in 1971–1972, American diplomats again agreed to cede total jurisdiction over the Canal Zone on a fixed date. But the Nixon administration, in deference to its conservative supporters, demanded that the United States maintain control of the canal for some fifty to eighty years.[4] General Torrijos of Panama regarded the "extension of American jurisdiction beyond the 1903 treaty's centennial as unthinkable," and he responded by publicizing previously confidential details of the negotiations, thereby derailing the talks.[5] Subsequently, Panama hosted a meeting of the U.N. Security Council and embarrassed the United States by persuading thirteen of the Council's fifteen members to support a resolution calling for recognition of Panamanian sovereignty in the Canal Zone.[6]

"The propaganda and political beating administered in the United Nations" transformed controversy over the Panama Canal "from a modest regional matter, which could be safely left in a state of stagnation, into a major priority."[7] With President Nixon distracted by Watergate, Henry Kissinger took the lead in trying to settle the matter. In February 1974 Kissinger visited Panama to sign a joint declaration of eight principles that would govern renewed negotiations. This Kissinger-Tack Agreement on Principles, signed on February 7, called for a treaty with a fixed termination date to replace the "perpetuity" clause of the 1903 treaty. The treaty would relinquish full control over the canal at the termination date, while in the meantime the two nations would share responsibility for operating and defending the canal.[8] Two weeks later Kissinger attended a meeting of foreign ministers from the Western Hemisphere "to collect the plaudits which this earnest of a 'new era' had won."[9]

Back home, however, there were few plaudits for Kissinger. The opposition in Congress immediately organized, and both Houses overwhelmingly passed resolutions opposing the negotiations. Meanwhile, the State Department stuck to a "tactical decision" to avoid campaigning to build support for the negotiations, despite the fact that even Pentagon officials were criticizing the talks. In the spring of 1975 Kissinger finally began speaking in support of the negotiations, but President Ford remained silent, hoping "to protect his conservative flank" in the upcoming presidential campaign.[10]

Then Ronald Reagan "discovered" the Panama Canal issue during the 1976 presidential primaries. Campaigning against President Ford, Reagan charged the administration with secretly negotiating to "give away" the canal. After audiences in New Hampshire and Florida proved enthusiastic, Reagan went on national television on March 31 with his call for an end to negotiations with the "pro-Communist" government of General Torrijos. Reagan articulated the antitreaty maxim that the Canal Zone was "sovereign U.S. territory every bit the same as Alaska and all the states that were carved from the Louisiana Purchase." Reagan's new issue reached full flower during the campaign for the Texas primary in April. While pointing out that President Ford's campaign statements on the issue differed from the principles animating administration negotiators, Reagan left no doubt where he stood: "We should tell Panama's tinhorn dictator just what he can do with his demands for sovereignty over the Canal Zone. We bought it. We paid for it. And they can't have it." When asked on May 2 how far he would go to keep the canal, Reagan responded: "How far would we go to stop someone from taking the State of Alaska?" [11]

The Panamanians seemed determined to aid Reagan's cause throughout the 1976 campaign. By establishing closer ties with Cuba and by threatening to attack the canal,[12] the Panamanians made Reagan's charges of anti-Americanism seem much more credible. Yet Reagan failed to really gain much from the issue, perhaps because his competition also adopted hard-line positions. During the televised presidential debate on foreign policy, President Ford claimed that the United States "must and will maintain complete access to the Panama Canal. The United States must maintain a defense capability of the Panama Canal. And the United States will maintain our national security interest in the Panama Canal." Even the challenger, Jimmy Carter, sounded much like Reagan, speaking in clear defiance of the principles governing the on-going talks: "I would never give up complete control or practical control of the Panama Canal Zone. But I would continue to negotiate with the Panamanians. . . . I believe that we could share more fully responsibilities for the Panama Canal Zone with Panama. . . . But I would not relinquish practical control of the Panama Canal Zone any time in the foreseeable future." [13]

General Torrijos responded to the American campaign rhetoric with additional threats. He seemed particularly incensed with Carter's remarks. "I want to tell Mr. Carter," he said, "that that word 'never' is a word that has been erased from the political dictionary by the struggles of liberation."[14] But Torrijos need not have worried about Carter. Upon assuming the presidency, Carter reversed his position and pledged to resume the negotiations on the basis of the joint statement of principles of 1974.[15] Renewed talks in February proved "inconclusive," but a "breakthrough" came in May, when Panama agreed "to accept a U.S. defense role after the termination of a new treaty" and the United States agreed "to set the year 2000 as the date for termination of the new treaty."[16] The talks subsequently hit another snag over financial arrangements; but on August 10, 1977, negotiators announced agreement "in principle" on two new treaties. Two days later President Carter announced the agreement to White House reporters.[17] The drafting of the treaties began, and by early September they were ready for signing.

The first of the two treaties, labeled the Panama Canal Treaty, acknowledged Panama's sovereignty over all of its territory, terminated all prior treaties, and governed the status of the canal until the turn of the century. Under its provisions, the United States retained the right to operate the canal and to exercise primary responsibility for its defense for the duration of the treaty. Management of the canal would be handled by the Panama Canal Commission, a new U.S. government agency composed of five Americans and four Panamanians. The commission would replace the Panama Canal Company and the Canal Zone government. Throughout the duration of the treaty, Panamanian workers were to be brought into all phases of the canal operation, and Panama was gradually to assume a greater burden in defending the canal. Upon expiration of the treaty, Panama would assume total responsibility for operating the canal. In addition, the treaty governed legal jurisdiction, established employment policies, provided for environmental protection, and committed the two countries to a joint study of a possible sea-level canal. The treaty also gave certain lands to Panama and increased payments to Panama to a fixed sum of $10 million per year plus additional monies from operating revenues.[18]

The second treaty, the Treaty Concerning the Permanent

Neutrality and Operation of the Panama Canal (the neutrality treaty), provided for a permanent regime of neutrality "in order that both in time of peace and in time of war [the canal] shall remain secure and open to peaceful transit by the vessels of all nations on terms of entire equality." In recognition of the contributions of the two nations, the vessels of Panama and the United States were entitled "to transit the Canal expeditiously," and both nations were to be responsible for maintaining the regime of neutrality. After the year 2000, only Panama was to operate the canal or maintain military installations in the area. The treaty provided rules for the regime of neutrality, including stipulations for operating the canal and levying tolls.[19]

President Carter hoped to introduce the new treaties dramatically and to push them through the Senate quickly. He began with an elaborate "Week of Panama" in Washington—a diplomatic extravaganza designed to build support for the treaties. Heads-of-state from all nations of the Western Hemisphere except Cuba witnessed the signing of the treaties and attended an orchestrated series of ceremonies, meetings, and parties.[20] Carter then sought help from Senate Majority Leader Robert Byrd in an effort to immediately begin Senate consideration of the agreement. But two major political problems delayed the debate. First, disagreements between Panamanian and American negotiators over the meaning of two provisions of the neutrality treaty came to light, prompting calls for additional talks to clarify the agreement. Second, the Senate balked at debating treaties so overwhelmingly opposed by the American people. Senate leaders demanded that Carter first take his case for the treaties to the public, hoping that he might shield treaty supporters from political damage.

The first problem—the problem of interpreting the neutrality treaty—was seemingly resolved on October 14, 1977. On that day Carter and Torrijos released a statement of understanding to clarify the interpretation of certain provisions in the neutrality treaty. It said, in part:

> Under the . . . [neutrality treaty], Panama and the United States have the responsibility to assure that the Panama Canal will remain open and secure to ships of all nations. The correct interpretation

of this principle is that each of the two countries shall . . . have the right to act against any aggression or threat directed against the Canal. . . .

This does not mean, nor shall it be interpreted as a right of intervention of the United States in the internal affairs of Panama. Any United States action will be directed at insuring that the Canal will remain open, secure and accessible, and it shall never be directed against the territorial integrity or political independence of Panama.

The Neutrality Treaty provides that the vessels of war and auxiliary vessels of the United States and Panama will be entitled to transit the Canal expeditiously. This is intended, and it shall so be interpreted, to assure the transit of such vessels through the Canal as quickly as possible, without any impediment, with expedited treatment, and in case of need or emergency, to go to the head of the line of vessels, in order to transit the Canal rapidly.[21]

The second problem demanded much more than a single public statement. Because of the State Department's refusal to campaign publicly for new treaties during the negotiations, opposition forces enjoyed a huge head-start in rallying public opinion. With the majority leader predicting "total disaster" if the Senate voted on the treaties with polls showing such widespread opposition,[22] Carter was persuaded to launch his own public relations campaign. But for some time, the administration focused more on lobbying Congress than on courting public opinion. Initially, the administration apparently thought it could secure ratification with direct appeals to uncommitted senators.

CHRISTMAS ON CAPITOL HILL

The Carter administration's lobbying for the Panama Canal treaties began long before the negotiations concluded, as the administration kept key senators informed of major breakthroughs in the talks. In May 1977 the White House's Robert Beckel began lobbying full-time for the Panama treaties, while Douglas J. Bennet, assistant secretary of state for congressional relations, pulled together a group of some thirty State Department liaison and information officers to concentrate exclusively on the issue. In "a meticulous round of briefings," the group concentrated on selected senators, beginning with members of the Foreign Relations Committee. Later they expanded the briefings to include many other senators and the leadership of the House. Treaty negotiators Ellsworth Bunker and Sol Linowitz joined the State Department staff at many of the briefings, as did a Pentagon representative—often George Brown, chairman of the Joint Chiefs of Staff. Within six weeks, about seventy-five senators had participated in at least one briefing and the chances for ratification seemed to improve.[23]

The White House joined more actively in the lobbying effort in August 1977. At that time, White House officials participated in a new round of "intensive, one-on-one" briefings during "a hectic, five-day period."[24] White House congressional liaison officers Robert Thomson and Dan Tate joined Beckel and Bennet in briefing more than forty senators on how to respond to questions on the treaties while back home during the summer adjournment. In addition, a White House task force under Hamilton Jordan sent wires to all 534 members of Congress urging them to keep an open mind on the treaties. President Carter joined in the effort by asking members of Congress not to take public positions before they had a chance to study the documents. Carter personally phoned more than a dozen congressional leaders, while all other members of Congress received letters. Once the administration formally announced the treaties during the congressional adjournment, Bennet's office sent copies of the treaties to all congressional offices. Later, the administration sent all members of Congress various background documents and samples of questions-and-answers on the treaties. They also distributed "fact sheets" and "an elaborate $100 set of maps." Bennet's office then sent new information packets to congressional offices every few days and began answering congressional mail on Panama within twenty-four hours instead of the usual seventy-two-hour turnaround.[25]

The White House took full charge in the final phase of the lobbying effort, and President Carter personally engaged in some old-fashioned horsetrading. Carter apparently won the vote of Senator Herman Talmadge by reversing the administration's position on the senator's bill to pay farmers $2.3 billion for acreage taken out of production. In another bid for a vote, the administration reversed its position on Arizona senator Dennis DeConcini's proposal to buy large amounts of copper for government stockpiles.[26] For those senators without pet policies to bargain with, Carter provided the "royal treatment." The "wooing" of Senator Edward Zorinsky of Nebraska included a personal invitation to a White House state dinner, invitations to the White House for 250 of his Nebraskan friends, tennis with treaty negotiator Sol Linowitz (Zorinsky won), and personal calls and briefings by the president, U.S. trade negotiator Robert Strauss, Secretary of State Cyrus Vance, National Security Advisor Zbigniew Brzezinski, Henry Kissinger, Secretary of the Treasury Michael Blumenthal, Vice President Mondale, Defense Secretary Harold Brown, Hamilton Jordan, and the Roman Catholic archbishop of Omaha, Daniel Sheehan. After Zorinsky still opposed the treaties and declined yet another invitation to the White House, Carter tried the indirect approach—Rosalynn Carter called Zorinsky's wife, Cece. Finally, Zorinsky agreed to one last meeting with the president on the day of the Senate vote on the first treaty. After the meeting, Zorinsky proceeded to Capitol Hill to cast his vote "no."[27]

Not surprisingly, many people criticized the lobbying tactics of the White House. Carter "shed some more of that evangelical sheen," Hugh Sidey wrote, by "orchestrating millions of dollars for a few votes, just like an oldtime pol." According to Sidey, Carter "resorted to shameless application of his Government expense account," as when "first-class limousine service was employed with abandon to cart the doubters up and down Pennsylvania Avenue." Some senators, especially those who risked their political fortunes by supporting the treaties early, reacted angrily. Senator Bob Packwood of Oregon argued that the presidency would be damaged if the "public thinks that the treaties were bought." The president, he said, should not conduct himself like the "master of ceremonies at 'Let's Make a Deal.'"[28] On occasion, Carter's generosity backfired when pro-treaty senators threatened to switch unless they too received

91

favors. Senator James Abourezk even threatened to oppose the treaties because he was unhappy with the administration's handling of policies regulating natural gas.[29] Most important, the strategy of "Christmas on Capitol Hill" expended much of the president's political capital. After the debate over Panama, Carter retained little to bargain with in future battles on Capitol Hill.[30]

Nonetheless, the lobbying campaign apparently did have some impact. The prospects for ratification, which seemed remote when Carter assumed office, improved considerably during the lobbying campaign. The campaign convinced some senators that the treaties should be ratified despite hostile constituencies. But others remained reluctant and continued to demand that the administration reshape public opinion on the treaties.

"Educating" the Public

The Carter administration's campaign to sell the Panama Canal treaties to the American people constituted, in effect, an indirect method of lobbying the Senate. With all the New Right's talk of "punishing" protreaty lawmakers at the polls, many senators remained reluctant to vote for the agreement as long as public opinion appeared so overwhelmingly opposed to it. As presidential aide Hamilton Jordan indiscreetly observed of the Senate, "some of those bastards don't have the spine not to vote their mail. If you change their mail, you change their minds."[31]

The State Department took the lead in the administration's campaign to change public opinion. State Department officials prepared and distributed statements and "fact sheets" and instituted a speaker's bureau specifically to promote the treaties. They reportedly charted the whole effort in "one of the most closely held, limited circulation documents in the State Department"—a weekly report known as the PITS, or the Panama Information Track Score. Complete with a "chatty column" of "weekly highlights" and "box scores," PITS tallied a total of 864 scheduled appearances by administration speakers as of the middle of February 1978—476 live speeches or debates with treaty opponents and 388 media interviews. PITS speakers addressed groups ranging from senior citizens in Miami, to the Arizona State Legislature, to Boy Scouts in Pennsylvania. Among the more than a dozen PITS speakers were Terence Todman, assistant secretary of state for Latin American affairs, treaty negotiator Ellsworth Bunker, and Gale McGee, U.S. representative to the Organization of American States. Between the signing of the treaties in September 1977 and February 1978, McGee alone appeared more than one hundred times in twenty-two states from the Deep South to the Far West.[32]

The State Department headquartered the PITS program in the Latin America Bureau's Office of Policy, Public Affairs and Congressional Relations. After nearly a year of planning and executing a strategy involving speakers and the dissemination of publications, the office resembled "a Pentagon war room," complete with charts and pinboards for each targeted state. Two full-time staff members and various part-time staffers handled a range of activities, beginning with sophisticated "market analyses" and studies of voting patterns of senators on "related types of issues." They also studied editorials from around the country, along with the level of public interest in Latin American affairs. The strategists then analyzed media markets to determine the best ways to disseminate their message in various locales, particularly in those states with senators predicted to remain undecided until the last moment. Then the office began training sessions for its speakers, replete with videotape practice sessions and lectures on audience psychology. Finally, the speakers were armed with six standard treaty speeches (including ones emphasizing military issues, commerce and business, Latin American relations, and "myths and realities" about the treaties) and sent on their missions to face specially targeted audiences.[33]

The efforts of the State Department, while extensive, constituted only one phase of a larger campaign centered in the White House and planned by Hamilton Jordan. In June 1977 Jordan drafted a twelve-page memorandum proposing a massive "educational" campaign on behalf of the treaties. He then conducted a series of strategy sessions which defined and coordinated not only the efforts of the State Department but also activities by officials of the National Security Council, the Departments of Defense and Commerce, and even the president himself.[34]

The White House played a significant role in Jordan's master plan as the setting for a series of some nineteen day-long briefings for more than fifteen hundred selected "opinion leaders" from around the country. In a "trickle down" strategy for persuading the public, the administration used the briefings to urge local community leaders to become advocates of the cause. The briefings were coordinated by Betty Rainwater, Jordan's deputy assistant for research, and as Ken Bode observed, they were "not run by second stringers." At each of the briefings the invitees heard from the president, Zbigniew Brzezinski, and George S. Brown, chairman of the Joint Chiefs of Staff. One of the two treaty negotiators, either Ellsworth Bunker or Sol Linowitz, would provide the basic protreaty case at each of the briefings.[35]

Participants in the White House briefings included local elected officials, educators, newspaper editors, heads of political organizations, labor leaders, and other influential people from some thirty states. The White House based the invitations on lists submitted by its own Congressional Liaison Office and by the Democratic National Committee. Protreaty senators hoping to minimize political damage back home apparently suggested many of the names. A typical group attended on September 21, when North Carolina and Tennessee were the targeted states. The seventy-eight invitees included Billy Ray Cameron, former commander of the North Carolina VFW; Frank Daniels, publisher of the *Raleigh News and Observer*; Wilbur Hobby, president of the North Carolina AFL-CIO and former candidate for governor; Tennessee governor Ray Blanton, a Democrat; former Tennessee governor Winfield Dunn, a Republican; Dr. H. Franklin Paschall, pastor of the First Baptist Church of Nashville; and Maxine Smith, executive secretary of the Memphis NAACP. In some cases the briefings also served to prepare groups for "citizens' fact-finding missions" to Panama. One such mission, sponsored by the National Committee on American Foreign Policy, included former top executives of CBS and NBC, a variety of other journalists, former and aspiring members of Congress, and leaders of Freedom House and the Appeal of Conscience Foundation. The White House strongly encouraged such missions because Panama's "genial despot," Omar Torrijos, proved a charming and persuasive spokesman for the treaties.[36]

In addition to the White House briefings, Jordan's strategy for selling the canal treaties included a series of activities featuring the president. Carter held a series of six "town meetings" in cities such as Riverside, California, and Springfield, Massachusetts. In January 1978 Carter also addressed local groups in New Mexico and Mississippi via special telephone hook-ups. On February 1 he devoted his second "fireside chat" to building support for the treaties. In another attempt to recruit local advocates, Carter sent letters to three thousand professional and business leaders asking them to "help us lay the facts before the public." In all, Carter officially devoted more than fifty presidential hours to selling the Panama treaties, along with untold hours of unofficial time. On one occasion, he even interrupted an important meeting with Israeli foreign minister Moshe Dayan to brief a group of private citizens on the treaties.[37]

The Iranian crisis and other problems could not yet be envisioned, but after his first year in office it could be said of Carter's efforts to sell the Panama treaties that there was "no other single foreign policy issue that, politically, consumed more of his time."[38] Yet Carter's public appearances accounted for only a few of the hundreds of appearances by administration spokesmen. Moreover, the administration's campaign itself constituted only one facet of a larger campaign promoting the treaties. A broad range of individuals and groups aided the administration in its efforts to sell the Panama Canal treaties.

COACT: The Semi-Official Ally

One of the most important allies in the administration's Panama campaign was a group called the Committee of Americans for the Canal Treaties (COACT). With Averell Harriman and Hugh Scott as its most recognizable leaders, this group emerged from a suggestion at a White House meeting on September 7 (the day the treaties were signed) that a "citizens' committee" be formed to conduct "an educational program supporting ratification."[39] COACT eventually boasted a roster that included former president Gerald Ford, Mrs. Lyndon B. Johnson, George Meany, Vernon Jordan, Henry Cabot Lodge, David Rockefeller, Nelson Rockefeller, Dean Rusk, Arthur Schlesinger, Jr., Theodore Sorensen, Stuart Symington, General Maxwell Taylor, Admiral Elmo Zumwalt, and even Theodore Roosevelt, IV. The committee, according to a spokesman, maintained only "loose cooperation" with the White House and was "totally independent" in its operations.[40]

In reality, however, COACT maintained close ties to the White House and served, in effect, as a tool for circumventing political and legal impediments to campaigning by government officials. Through Landon Butler, an aide to Hamilton Jordan, COACT coordinated its activities with the administration campaign, and many of its appeals depended entirely upon its White House connection—sometimes in rather questionable ways. One COACT fund-raising letter promised a reception at the home of President Carter's chief trade negotiator, Robert S. Strauss, and a dinner at the White House for anyone who raised or donated fifteen thousand dollars or more. COACT's status as a technically independent group also allowed it to advertise and to distribute campaign materials prepared by the administration with funds solicited from such corporations as Braniff Airways, Occidental Petroleum, and others doing business in Latin America.[41] While administration officials worried about violating a 1926 criminal statute prohibiting the use of appropriated funds to influence a vote of Congress, COACT distributed protreaty materials, even at White House briefings, without fear of legal or political repercussions.[42]

COACT's major product was a 140-page handbook and "how-to" kit distributed at White House briefings. Designed to aid local "opinion leaders" in conducting their own local campaigns, the handbook reflected the White House's effort to maximize the return on campaign expenditures by recruiting an army of advocates at the grass-roots level. COACT supplied a comprehensive set of instructions and materials for the local campaigner; its handbook provided everything needed for advertising, free publicity, and local meetings and rallies in support of the treaties. It encouraged supporters to "take an active role in disseminating the information."[43]

For protreaty public speaking by local supporters the COACT handbook provided a sample speech, apparently prepared by the State Department, in both outline form and as a complete text. It advised supporters to seek invitations for presenting the speech from local clubs and organizations like the Chamber of Commerce, Kiwanis, Lions, Rotary, Elks, and the PTA. In a note on the "content and use" of the speech, COACT advised:

> This speech is intended for a heterogeneous audience of citizens representing no particular interest constituency. It is tailored for a situation in which the format calls specifically for a presentation on the Panama issue, without further limitation. The presumption is that most of the members of the audience have not been previously briefed on the treaties.
>
> This is a basic presentation summarizing what we hold to be the key points in the positive brief for the treaties. A speaker would have to be prepared to answer further questions on the details of matters raised in the speech, or other related issues not raised, and on key points often raised by opposition forces but not sufficiently relevant to the real issues to address in the prepared remarks.

In preparing the supporter for questions, the handbook provided answers for thirty-five common questions grouped in such categories as "defense" and "economic provisions." The kit also provided a handy collection of statements by notable persons and groups (including General George S. Brown, Senate Majority Leader Robert Byrd, George Meany, Benjamin Hooks of the NAACP, William F. Buckley, Jr., John Wayne, the National Council of Churches, and the National Women's Political Caucus) so that the speaker could select credible testimony for use before virtually any audience.[44]

The COACT handbook's treatment of advertising was equally detailed and comprehensive, providing instructions and materials for advertising on a variety of media. It provided sample copy for advertising in newspapers, complete with five possible headlines. One headline emphasized a common analogy to Vietnam: "Let's Not Make the Canal Zone Another DMZ Zone!" Others used slogans associated with Theodore Roosevelt: "America: Speak Softly but Carry a Big Stick," and "Bully for America? Or America, the Bully?" A fourth headline emphasized the need to maintain harmony in U.S.–Latin American relations: "Vote Down the Panama Canal Treaty and We Might as Well Kiss Our Good Neighbors Goodbye." And the final headline attacked the antitreaty characterization of the agreement as a "giveaway": "The Panama Canal Treaty is not a Giveaway, It's a Give Back." [45]

For advertising on the electronic media, the handbook provided a complete package of twenty-three prepared radio and television announcements in sixty-, fifty-, forty-five-, and thirty-second formats. Each ad centered around a statement by a noteworthy supporter of the treaties and was printed on a separate, perforated page which could be removed from the kit and sent directly to stations. COACT noted that the ads were "prepared for voice delivery" but could be "embellished with music and sound" on radio or "adapted for video if the television station will add visual matter." COACT urged supporters to try to convince stations to air the spots free as public service announcements or, more realistically, to "try to find a business sponsor who would donate air time for this purpose." [46]

Elsewhere in its handbook COACT described a variety of techniques for generating free protreaty publicity in local media. "In almost every community in the United States," the handbook stated, radio and television stations have interview or talk programs which "welcome guests and usually appreciate the offer of participation." It suggested that supporters "contact the manager, program director, or news director of the local station" and offer to appear, but only after absorbing "enough of the information to make an educated presentation." If no such program existed, or if supporters did not want "to appear personally on a program," COACT urged them "at the least" to "find a telephone/talk program at one or more of your local stations, call in and open a discussion about the Treaties, offering your positive position." COACT also touted letters-to-the-editor and Op-Ed columns as means of free publicity and provided samples of each. Concerning its sample letter-to-the-editor COACT advised: "You can, of course, modify it to suit your own style and thinking. Use this method with some prior thought. Should there be an article in the newspaper taking the other position, or should there be an editorial for or against the Treaties, or should there be some national movement in either direction covered by the newspaper, your Letter-to-the-Editor will stand a fairly good chance of being published." Along with its sample Op-Ed column the handbook also provided an explanation: "This is something reasonably new with newspapers. Usually the Op-Ed column will appear either on the editorial page or next to it. This is a means by which a citizen can have an editorial printed in the newspaper. Obviously, even if the newspaper carried one Op-Ed column a day, only a small portion of those submitted will be carried. However, with the Panama Canal Treaties so hot an issue, you stand a better possibility. . . . Again, feel free to modify [the sample] to suit your own style."[47]

COACT's expectations for campaigns by local supporters rose to seemingly ridiculous levels in a final lesson: how to conduct protreaty rallies and local versions of the White House briefings. In advice that one suspects few supporters followed, COACT recommended that protreaty rallies be conducted in local shopping centers because they had become "the equivalent of the Town Square of years ago." COACT urged that the rallies be "tastefully done with appropriate signage and some hand-out material," yet at the same time it suggested using one's "imagination" to come up with "gimmicks" to "attract attention." COACT itself recommended several such "gimmicks": "relief maps of the Canal Zone area, photographs of the area, attractive people to man the display," and the ever tasteful "high-school band" putting on "a patriotic concert." For local versions of the White House briefings, COACT urged supporters to persuade "one or more leading figures in the community" to "make his or her home available for some sort of reception, luncheon or dinner." On the purpose and methods for conducting the briefings, COACT explained: "There can be a four-fold purpose to such meetings: dissemination of information, fund raising, further exposure of the positive side, and the generation of letters to senators. The meetings are easy to orchestrate. All it takes is the catalyst in the person who will host. You can serve as the briefer, or, if the event warrants, we will do our best to supply one. We can assist with hand-out material if we are given sufficient notice. There should be hand-out material so the participants carry something away." The money raised at such briefings, the handbook judiciously advised, could either be "diverted to COACT for use in national advertising or . . . retained."[48]

Finally, the COACT handbook pleaded for supporters to contact their congressmen to help counter the flood of anti-treaty mail generated by the New Right's campaign. COACT admitted that senators had been "inundated with mail against ratification" but insisted that most of the mail had not been "of an individualized nature"; it consisted of "mass produced letters which are all the same and a great number of post cards." A "personal letter" would have "much more impact," COACT suggested, and the group also recommended other personal means for contacting one's lawmakers. It suggested that Western Union "Public Opinion" telegrams were a bargain at only $2.00 for fifteen words or less, and it noted that one could order a Western Union "Mailgram" by phone for only $2.75 for a hundred words or less. Finally, COACT suggested that supporters might call their senators directly and provided the office phone number for every member of the U.S. Senate.[49]

COACT had high expectations at the outset. But the group ultimately raised only $350,000 of a projected $1 million and could not afford to implement much of its plan for media campaigning. COACT did sponsor some newspaper advertising and some three hundred thousand pieces of direct-mail. But even George Moffett, III, COACT's former research director, admits that it never proved "effective" and never generated "a broad political base."[50] In the end, COACT's impressive list of "establishment" supporters, combined with its apparently min-

imal impact at the grass-roots level, did little more than re-
inforce the impression that powerful elites and "the people"
disagreed fundamentally about the Panama Canal treaties.

BUSINESS AND RELIGIOUS ALLIES

The resources available to the White House for shaping
public opinion extend well beyond the president's instant access
to the media and to the various governmental offices of public
relations. As shown by the formation of COACT, the president
also can use the prestige of his office to entice private citizens to
campaign on behalf of the administration's initiatives. In addition, the president may persuade special interest groups to
lend their influence and their established machinery of public
relations to an administration cause. This is perhaps the most
valuable resource of a sitting administration, for not only do
special interest groups have experience and ongoing programs
of public relations, but they also have great credibility within
large, permanent constituencies.

Two categories of special interest groups played major roles
in the Carter administration's Panama campaign: business
groups and religious organizations. These two types of special
interest groups were potentially very valuable, not only because of their campaign resources, but also because they could
speak with special expertise in two areas of heated controversy
in the debate over Panama. Business groups proved useful allies
when debate focused on the economics of the treaties. When
critics of the treaties predicted that the agreement would fuel
inflation or disrupt America's international trade, the administration could trot out leaders of major international trade
associations or multinational corporations to refute the accusations. Meanwhile, the religious groups led the moral indictment of America's history in Panama, emphasizing America's alleged "colonialism" or "imperialism" in Panama.

The Commerce Department led the administration's re-
cruitment of business support for the Panama treaties, and the

effort initially met with considerable success. Individual business executives flooded Capitol Hill with "testimonial letters" solicited by the administration, and by September 1977 the list of endorsements was impressive: Max M. Fisher, chairman of United Brands (Panama's largest corporate taxpayer); Howard L. Clark, chairman of American Express; Richard M. Furland, chairman of Squibb Corporation; John W. Brooks, chairman of Celanese Corporation; James H. Evans, chairman of Union Pacific; and Robert O. Anderson, chairman of Atlantic Richfield.[51]

The White House also counted on support from a number of business organizations. An ad hoc group called the Business and Professional Committee for a New Panama Canal Treaty was formed at the invitation of the State Department and Senator Gale McGee. It included representatives from more than two dozen U.S. multinational corporations. Convening at the State Department in the fall of 1975, the group mapped strategy for congressional lobbying and for a public relations campaign. The group also agreed on an initial operating budget of a half million dollars. Corporations supporting the effort included Kodak, Chase Manhattan Bank, Bankers Trust, Gulf, and Shell. However, the Business and Professional Committee for a new Panama Canal Treaty disbanded soon after its founding, apparently because its chief organizer, former Commerce Department official Richard Eisenmann, had a change of heart. Testifying before the Foreign Relations Committee in October 1977, Eisenmann claimed that he had been "misled" into supporting the treaties and condemned the agreement for perpetuating the "brutal rule of one of the most corrupt and arbitrary dictatorships in Latin America."[52]

The administration had similar luck with several standing business organizations, including the Business Roundtable, the National Association of Manufacturers (NAM), and the Chamber of Commerce. The leaders of both the Roundtable and the NAM were early "personal advocates" of the treaties and both campaigned for formal resolutions of support from their organizations. The leadership of the Chamber of Commerce also endorsed a new treaty early in the controversy, with its directors voting in 1975 to support renegotiation of the 1903 pact.[53] But

102

again, the early support of each group withered as rank-and-file members rebelled against their leaders. Both the Roundtable and the NAM failed to pass resolutions supporting the treaties, and the Chamber of Commerce backed off from its early support after polls of its membership revealed overwhelming opposition to a resolution of endorsement.[54]

These problems ultimately left organized business support for the treaties to the Council of the Americas—an organization composed of over two hundred major corporations accounting for about 90 percent of all U.S. private investment in Latin America and the Caribbean. In January 1978 the administration courted the group by inviting its board of trustees and staff to a meeting in the Cabinet Room of the White House with President Carter, Zbigniew Brzezinski, Ambassador Bunker, and Dr. Robert Pastor of the National Security Council. The Council of the America's support for new treaties, however, began long before this meeting. In January 1977 the group wrote to each U.S. senator requesting that any resolution which might derail the negotiations be rejected. They further established a Work Group on Panama consisting of forty-five senior executives to counter the early efforts of antitreaty groups. The Work Group published six thousand copies of a thirty-six-page pamphlet entitled *United States, Panama, and the Panama Canal: A Guide to the Issues*, which it distributed to six thousand national, state, and local organizations, as well as to the council's membership and to U.S. senators. The group also sent a shorter statement supporting the treaties to twenty-five hundred corporate executives around the country. In addition, it monitored the activities of opponents of the treaties and compiled a list of twenty antitreaty organizations. The Work Group carefully limited its strategy to meeting with key senators, testifying before the Senate Foreign Relations Committee, and persuading "opinion leaders." Both the White House and the Council of the Americas believed that the political clout of business could be crucial in the campaign, but they feared creating the public perception that the treaties were "written by Wall Street" for the benefit of big business.[55]

Organized religious groups were also very active in debate

over the Panama Canal treaties. As early as October 1974, General Torrijos hosted a special thirty-seven member ecumenical group in a "citizens' fact-finding mission" to Panama. In the fall of 1977, seventy-five Protestant, Catholic, and Jewish representatives attended their own White House briefing.[56] Religious leaders followed these events with countless resolutions and publications supporting the treaties. The administration praised the religious groups for their political involvement, as when Ambassador Andrew Young spoke before the semiannual meeting of the National Council of Churches Governing Board in November 1977. After the group passed a resolution supporting the treaties, Young proclaimed that "nothing really gets done until the churches get behind it. . . . What you are doing is crucial." Later, President Carter sent a personal letter to National Council president William P. Thompson thanking him for the group's support.[57]

The administration's gratitude was understandable. Even before the White House began its own campaign, the religious community had projected "through its official leadership a remarkable unanimity in support of the treaties." According to James Wall, the Panama treaties became for the church leaders "one of those national issues that challenge the capacity of our religious institutions to sway public opinion, both within and outside their own constituencies."[58] Not since the Civil Rights movement had the churches been so involved in a national political cause.

The National Council of Churches (NCC), consisting of thirty Protestant and Orthodox denominations, began its pro-treaty campaign in October 1975 when its governing board adopted a protreaty resolution and urged member churches to "undertake educational programs concerning the urgent need for a new relationship" with Panama. The NCC also encouraged member churches to "send delegations to the Republic of Panama to discuss with appropriate groups there the present reality and their hopes for the future, for the purpose of increased awareness and informed action within the churches."[59] In April 1976 the NCC sent its own delegation to Panama. This delegation issued a statement calling for a new treaty to rectify the "serious injustice" of the existing situation and to improve relations with Latin America and the rest of the world. Calling "the struggle of the Republic of Panama and its people to assert sovereignty" a "struggle against colonialism and its inherent racist oppression," the statement also argued that "U.S. churches have a responsibility to inform and educate their constituencies about the facts concerning U.S. involvement in Panama so that they may take appropriate actions as aware Christian citizens."[60] In 1977 the NCC Executive Committee approved a resolution commending the new Panama Canal treaties and urging the U.S. Senate "to ratify them at an early date." Council president William Thompson capped off the NCC's two year campaign by testifying before the Senate Foreign Relations Committee in mid-October 1977.[61]

The United States Catholic Conference (USCC), claiming the allegiance of some 330 bishops and their fifty million followers, also campaigned long and vigorously for new Panama Canal treaties. As early as February 1975 the administrative board of the USCC adopted a resolution supporting the concept of a new treaty relinquishing control over the canal and saying that a "new and more just treaty" was "a moral imperative—a matter of elemental social justice."[62] In November 1976 the USCC, at its general meeting of bishops, adopted a second statement calling for a new treaty to dissolve "the vestiges of a relationship which more closely resembles the 19th century, than the realities of an interdependent world of sovereign and equal states."[63] The USCC reprinted these two statements in a number of publications and they formed the basis of testimony by John Cardinal Krol, archbishop of Philadelphia, before the Senate Foreign Relations Committee on October 12, 1977.[64] The USCC also sponsored various publications supporting the treaties, including articles in its magazine, *Origins*, and a collection of protreaty materials entitled *The Panama Canal and Social Justice*. In addition to various statements by the USCC, the NCC, and individual church leaders, *The Panama Canal and Social Justice* contained a one-act play critical of the history of U.S.

105

involvement in Panama and a guide for conducting community discussion groups on the Panama issue with an emphasis on biblical themes.[65]

Both the NCC and the USCC financed a more strident campaign against American involvement in Panama conducted by two special interest groups—the Washington Office on Latin America and the Ecumenical Program for Inter-American Communication and Action (EPICA). Established in May 1974 and expanded in January 1975, the Washington Office on Latin America published a regular bulletin and a "Special Update on Panama." It also claimed to inform "Congressional and other government personnel of the churches' concerns for human rights and social justice where U.S. aid to Latin America is concerned."[66] EPICA developed a multi-faceted campaign of community "education and mobilization" against American "colonialism" in Panama. Among EPICA's projects were a single-page flyer headlined "Six Myths About Panama," a slide show on Panama, and a brochure entitled "Americans on a Solidarity Visit to Panama." EPICA's more substantial publications included a 127-page collection of articles, poems, and other materials, most by Panamanian leftists, entitled *Panama: Sovereignty for a Land Divided*, and a "special-issue pamphlet" of twenty-two pages called *Treaty for Us, Treaty for Them*. The latter publication, according to an advertising flyer, did not "pretend to have all the answers" but merely presented "two penetrating, clarifying analyses of the Panama Canal treaties—one from a North American perspective, the other from a Panamanian point of view."[67]

Available from either EPICA or the Washington Office on Latin America was a package containing an "Action Memo on the New Canal Treaty," along with an "educational primer" entitled "Uniting Panama: A New Canal Treaty." A "mobilizing packet," including a primer entitled "Panama's Struggle for Independence," could also be obtained from either group. In addition to miscellaneous articles and documents, these "community mobilization" packets included advice on how to organize popular support and how to approach key legislators. Finally, EPICA established a National Committee for Panamanian Solidarity—an outreach program designed to establish affiliated local groups across the United States.[68]

While the official rhetoric of the NCC and the USCC echoed the moderate tone of the Carter administration, EPICA spoke the language of self-proclaimed leftist "revolutionaries." In *Treaty for Us, Treaty for Them*, the Reverend Philip Wheaton, EPICA's director, actually attacked the new treaties, claiming that they would be "good *for us,* which is precisely the problem with the Treaty of 1903 and the colonial environment of the Panama Canal Zone: good for some Americans but extremely prejudicial to the Panamanian people." According to Wheaton's analysis, "all the arguments for or against the Treaties" were "upper class reasons." He called for a "critical analysis," pointing out how the new treaties would in fact "create a *neo-colonial relationship* advantageous to the United States." Instead of endorsing the treaties he called for a continued "solidarity commitment with the Panamanian people in their historic and legitimate struggle to regain full sovereignty over the Canal Zone."[69]

Similarly, EPICA's *Panama: Sovereignty for a Land Divided* told the "true" history of America's abominations in Panama—a history seemingly planned by "Satan and his imposters." In shrill "revolutionary" poetry translated from Panamanian sources and in revisionist historiography, EPICA'S major publication on the treaties convicted the "gringos" of crimes ranging from "the slaughter and exploitation of [Panama's] people" to crossing "the sidewalk of the nearby zone line to take [its] women."[70] The NCC and the USCC did not publicize their financial support for EPICA, of course. Most churchgoers remained unaware that American collection plates supported EPICA's crusade against American "colonialism" until the CBS News magazine *Sixty Minutes* exposed the group's political activities in 1983.[71]

Among other, less inflammatory protreaty religious groups, the Synagogue Council of America, representing the three branches of American Judaism and more than four million American Jews, sent a statement to all its members deeming the Panama treaties "in the best interest of the United States and far-sighted in terms of our relations with other nations."[72] The Church of the Brethren, representing some one thousand Protestant congregations, announced at its 1976 annual conference an "educational program" called "In Support of a New Relationship with Panama" and sent out several hundred "study packets" to member churches.[73] The Christian Church (Disciples of Christ) used resolutions and its newspaper to urge its congregations to "undertake educational programs concerning the urgent needs for new Treaties with Panama" and to "inform . . . elected officials of their support for the Treaties."[74] Undoubtedly the most unorthodox religious support for the treaties, however, came from one of the country's top gospel disk jockeys, the Reverend J. Bazell Mull of Knoxville, Tennessee. The sixty-three-year-old Mull showed his appreciation for an invitation to a White House briefing by airing the protreaty case nationwide on (among other outlets) the 150,000-watt, clear-channel AM station, WWL in New Orleans. Interrupting his programs of gospel music, Mull delivered the protreaty case with evangelical fervor, and he personally tried to persuade Senator Howard Baker to support the agreement. Not since his fight against the repeal of Prohibition had Mull become so involved in a national political controversy.[75]

POLITICAL ALLIES

In addition to help from COACT and from the business and religious establishments, the Carter administration benefited from protreaty campaigns by a variety of other individuals and organizations. Some of these supporters promoted ratification for obvious political reasons, while others had only a vague ideological affinity for Carter's "new" approach to Latin American policy. Whatever their motivation, several of these efforts deserve mention because of their special contributions and because they illustrate the range of interests involved in the protreaty effort.

Undoubtedly the most significant political ally of the Carter administration was a group called the Commission on

United States–Latin American Relations. Boasting a roster of over twenty prominent businessmen, academicians, media figures, and lawyers, this group contributed significantly to the intellectual substance of the protreaty cause with elaborate reports on the need for change in America's "basic approach to Latin America and the Caribbean" and with other presumably nonpartisan efforts to "build understanding in the United States of the other nations in the Western Hemisphere." Treaty negotiator Sol Linowitz chaired the commission, and it was founded and sponsored by the Center for Inter-American Relations—a "nonprofit, tax-exempt, membership corporation financed by foundation grants, membership dues, individual and corporate contributions." Funding for the commission came from the Ford Foundation, the Rockefeller Brothers Fund, and the Clark Foundation. The Center for Inter-American Relations claimed that the center's "fundamental aim" was to provide forums "for those concerned with political, social, and economic activity in the Americas," but it definitely limited its definition of "those concerned" to proponents of new treaties with Panama—the "most urgent issue" in U.S.–Latin American relations. In its 1975 report the commission "strongly [supported] the signing and ratification of a new Panama Canal treaty based on the Statement of Principles" of 1974.[76]

The Panamanian government, of course, was another political entity concerned with promoting the treaties, although it strived to conceal its involvement in the American political debate. Instead of directly participating, the Panamanians hired a New York public relations firm called Public Affairs Analysts to make its case. The agency, headed by former presidential campaign aides of Senators Barry Goldwater and Hubert Humphrey, began working for the treaties in January 1977. After six months, Panama's bill totaled an estimated $150,000 to $200,000. Like the White House, Public Affairs Analysts focused on selected "opinion leaders" rather than on public opinion. The firm sent "thick, neatly arranged packets of pro-treaty material" to six thousand influential politicians, journalists, academicians, and business people. In addition, it monitored the activities of various groups opposing the treaties. Public Affairs Analysts did not directly lobby senators and they denied that they engaged in "propaganda" activities. The Panamanian government hoped to avoid accusations of meddling in American political affairs— a concern that prompted the Panamanians to reject earlier proposals by American firms for a national billboard campaign and full-page newspaper ads headlined "Isn't It Time for Uncle Sam to Ante Up?"[77]

Other groups campaigned for ratification of the Panama Canal treaties simply because they symbolized—as they did for New Right opponents—a particular philosophy of foreign affairs. A self-professed "citizen's lobby" called New Directions supported the treaties as part of its effort to become a permanent foreign policy organization based on the model of Common Cause. Founded in 1976, New Directions enlisted support from a number of standing organizations like the AFL-CIO, the Democratic National Committee, the United Auto Workers, the Americans for Democratic Action, and the Washington Office on Latin America. Its task force, called the Committee for Ratification of the Panama Canal Treaties, printed a booklet about the treaties and paid travel expenses for field organizers dispatched by member organizations to rally support in a dozen targeted states. New Directions also sent out over one million letters to "known liberals" like the members of Common Cause. The letter, signed by New Directions chairman Margaret Mead, was accompanied by a handsome brochure listing "myths and facts" about the Panama Canal. Copying a technique of New Right direct-mail experts, New Directions enclosed postcards to be sent to members of the Senate and urged readers to send money to "help make the voice of reason and responsibility heard." The group quickly learned, however, that few Americans would rally to liberal causes out of support for the treaties. Instead of building its support with the Panama campaign, New Directions collapsed under the financial burden of its direct-mail effort.[78]

Farther to the left and more ideologically dogmatic than New Directions was a group called the U.S. Committee for Panamanian Sovereignty (USCPS). This organization, which emerged out of a visit to Panama by a group of forty "North

American anti-imperialists" in 1975, became a "clearing house for information on Panama" and distributed slide shows, films, buttons, and a variety of printed material proclaiming "solidarity with the Panamanian people's struggle." Through its "educational campaign," national speaker's bureau, and local chapters, USCPS claimed to unite oppressed "working people" in the United States with others involved in the world-wide "struggle against imperialism." In fact, USCPS appealed primarily to leftist academicians and other elites. In a letter to "specialists in Latin American studies," Professors E. Bradford Burns (Latin American history, UCLA) and Sheldon B. Liss (Latin American history, University of Akron) urged "lobbying with elected officials, lecturing in your local communities or nationally, imparting your knowledge to local media, and . . . encouraging your students to understand the Panama situation and to discuss it with others." The professors called on their colleagues to correct the mistaken impressions left by "politicians and organizations" with "little concern for the people of Panama, scant knowledge of the situation, and a mistaken understanding of the broader interests of the U.S. people."[79]

Some of the remaining organizations aiding the protreaty cause of the Carter administration came from the ranks of organized labor. Labor groups endorsing the treaties or engaging in some other protreaty activities included the AFL-CIO, the Communication Workers of America, the American Federation of State, County and Municipal Employees, and the United Auto Workers. Additional support came from ethnic organizations, including the NAACP, the National Conference of Black Mayors, the Mexican-American Legal Defense Educational Fund, the League of United Latin American Citizens, the National Council of La Raza, and El Congreso Nacional De Asuntos Colegiales. Other standing organizations supporting the treaties included the American Friends' Service Committee, the Sierra Club, the National Women's Political Caucus, the New Democratic Coalition, the American GI Forum, the Americans for Democratic Action, the American Jaycees, and the Democratic National Committee. Foreign policy interest groups like the Coalition for a New Foreign and Military Policy and the

Council on Hemispheric Affairs also endorsed the treaties. Of course dozens of major media editorialized in support of the treaties, and innumerable politicians, military leaders, academicians, and other influential individuals supported the protreaty cause. Among the most cherished of these individual supporters were the prominent "defectors" from the right: columnist William F. Buckley and actor John Wayne. COACT mentioned Buckley and Wayne to refute charges that only "bleeding hearts" supported the treaties, while General Torrijos poked fun at Ronald Reagan by claiming that Wayne was the better actor.[80]

With all the resources of the presidency and its broad range of allies, the Carter administration seemed well-equipped to shape public opinion on the Panama Canal treaties. But the administration got a late start in campaigning, and many early supporters in business, religion, and politics proved less devoted to the cause as the debate progressed. Furthermore, the administration and its allies focused more on shaping elite opinion than on public opinion at the grass-roots level. Protreaty advocates presumed that "opinion leaders" would carry their message to the public at large. But intellectual agreement may not motivate people to take action. Few "opinion leaders" seemed sufficiently inspired by the protreaty case to devote time and money to the cause, and many seemed unwilling to risk confrontations with already hostile constituencies.

The administration often portrayed the "emotionalism" of the opposition as a vulnerability; they argued that the "facts" of their case would change antitreaty opinions grounded in fear or national chauvinism. Yet emotionalism is also a motivator, and neither administration advocates nor many of their allies seemed particularly aroused over the need for a new agreement with Panama. Moreover, the protreaty claim to a monopoly on the "facts" should be recognized as a dubious and self-serving rhetorical ploy. The administration's claim to superior logic is not necessarily sustained by analysis of the arguments in the debate.

The most obvious obstacle to the success of the protreaty campaign, however, was the formidable opposition campaign conducted by the New Right. In the contest for public opinion on the Panama Canal treaties, the New Right demonstrated the ability to campaign effectively on an issue it holds dear. It became clear during the debate that there was indeed something new about the New Right: its ability to make a difference.

5

The New Right's Crusade

American conservatives greeted President Carter's effort to relinquish the Panama Canal with mixed emotions. They opposed the treaties, of course. For many conservatives the Panama Canal is the preeminent symbol of a lost era of American international greatness, and they think that the waterway still has great economic and military value. But many conservatives, particularly the "neo-populists" of the so-called New Right,[1] welcomed Carter's initiative as a political opportunity. With an eye on polls showing overwhelming public opposition to relinquishing the canal, they believed that they could exploit the issue to build their popular support. They envisioned the dawning of a new age in American politics—an era in which conservatives championed the interests of "average citizens" against a liberal establishment controlled by special interests. New Rightists viewed the debate over Panama as a major chance to demonstrate that there was indeed something "new" about the New Right.

Yet there was little new in their message. Nostalgia for an idealized past, appeals to "old-fashioned" religious, social, and political values, and conspiratorial logic have been persistent strains in American right-wing political rhetoric. Even New

114

Right guru Richard Viguerie admits that "there aren't that many new conservative ideas. Most of the ideas have been around for a long time."[2] Nevertheless, the New Right *seemed* new in the late 1970s because it had learned how to recruit, how to organize, and how to successfully market old conservative ideals. "The old right were talkers and pamphleteers," presidential assistant Lyn Nofziger observed in distinguishing the New Right from the Old. "They would just as soon go down in flames as win."[3] By contrast, New Rightists disavow martyrdom. They seek political victories through mastery of advanced communicative technologies and through new, more successful techniques for exploiting established mass media. In the 1970s the New Right became a force in American politics because it learned new methods for packaging and marketing an old political product.

The debate over the Panama Canal treaties played a major role in the political maturation of the New Right. New Rightists approached the fight as an old-fashioned crusade, but they displayed the state-of-the-art in modern campaigning. The campaign against "giving away" the canal coalesced previously isolated conservative organizations in America and displayed for the first time the New Right's potential for deploying a large number of advocates, for raising and spending large amounts of money, and for executing sophisticated media strategies. In its Panama campaign the New Right revealed three major reasons for its unprecedented impact on the national political dialogue in the late 1970s: its emphasis on organization, its mastery of new political technologies, and its new, more positive attitude toward the established mass media in America.

Organizing the Network

The New Right did not campaign against the Panama treaties in a single-issue, flash-in-the-pan uprising. Rightists considered the Panama campaign a pivotal event in their long-range plan for building a new, more effective conservative political coalition. As *Newsweek* reported, the New Right hoped "to use the canal treaty to rally public support for other conservative causes, build a bigger conservative block in Congress—and take control of the Republican Party." Richard Viguerie, who already had established his credentials as the leading conservative fund-raiser, seemed almost unconcerned with winning the Senate vote on the treaties. According to Viguerie, the issue's importance stemmed from its long-term potential for serving conservatives politically as Vietnam had served liberals:

> This is a cutting issue. . . . It's an issue the conservatives can't lose on. If we lose the vote in the Senate, we will have had the issue for eight or nine months. We will have rallied many new people to our cause. We will have given our supporters an issue, a cause to work for. The left has had this over the years and the right hasn't. They've had their civil rights causes and their Vietnam war protests and ecology. People get involved in these causes for a particular reason and first thing they knew they were involved in all kinds of liberal activities. . . . Now conservatives can get excited about the Panama Canal giveaway and they can go to the polls, look for a person's name on the ballot who favored these treaties and vote against him. . . .
>
> Conservatives have one weapon the White House really doesn't have—the ability to *punish*. . . . We're going to look *very* carefully at the votes when all this is over and do an *awful* lot of punishing next election.[4]

The Carter administration tried to reassure potential supporters of the treaties that Viguerie and company could not "punish" them. The president's "resident political scientist," Mark Siegel, argued that the New Right would have little impact "in the long term," while Carter's pollster Patrick Caddell sounded a theme reminiscent of White House statements on antiwar protests in the Vietnam era: "Their people are intense, loud and noisy, and they write letters, but that's because they can't succeed in the voting booths."[5]

In the long run, however, the issue apparently did serve the New Right as Viguerie had predicted. The Carter administration won the debate over Panama in the most obvious, short-term sense: the Senate finally ratified the treaties. But, as Viguerie put it, the campaign eventually showed "how much you can win even when you lose."[6] New Rightists could claim justifiably that they "won" the contest for public opinion on the treaties, and they exploited the issue for several years after ratification to recruit new supporters, to raise large amounts of money, and to hurt the reelection chances of incumbents on their "hit lists." New Rightists had good reason to brag that they had "won" on Panama, and much of the credit must be given to their organizational innovations during the debate.

Nowhere is the contrast between the Old Right and the New Right more evident than in ideas about organization. Old Rightists typically viewed themselves as individualists, proudly bucking the "liberal establishment," and refusing to compromise their cherished principles for reasons of political expediency. They could be found predominately in the Republican party, but they really had no party or significant national organizations they could call their own. The emergence or resurgence of groups like the John Birch Society, the Ku Klux Klan, the American Nazi party, and the Liberty Lobby sent American liberals into fits in the 1960s and 1970s. But these groups were so extreme or so eccentric that nationally prominent conservative leaders disowned them, and their followings were so small that politically they were irrelevant. In the world of real political influence, the old "radical right" was a "mythical bogey, a vapor of the perfervid liberal imagination."[7] Radical rightists controlled no positions of power and they had no legitimacy; they could never manipulate large blocks of voters to win political influence, much less to win elections. They engaged in political theater, not political campaigning. Indeed, the "radical right" may not have been newsworthy at all had it not been for the hysteria of American liberals.

The New Right, by contrast, has become virtually synonymous with organization. "Organization is our bag," proclaims Paul Weyrich of the Committee for the Survival of a Free Congress. "We preach and teach nothing but organization." The result can be seen in a proliferation of New Right groups, each with specific purposes, but all contributing to the cause. As Alan Crawford has observed, the New Right has learned

117

that political influence takes many forms in America, and it has developed organizations to cover all bases:

> The New right affiliates include large, multi-purpose umbrella groups like the American Conservative Union and the Conservative Caucus; organizations, like Young Americans for Freedom, designed to train young leaders; educational "think tanks" like the Heritage Foundation; periodicals and publishing houses like *Conservative Digest* and Green Hill Publications; tax-exempt legal foundations and public-interest law firms like the Washington Legal Foundation; congressional lobbies like Christian Voice; research arms like the National Conservative Research and Education Foundation; groups to provide research for right-wing state legislators, like the American Legislative Exchange Council; and, on the fringes, a vast array of single-issue groups, ad hoc or long-run, that work on an informal basis with the more established political bodies. The New Right also includes numerous political action committees (PACs) dedicated to financing the political campaigns of like-minded candidates and wrecking those of moderates or liberals.[8]

Many of these New Right groups, especially those emphasizing fund-raising and public relations, first realized their political clout in campaigns against the Panama Canal treaties. The American Conservative Union (ACU), claiming three hundred thousand members in over forty state chapters, sent out 2.4 million pieces of mail and spent $1.4 million in just its first year of campaigning on the issue. Another major New Right group, the Conservative Caucus, sent out over 2 million pieces of mail on the treaties and raised over $800,000 by January 1978. The Caucus marshalled sufficient resources to sponsor a national billboard campaign, fifty-three organizational training conferences in individual congressional districts, rallies in all fifty states, and a "fact-finding mission" to Panama for New Right leaders. The Caucus also purchased time on nearly five hundred radio stations for advertising featuring Ronald Reagan, and it distributed a cassette tape featuring Senator Orrin Hatch telling "the whole story about why turning over the Canal to a Castroite Dictator—and paying him $80 million a year to boot—[is] bad for America." Still, the Conservative Caucus could afford to cap off its campaign with a radio and television blitz on the eve of the Senate debate.[9]

Among other New Right affiliates, Terry Dolan's National Conservative Political Action Committee sponsored almost half a million letters, John Fisher's American Security Council sent out some two million letters, and the Council on Inter-American Security (directed by Ronald Docksai and L. Francis Bouchey) mailed two million letters and purchased radio advertising in thirteen states. Even the New Right's cadets, the Young Americans for Freedom, conducted a significant campaign against the treaties. Many of YAF's fifty-five thousand members joined in circulating petitions, distributing literature and bumper stickers, sponsoring debates and campus speakers, and distributing a free "Panama Canal Activist's Kit." By February 1978, the YAF's petition drive had secured approximately thirty-five thousand signatures—enough to prompt the Senate Foreign Relations Committee to invite the YAF's National Projects Director Kenneth F. Boehm to testify about the group's opposition to the treaties.[10]

The Panama campaign marked the first time these and other New Right affiliates acted in a coordinated fashion and effectively pooled their resources. As Viguerie observed, the crusade against "giving away" the canal became the New Right's greatest lesson in organization—"an exercise in coalition building none of us will ever forget."[11] Through two ad hoc umbrella groups, one called the Committee to Save the Panama Canal and the other called the Emergency Coalition to Save the Panama Canal, the New Right coordinated for the first time some twenty national conservative organizations, including the American Conservative Union, the Conservative Caucus, the American Security Council, Citizens for the Republic, the Committee for the Survival of a Free Congress, the Council on National Defense, the Council for Inter-American Security, the National Conservative Political Action Committee, the Campus Republican Action Organization, the Committee for Responsible Youth Politics, the Young Republicans, and even STOP ERA.[12]

The umbrella groups provided important benefits lacking

119

in previous New Right crusades. Not only did they allow the New Right to circumvent restrictions on activities by their standing political groups imposed by election, lobbying, and tax laws,[13] but they also unified opposition to the treaties and prevented duplicated effort. With regular meetings, the heads of the various organizations planned and coordinated strategy and divided tasks. They taught each other lessons learned in earlier campaigns, and they pooled their resources to sponsor projects beyond the means of individual groups. This coordination produced the first large and sophisticated New Right campaign—a campaign which also displayed the New Right's mastery of new communicative technologies.

THE NEW POLITICAL TECHNOLOGY

It seems inevitable that rightists would oppose the new Panama Canal treaties. Rightists have opposed the concept embodied in the treaties—the notion that America should relinquish its control over the waterway to atone for historical sins—since Franklin Delano Roosevelt agreed to a number of concessions to Panama under the treaty of 1936. But Old Rightists and New Rightists opposed the "appeasement" differently. The New Right displayed a mastery of technologies like direct-mail and telephone solicitation, and they executed slick television fund-raising and persuasive strategies.

Direct mail is the most notorious "new" technology employed by the New Right. Yet the New Right did not discover direct-mail suddenly in the 1970s. They had been refining their mailing lists and their "personal" direct-mail rhetoric for over a decade prior to the Panama campaign. In 1964 rightists first disproved the theory that large amounts of money could not be raised by direct-mail. With more than fifteen million direct-mailings, the Goldwater campaign raised $5.8 million from 380,000 responses at a cost of slightly more than $1 million. In 1968 Richard Viguerie came to the forefront of the conservative direct-mail industry by raising an estimated $6 million for the presidential campaign of Governor George C. Wallace. Direct mail accounted for 76 percent of the income for Wallace's campaign. By 1976 Viguerie was raising more money for conservative political action committees than the total revenues of the Republican National Committee and its congressional campaign committees combined.[14] No longer did anybody doubt that he had "the most extensive and fecund political mailing list in the country."[15] At his windowless, high-security headquarters in Falls Church, Virginia, he presided over a sophisticated computer system and thirty-three hundred closely guarded reels of magnetic tape. The tapes contained the names of 30 million Americans, including about 4.5 million who already had contributed to at least one rightist cause.[16]

By November 1977 Viguerie had sent out some two million skillfully computer-personalized pieces of mail on the Panama Canal treaties.[17] As always, they were designed to do three basic things. First, of course, they aimed to raise money. Even New Rightists were surprised at how well letters on the canal treaties did the job. One five-thousand-piece mailing intended to raise $50,000 instead brought in $110,000 in just two weeks.[18] Second, they promoted *action* to bring public pressure on fence-sitting senators. Mailings on Panama called upon readers to contact their senators to voice their opposition to the treaties, and they typically expedited the task by providing postcards to be signed and mailed. The result could be seen in an unprecedented volume of mail opposing the treaties. A compilation of Senate mail by the American Conservative Union showed that some senators received as many as four thousand communications in a single week, with opposition to the treaties running from 90 to 100 percent. As of August 1977, Senator Orrin Hatch alone had received three thousand communications, only three of which expressed support for the treaties.[19] Finally, the mailings aimed further to persuade recipients about the evils of the treaties. New Rightists value direct mail because it allows complete control over the message communicated to its audience. They consider direct mail a "vehicle to carry [their] message to the voters without going through the filter of the liberal-leaning news media."[20] In the Panama campaign they used this freedom to raise seemingly wild and emotional charges concerning conspiracies to "give away" the canal or concerning the communist ties, atrocities, or drug-dealings of Panama's leaders. The New Right's mailing lists are filled with people who have demonstrated their responsiveness to frenzied, conspiratorial logic and sordid accusations, and direct-mail allows messages to be tailored to these people without the intervention of "liberal" judgments about what is "newsworthy" or "proven."

Examination of a mailing sent to 250,000 Americans by the Conservative Caucus reveals the virtual formula for direct-mail which has proven so successful for the New Right. First, the "personal" letter, signed by the late Representative Larry McDonald, created a "devil" conspiring to give away the canal. According to McDonald, a seemingly omnipotent alliance was behind the "sellout": Big Labor, Big Business, Big Media, Big Banks, and Big Government Bureaucrats. Of course, one could hardly expect "Big Media" to have reported this "fact" to concerned, conservative Americans. Second, McDonald asked for a pledge of action—a permanent commitment to vote against politicians who supported the "Big Boys." He proclaimed: "It's our job—yours and mine—to make Senators know that hundreds of thousands of patriotic Americans will pledge now to vote forever against any elected official who supports the Panama Canal sellout." The reader was then to take the pledge: "I PLEDGE ALLEGIANCE TO THE UNITED STATES OF AMERICA. I PLEDGE NEVER TO CAST MY VOTE FOR ANY ELECTED OFFICIAL WHO SUPPORTS THE SURRENDER OF U.S. SOVEREIGN JURISDICTION AND CONTROL OVER THE AMERICAN CANAL AND ZONE AT THE ISTHMUS OF PANAMA." The letter continued its call for action and personal involvement in the campaign by instructing the reader to sign two enclosed copies of the personal pledge—one for each senator—and to "put them in the mail at once." Finally, the letter asked for money, but as always it promised something in return. For a contribution of $25 or more, McDonald's audience received Philip Crane's book, *Surrender in Panama: The Case Against the Treaty*.[21] The book was written specifically to provide more propaganda for the campaign, of course, and it may have encouraged additional contributions. Nonetheless, it also may have made respondents feel they got something more for their money than the satisfaction of standing up to the "Big Boys."

Whatever one may think of the New Right's melodramatic formula for direct-mail rhetoric, the fact remains that it works. Indeed, the more emotional the letter—the more urgency, fright, or hatred it fosters—the more it apparently motivates its already sympathetic readers to go beyond merely believing and to send money.[22] Conservatives claim to be eight to ten years ahead of liberal direct-mail experts for very good reason. Nearly 85 percent of all political direct-mail experts in the United States work for conservative causes; Viguerie estimates that forty to forty-two of the fifty political direct-mail experts in the United States are conservatives.[23] During the Panama campaign, liberal direct-mail expert Thomas R. Mathews summarized the political significance of the conservative direct-mail industry: "The Canal treaties are not in trouble. All you have to do is stop Viguerie."[24]

The New Right's mastery of new communicative technologies goes beyond its skill with direct mail. During the Panama campaign the New Right also displayed and refined its skills in paid political advertising, telephone solicitation, the use of cassette recordings and mailgrams, and other marketing gimmicks. The greatest advances came with the application of lessons learned about direct-mail to telephone solicitation and to paid political advertising. Indeed, the telephone and the television have become so important to the New Right that some direct-mail experts have begun to call themselves "direct-response" professionals to emphasize their use of these other media in their fund-raising campaigns.[25]

The most subtle application of direct-mail techniques to other media may be seen in the New Right's paid political advertising during the Panama campaign. Although paid political advertising cannot be targeted at potential supporters as efficiently as direct mail, it does provide another mechanism for communicating unfiltered messages. During the Panama campaign, the New Right disseminated over a variety of media the same emotional, provocative messages that proved so effective in motivating regular direct-mail contributors to reach for their

123

wallets. On billboards and leaflets the New Right spread emotional rumors about the "crimes" of Panama's leaders—messages like a "Wanted Poster" of Panama's allegedly murderous, drug-dealing leader, General Omar Torrijos. In newspaper and magazine advertising and in spot ads on electronic media, the New Right practiced another lesson from its direct-mail experience: urging supporters to take action to put pressure on lawmakers. The typical print ad proclaimed in eye-catching type: "WRITE, PHONE, WIRE OR VISIT YOUR U.S. CONGRESSMAN, SENATORS AND THE PRESIDENT, EXPRESSING YOUR OPPOSITION TO GIVING AWAY THE CANAL!" One such advertisement in the *Nashville Banner*, paid for by the American Conservative Union, generated some thirty-six hundred pieces of mail in Senator Howard Baker's office in only a week. Meanwhile, a radio and television blitz promoting the Conservative Caucus' "pledge card" campaign flooded Senate mailrooms with the prefabricated, yet signed threats to "never" vote for a treaty supporter.[26]

A more obvious application of the New Right's experience with direct-mail could be seen in its use of telephone solicitation. In the past, telephone solicitation was seen as an expensive, inefficient tool of political campaigning. But in combination with the lists of known contributors developed in direct-mail campaigns, telephone solicitation becomes not only competitive with mailings but strikingly superior. Using lists tested in earlier campaigns, Bruce W. Eberle and Associates developed a program of telephone solicitation for the Council for Inter-American Security's campaign against the Panama treaties that produced a response rate some five times greater than the typical direct-mailing. With a script of only ninety-eight words, Eberle's trained callers prompted more than half of all those reached to pledge money (as compared to the typical direct-mail response rate of 8 to 12 percent) and 70 percent of those pledges were paid in full.[27]

A further application of the telephone combines paid political advertising with pledges by phone. In this technique, pioneered by conservative television evangelists like the Reverend Jerry Falwell, a toll-free number appears on the television screen while the spot or program urges the audience to make a pledge. The advantage for the contributor, of course, lies in its convenience. Rather than writing down an address, writing out a check, addressing an envelope, purchasing a stamp, and mailing a letter, contributors can simply call in pledges and charge them to major credit cards (since the Federal Election Commission approved the practice in 1978) or wait for an addressed, post-paid return envelope to arrive at their home. The method is even more advantageous for the campaigner, however, since it promotes emotional, impulsive contributing, provides instantly available funds, and generates lists of contributors for future direct-mail or telephone contacts.[28]

This combination of television advertising and telephone solicitation proved most effective in the American Conservative Union's taped "telethon" on the Panama Canal treaties. As a fund-raising tool, and as a vehicle to convey the New Right's "urgent" message about the treaties without outside interference, the ACU's glossy, thirty-minute videotape proved perhaps the best example of the right's new media savvy. Entitled "There Is No Panama Canal; There is an American Canal in Panama," the program began with a characteristically urgent tone: "This may be the most important TV program you have ever watched." Fulfillment of this startling promise depended on one's opinion of antitreaty testimony from Senators Jesse Helms, Paul Laxalt, Jake Garn, and Strom Thurmond, along with retired Canal Zone Federal Judge Guthrie F. Crowe, Phelps Jones of the VFW, and Major General J. Milnor Roberts, Jr., of the Reserve Officers Association. Like the direct-mail campaign, the program emphasized pressuring Congress and raising more money to fight the treaties. Host Philip Crane gave detailed instructions on how to write one's senators, and he interrupted the show six times with a plea for money: "Make a pledge of ten dollars or more to our emergency fund to save the canal, so that we can telecast this program in other parts of America. Right this moment, you can phone a toll-free number and make a pledge of ten dollars or more. The number to call is: 1-800-325-6400." The program thereby made it easy to make a pledge via a simple phone call and it explained exactly how the money was to be used. It also promised something in return for a contribution and made it easy to send the money quickly: "An operator will record your name, address and pledge—and your pledge will be confirmed within thirty-six hours by a personal mailgram from me delivered to your home. A return envelope will be provided for your check or money order."[29]

After initial showings in three southern states with strong antitreaty sentiment, the return envelopes began pouring in, providing the ACU with financing to sponsor showings in additional states. With the first fifty thousand pledges raising $240,000, the program quickly became self-supporting, allowing the ACU to broadcast the tape in almost every state. The program ultimately reached an estimated ten million viewers and raised $1 million for the ACU, thus providing a very good return on a program that cost only $20,000 to produce.[30]

The New Right's success with the new political technology—the direct-mail campaign, the slick political advertising, the phone banks, and the mailgrams—does not completely explain how the New Right differs from the Old Right. Perhaps just as important as the new technology is a new positive attitude, particularly toward the established news media. New Rightists, like Old Rightists, do not trust the reporters and news organizations that cover American politics. But they have learned how to attract more coverage and, to a lesser extent, to shape more favorable coverage through cooperation rather than conflict. This new attitude toward the established news media, as much as anything else, reveals what is "new" about the New Right in America.

MAKING THE NEWS

As Sidney Blumenthal has observed, Richard Viguerie is "an apt pupil of George McGovern, the New Left, and the AFL-CIO, all Satan incarnate to old rightists." Viguerie himself boasts that "we just learned how the Left did it and were good copiers." He admits to adopting "close to 100 percent of the left's tactics." "What we're doing is what they did," he says. "We're into making a list of all the things they do and doing the same things."[31] Among the most important lessons Viguerie learned from the New Left of the 1960s were strategies for "making the news." Like the New Left, the New Right has learned about staging "media events" and about cooperation with the news media. In the Panama campaign New Right leaders were especially good at exploiting the news media's obsession with drama, conflict, and the bizarre, and they surprised many reporters by pandering to their desires for "inside" stories about the New Right.

Demonstrations in the streets have not been associated with conservative politics historically in America, but they have become an important part of the New Right's strategic philosophy since the Panama campaign. Just as the New Left proclaimed itself the "voice of the people" in its antiwar protests, the New Right claimed to speak for "the people" in the Panama debate, and it carefully orchestrated demonstrations to produce "newsworthy" conflict with the presumably unresponsive "establishment." The dramatization of the New Right's Panama rallies began with promotional rhetoric promising such left-like displays as a "March on Washington," and conflict with the "establishment" was assured by scheduling the march and other demonstrations during the president's "Week of Panama." The New Right also promised "newsworthy" conflict by stationing protestors on the steps of the U.S. Capitol and by scheduling numerous local rallies in "key states" with wavering or uncommitted senators. Whether at home or in Washington, senators could not avoid confrontations with noisy, boisterous protestors and attention from reporters who came out for the show. In addition, the New Right mimicked the highly publicized "teach-ins" of the antiwar movement with fifty-three "training conferences," and it seemingly modeled its "fact-finding mission" to Panama after headline-grabbing trips to Vietnam by well-known antiwar leaders. One New Right "media event," called "Headlights on to Save the Canal," aimed to demonstrate antitreaty sentiment across the country with flashing headlights at the moment the treaties were signed in Washington—a demonstration reminiscent of days designated for local antiwar prayer vigils or for wearing armbands. In its search for the perfect media event, the New Right even invented new ways of exploiting the media's equation of "newsworthy" with "bizarre." While taking his seat at a University of Tennessee football game, Senator Howard Baker was embarrassed on his home turf when some eighty thousand of his constituents and the Tennessee media observed a light plane circling the stadium with banner in tow: "Save Our Canal: Write Senator Baker."[32]

The New Right also exploited the news media in more traditional fashion by offering reporters the opportunity to cover its leaders "barnstorming" as the "Panama Canal Truth Squad." Accompanied by representatives of all three networks, Metromedia, and a score of newspapers—some thirty representatives of the national news media in all—a group of some two dozen antitreaty congressmen and retired military personnel crisscrossed the country in a chartered Boeing 737, appearing in key states with wavering or uncommitted senators. The Truth Squad brought the sort of comprehensive, daily coverage typical of a presidential campaign, and its appearances in various cities brought local coverage to supplement the reporting of the national traveling press. The Truth Squad did not leave even the local coverage to chance. In Portland the group split into smaller groups for visits to newspaper offices and to radio and television stations, while in Denver it assured local coverage by adding Ronald Reagan to its list of attractions. In the end, Richard Viguerie estimated that the Truth Squad reached over ten million people through media coverage of its appearances in only four major cities. As usual, the New Right made the most of its campaign dollars.[33]

Barnstorming, of course, is nothing new in American politics, even for advocates of the Old Right. But Old Rightists barnstormed to circumvent the media; they sought to reach out directly to the public without going through the filter of the "left-leaning media." By contrast, the Truth Squad was first and foremost a media attraction. Rather than shun the media out of fear of adverse coverage, the Truth Squad claimed political legitimacy by virtue of its members' political or military credentials, and it demanded the same serious coverage accorded other traveling political dignitaries. In this sense, the Truth Squad provided a good example of the Right's new positive attitude toward the news media—an attitude which, like many

New Right innovations, can be traced to the strategic thinking of Richard Viguerie.

Viguerie recognized long ago the need for conservatives to treat the news media, not simply as an enemy, but as an institution which could be influenced. This is not to say that Viguerie does not share the age-old right-wing view that the major media in America have a liberal bias. Like virtually all conservatives, he complains that liberals have a virtual monopoly on the major media and that they ignore conservatives or portray them unfavorably. But Viguerie, unlike a Joseph McCarthy or a Spiro Agnew, does not try to change that fact through threats or intimidation. Instead, he suggests that rightists try some old-fashioned flattery or that they exploit reporters' desires to find news which will make the front page or the nightly newscasts. Viguerie himself flatters reporters by calling them "good, decent men and women who are trying to do a professional job," and he likes to tell the story of how he learned to seduce even hostile reporters into providing more favorable coverage:

> I remember one day a fairly well known writer for a major newspaper called and wanted an appointment to come and talk to me.
>
> I was a little short of terrified. I told my secretary to tell him I'd get back to him.
>
> I then called some of my conservative associates and asked what I should do. Almost all advised me to avoid the reporter.
>
> The advice went something like this—that newspaper is no friend of the conservative movement, that reporter will try to do you in, etc., etc.
>
> But then I got to thinking. I and my conservative friends are not playing in the big leagues—but we want to. . . .
>
> I called the reporter back and said, "Why don't you come over and, if you've got time, why don't we have lunch?"
>
> Well, I spent an enjoyable three hours with the reporter. He wrote a basically fair and accurate story (although it wasn't as fair and objective as my mother would have written).
>
> And from that day forward, I felt that I and other conservatives had to change our view of the press.[34]

The recognition that media coverage is determined by definitions of "news" as well as by political ideology is indicative of the Right's political maturation. It suggests another major reason why the New Right has enjoyed unprecedented success in promoting old conservative ideals. By producing "newsworthy" political drama and conflict, and by cultivating more cordial, personal relationships with members of the press, the New Right has increased the quantity and improved the quality of its media coverage. The New Right, like the New Left of the 1960s, is in fact a fringe political movement, commanding the devout loyalty of only a small slice of the American polity. But because they have promoted themselves effectively and have attracted inordinate attention from the established media, New Rightists *seem* more important politically than their numbers may warrant. It may well be that the New Right's claim of speaking for "the people" is an illusion created by its own rhetoric and by a gullible news media. But perceptions that exaggerate the New Right's importance may intimidate elected officials and influence public policy debate.

With virtually the entire political establishment—both Democratic and Republican—supporting the Panama Canal treaties, the New Right alone "talked sense" to such large, wealthy, and influential groups as the American Legion (4 million members) and the Veterans of Foreign Wars (2.4 million members).[35] One can only speculate about how alliances with these and other special interest groups during the Panama campaign contributed to the New Right's quest for greater political status in the years that followed.[36] But one can state with some certainty that the antitreaty coalition proved a serious challenge to the Carter administration and signaled a new approach to conservative politics. During the Panama campaign the New Right entered the world of modern, scientific public relations. It executed a sophisticated strategy based on advanced direct-mail technology, paid political advertising, and exploitation of the established news media. New Right groups eventually sent out approximately nine million cards and letters and spent several million dollars campaigning against the treaties. They demonstrated convincingly that they had acquired the wherewithal to be a serious voice in the national political dialogue.

Still, the New Right could not match the resources of protreaty campaigners. Backed by the entire executive branch and aided by most of the political, business, and religious establishment, the administration enjoyed numerous advantages. But protreaty advocates seemed less concerned with public opinion than did their opposition. While the New Right cultivated grassroots opinion, the administration emphasized lobbying Congress and persuading elites. The New Right also seemed more highly motivated than its opposition. As their critics often charged, New Rightists became emotional about the Panama Canal treaties. But that emotion seemed to inspire them to work harder than their more numerous and prestigious opponents.

Above all, the New Right was able to mount an effective challenge to the Carter administration because its message was persuasive to many Americans. For the most part, scholars and political commentators have overlooked this simple fact, assuming that the broad coalition of elites supporting the treaties *must* have made the better case in the debate. But as William Schneider has written, the fact that "virtually the entire political elite" supported the Panama Canal treaties does not mean that they were "right,"[37] much less that their arguments persuasively addressed the public's questions and concerns about the treaties.

Part 3
The Arguments

6

Interpretations of History

Argument from history is common in deliber-
ative debates, as advocates routinely look to the past for legal
precedents, parallel situations, or traditional wisdom to justify
policies. Perhaps, as Ernest May suggests, looking to the past is
basic human nature—a "habit" of thinking.[1] But certain issues,
by their very nature, demand argument from history. Two general issues in the debate over the Panama Canal treaties illustrate how history may impinge upon deliberations about the
future.

First, controversy over sovereignty in the Panama Canal
Zone led both sides to the historical record. Hoping to convince
Americans that relinquishing the Panama Canal would be a
radical action akin to returning Alaska to the Russians or the
Louisiana Purchase to the French, opponents of the treaties
argued that the United States acquired full sovereignty and
ownership of the Canal Zone in 1903. Those favoring the treaties,
on the other hand, tried to minimize the significance of acknowledging Panama's sovereignty over the Canal Zone. They
insisted that history proved that the United States never had
sovereignty or rights of ownership in the area. They claimed
that the new treaties merely acknowledged sovereignty Panama

had always possessed. They thereby portrayed the treaties as merely a symbolic concession with little substantive impact.

Second, ethical questions concerning America's presence in Panama led both sides in the debate to weigh the evidence of history. Opponents of the treaties rejected the notion that the United States had "stolen" the canal and needed to atone for its history of "colonialism." They argued that the United States legitimately secured sovereignty over the Canal Zone and bestowed great benefits upon the Republic of Panama. Those favoring the treaties challenged this portrait of America's historical benevolence. They cited a record of unfair advantages for the United States and offered the proposed new treaties as medicine to soothe the national conscience.

Neither side necessarily lied or distorted historical fact in the debate over Panama. The history of relations with Panama, like all historical processes, is complex and multi-faceted, combining elements both favorable and unfavorable to any particular viewpoint. Each side in the debate selectively recalled historical facts, and each side interpreted the facts in terms of their distinctive ideological framework. But, as a rule, neither side told historical untruths in the debate. Each side presented an incomplete but generally accurate slice of America's history in Panama.

The matter of who "won" the debate over historical issues is more a question of persuasiveness than of truthfulness. Which side in the debate presented the most consistent, believable, and appealing case? That question is relatively easy to answer, for those opposing the treaties had numerous advantages. In debating the issue of sovereignty, opponents of the treaties enjoyed the benefits of defending the standard interpretation of America's history perpetuated by textbooks and political folklore. Meanwhile, protreaty forces sought to convert Americans to a less authoritative, seemingly contradictory "revisionist" history. On questions of the morality of America's historical presence in Panama, opponents of the treaties defended the honor of Theodore Roosevelt and emphasized U.S. benevolence toward Panama. Meanwhile, the administration alienated both conservatives and liberals by mixing moral condemnation of America's history in Panama with praise for Roosevelt's generation. Moreover, antitreaty advocates presented a version of history that most Americans *wished* to believe, for they recalled a story of national righteousness and glory. By contrast, protreaty advocates presented a fundamentally negative portrayal of American history, albeit they sought to mitigate the indictment with claims of patriotic pride in America's accomplishments in Panama.

THE DEBATE OVER SOVEREIGNTY

As James Busey observed in 1974, "directly or indirectly, the question of sovereignty lies behind virtually all the issues, and certainly the most heated ones, that have plagued U.S.-Panamanian relations since 1903."[2] For both Panamanians and Americans sovereignty had long been a powerful symbolic issue. But it also raised complex legal issues. In the United States these issues became a major battleground in debate over new Panama Canal treaties, as both sides looked to history for legal texts, official interpretations, and precedents to sustain their claims about sovereignty in the Canal Zone.

Opponents of the Panama Canal treaties enjoyed the advantages of defending the interpretation of sovereignty in the Canal Zone that had guided American policy for at least half a century. That Panama possessed, if anything, only "titular sovereignty" constituted the standard interpretation found in such basic sources as the *Encyclopaedia Britannica,* and this view already had widespread currency within Congress and the general public.[3] For this reason, antitreaty advocates welcomed debate over sovereignty in the Canal Zone; they believed the historical record unmistakably sustained their point of view.

Treaty opponents began their case by citing the Hay-Bunau-Varilla treaty itself. John McGarret observed that the 1903 treaty granted the United States all sovereign rights in the Canal Zone "to the entire exclusion of the exercise by the Republic of Panama of any such sovereign rights, power or authority." In *Surrender in Panama,* Philip Crane called this passage "clear and in-

137

controvertible language" granting the United States "exclusive, sovereign rights over the Canal Zone from the outset." Ronald Reagan interpreted the text both in terms of the intent of the framers and in terms of international law. The U.S. government, he argued in his nationally televised address on the treaties, "intended to acquire a firm, unshakable legal basis for building, operating and defending the canal." And in a symposium with treaty proponent Gale McGee, he explained: "Historically, . . . it has been the case that only one nation can exercise sovereign rights over a given piece of land at a given time; and the 1903 treaty made it clear that the United States—not the Republic of Panama—would do so in the Canal Zone."[4]

Opponents of the treaties added that the American government owned the territory in "fee simple." Before building the canal, they argued, the United States went to great expense to acquire undisputed title to the land. First, the United States paid the government of Panama $10 million for "the full rights of sovereignty in perpetuity over the Zone." Then "the United States . . . acquired all the privately owned land and property in the Canal Zone in what would be called in domestic law 'title in fee simple.'" As Robert S. Strother noted in the *National Review*, "the United States spent nearly $162 million to acquire title to the Canal Zone's 647 square miles."[5] Even squatters were paid for their holdings. And just to be sure, the United States also paid the French for their rights and abandoned equipment and later paid Colombia, "from which Panama had seceded." In all, observed retired federal judge Guthrie F. Crowe in the ACU "telethon," the United States "paid almost $170 million to get a clear title to the land."[6] This made the Canal Zone "by far the most expensive of America's territorial purchases."[7] According to Robert Strother, America's title to the land was "as valid as its rights to Alaska, . . . or to the states carved out of the $15-million Louisiana Purchase." Ronald Reagan summarized the antitreaty case on America's rights in the Zone: "We not only have the rights of sovereignty; we are the owners of the real estate."[8]

Treaty opponents did not dispute that the United States historically had recognized Panama's "titular" or "residual" sovereignty in the Canal Zone.[9] But they claimed that such sovereignty was substantively meaningless. They commonly quoted at length from "the first interpretation" of the 1903 treaty by Secretary of State Hay in 1904. Any "titular" sovereignty which "could or should be admitted," Hay said, had been "mediatized" (i.e. converted) by Panama's "own act, solemnly declared and publicly proclaimed by treaty stipulations." Treaty opponents also quoted Secretary of War William Howard Taft's interpretation of "titular sovereignty" before the Committee on Interoceanic Canals in 1906. "Titular sovereignty," he said, was a "barren ideality" with meaning only to "poetic and sentimental" Latin Americans who dwelled "much on names and forms." Finally, they cited Secretary of State Charles Evans Hughes' response to Panamanian protests in 1921–1923. At that time, Hughes proclaimed it "absolute futility for the Panamanian government to expect any American Administration . . . ever to surrender any part of these rights, which the United States has acquired under the Treaty of 1903."[10]

Opponents of the treaties insisted that the treaty revisions of 1936 and 1955 actually "renewed," "reaffirmed," or "reemphasized" the original grant of sovereignty to the United States.[11] According to Crane, these treaties constituted "major revisions," but they in no way "amended or modified Articles II and III of the original agreement, the crucial passages conferring power of sovereignty on the United States in perpetuity." Crane made much of the remark by the State Department's Henry Holland that the 1955 treaty could not be "interpreted as implying any admission by the United States that we possess and exercise anything less than 100 percent of the rights of sovereignty in this area."[12]

Treaty opponents also cited decisions by American courts supporting their interpretation of sovereignty in the Canal Zone. They cited the 1907 Supreme Court case of *Wilson v. Shaw* as recognizing "the Canal Zone as official territory of the United States." A treaty with Panama "ceding the Canal Zone," the Court had ruled, had been "duly ratified."[13] The Court had called it "hypercritical to contend that the title of the United States to the Canal Zone is imperfect and that the territory described does not belong to this nation."[14] This decision, Donald Dozer noted, "has never been overruled but was reaffirmed by the Supreme Court as recently as 1972." In 1972, Dozer and others observed, the Court referred to the Canal Zone as "unincorporated territory of the United States" over which Congress exerted "complete and plenary authority."[15]

Treaty opponents admitted that Congress, in exercising authority over the Canal Zone, had not always treated the area as part of the United States. Specifically, customs and tariff legislation treated it as outside the United States, and children born to Panamanian parents in the zone were excluded from U.S. citizenship. Furthermore, the U.S. Constitution did not apply automatically within the zone; the governor had deportation powers, Congress enacted a separate Bill of Rights for the Canal Zone, and only certain categories of people could live there. But opponents of the treaties had answers to all these objections. In addition to noting that other legislation *did* treat the Canal Zone as territory of the United States, they argued that the very act of excluding the Canal Zone from some U.S. law constituted an exercise of sovereignty. As Maechling argued, "each inclusion or exclusion of the zone from the application of U.S. law, and each narrowly limited cession of jurisdiction, is itself the product of U.S. congressional legislation or executive order. Each limited transfer of jurisdiction has been an assertion of U.S. sovereignty, not a denial of it." Or, in Philip Crane's words, "the very yielding to Panama of certain small pieces of control proves that the United States has full control—defacto sovereignty—in the first place."[16]

Finally, those opposed to the Panama Canal treaties denied Panama's claims that the annuity paid by the United States constituted rent and was therefore an admission that the United States held only tenancy in the Canal Zone. Some of them looked to the historical record for the original purpose of the payments and concluded that the United States had agreed to pay for the use of the Panamanian railroad.[17] Most, however, simply went back to the text of the 1903 agreement and noted that "the terms 'rent,' 'lease,' or their equivalents" were not found "anywhere in the Treaty." "Read the 1903 treaty a thousand times," urged Ronald Reagan, "and you'll never once see the words 'rent' or 'lease.'" This was no accident, Donald Dozer argued, for the United States had rejected an early draft of the 1903 treaty precisely because it contained the word "lease" rather than "grant," and the United States had refused to allow the words "lease" or "rent" in any subsequent treaty.[18]

Those opposed to the Panama Canal treaties displayed remarkable unanimity in arguing that American sovereignty in the Canal Zone was historically secure. The American people heard a strong, unified case, and that case was grounded in the statements of American leaders and American courts. Antitreaty advocates seemed confident in debating legal issues, for they defended the standard interpretation. They believed that the American people would agree that the new treaties called for a forfeiture of ownership and sovereignty over some of America's most valuable real estate. Such an interpretation made the treaties appear radical indeed.

By comparison, the protreaty case on sovereignty seemed weak—even contradictory—and relied upon little authoritative testimony. Indeed, by sidestepping the question of sovereignty or by denying its relevance to the debate, those favoring the treaties often admitted implicitly that they could not refute their opponents. The Committee of Americans for the Canal Treaties (COACT) provided supporters with a sample speech claiming that "these old arguments about the past are less important than our nation's real stake in the canal's future." Secretary of State Cyrus Vance proclaimed that historical controversies did little more than "resurrect old grievances or reopen old wounds." Treaty negotiator Ellsworth Bunker told the Des Moines Chamber of Commerce and Rotary Club that "the historical and legal questions which many treaty opponents raise are interesting," but he insisted that they should not divert attention from "the realities we face."[19]

When they did address the issue of sovereignty, treaty proponents often disagreed among themselves. Even "official" administration advocates contradicted each other, even though they undoubtedly had ample opportunity to coordinate their arguments. In addition, their case had the marks of an underdeveloped revisionist history. Protreaty advocates simply seemed unsure of their arguments about sovereignty in the Canal Zone. They seemed tentative, defensive, and rather confused.

The confusion in protreaty rhetoric on sovereignty began at the top. On at least two occasions President Carter suggested that Panama and the United States somehow shared sovereignty over the Canal Zone. During a call-in show broadcast on March 5, 1977, Carter told a caller: "As you may or may not know, the treaty signed when Theodore Roosevelt was president gave Panama sovereignty over the Panama Canal Zone itself. It gave us control over the Panama Canal Zone as though we had sovereignty. So we've always had a legal sharing of responsibility over the Panama Canal." At a town meeting in Yazoo City, Mississippi, Carter expounded on the curious notion of shared sovereignty: "So even in the time of Theodore Roosevelt the agreement was that we and the Panamanians both, in effect, have sovereignty over the Panama Canal Zone." Yet during his call-in show, Carter also asserted that Panama had always been the sole sovereign in the Canal Zone. Ultimately, the president tried to retreat from his confusion by joining those who simply dismissed the issue: "As far as sovereignty is concerned, I don't have any hangup about that."[20]

Others sought to rescue Carter with more consistent and tenable interpretations of the 1903 treaty. Most of Carter's allies argued that the 1903 treaty "retained sovereignty in Panama" by noting that America was only granted rights "as if it were sovereign."[21] The 1903 treaty, stated a State Department publication circulated on Capitol Hill, "gave us power 'as if sovereign' over the Zone, but did not make the Zone part of the United States." From the wording of the 1903 treaty, COACT surmised that the framers never intended a transfer of sovereignty: "If the intent had been to give us sovereignty, there would have been no need to write the Treaty in this way."[22]

Differences of opinion continued to emerge as treaty supporters addressed the question of whether the United States owned the territory in the Canal Zone. On a couple of occasions, Carter maintained flatly that "we have never owned the Panama Canal Zone. We've never had title to it." The State Department, however, seemed far less certain. In a "fact sheet" distributed to Congress, the State Department concluded only that "the exact status of the title to much of the land in the Zone is cloudy." According to the State Department, it was "practically impossible to determine from the available records the precise state of the title to any particular parcel of land in the Zone," although it admitted that the United States held clear title to at least one-third of the land. Hence, while treaty proponents never granted their opponents' claim that the United States owned the Canal Zone, they did not strongly make the counterargument. Again, President Carter tried to skirt an important issue by claiming "it's not so important who actually owns the canal."[23]

Treaty proponents seemed a bit more confident discussing court and legislative actions pertaining to sovereignty in the Canal Zone. President Carter, for instance, firmly asserted that the Supreme Court had "confirmed since [1903] that this is Panamanian territory," although he cited no decisions to that effect.[24] Treaty negotiator Sol Linowitz offered some evidence, telling the American Legion Convention that *Wilson v. Shaw* called the Canal Zone U.S. territory only for the "limited, specific purpose" of expending funds for construction. Linowitz also noted that in 1948 the Court described the Canal Zone as "admittedly territory over which we do not have sovereignty."[25]

In addressing congressional legislation, treaty supporters presented a list of actions suggesting that Congress considered the Canal Zone as something other than U.S. territory. They noted that children born to non-American citizens in the Canal Zone had never been granted U.S. citizenship as they would have been in sovereign American territory.[26] They also noted that goods coming from the Zone into the United States passed through customs and were subject to duty just as though they had come from a foreign country.[27] And they noted that the U.S. government considered Canal Zone ports as foreign ports for the purpose of transporting U.S. mail.[28] The Canal Zone thus contrasted with territorial acquisitions such as the Louisiana Purchase, the purchase of Alaska, and the purchase of land from Mexico.

Above all, treaty proponents emphasized how the agreement to make regular payments to Panama demonstrated that the United States never claimed sovereignty over the land. As President Carter said in his fireside chat: "You do not pay rent on your own land." COACT displayed less certitude, treating the payments as merely analogous to rent. On one occasion, COACT referred to the payments as "rather like a rental payment," while COACT's sample speech claimed that the annuity payments "can be considered as a kind of rent—similar to the rent that we would pay a landowner if we leased a vacant lot and put a building on it." According to the sample speech, the payments most resembled legally the payments to Spain, Greece, and other nations for the maintenance of military installations in their territory.[29]

Treaty supporters, like their opponents, cited historical testimony and the language of the various treaties with Panama to support their claims about sovereignty in the Canal Zone. They especially emphasized the reference in the 1936 treaty to "territory of the Republic of Panama under the jurisdiction of the United States."[30] But the fact remained that they failed to refute convincingly the case on sovereignty developed by their opponents. Throughout the debate treaty proponents seemed unable to present a clear, consistent, and well-documented case on the issue of sovereignty.

Supporters of the treaties no doubt recognized their disadvantage in a historical debate over the legal status of sovereignty. Perhaps their attempts to dismiss or to diminish the importance of the issue should be viewed as a strategic retreat. No logic dictated that one who favored affirming Panamanian sovereignty over the Canal Zone under the new treaties had to insist that they had possessed it all along. So why did treaty proponents even debate the issue at all? Why did they not just grant that the United States had possessed sovereignty historically and emphasize that times had changed?

The answer lies in fears that the new treaties would seem "radical" if they could be portrayed as analogous to "giving away" a state. To the extent that Americans perceived the canal as valuable real estate owned by the United States, they demanded more in return than promises of good will and harmony. Not surprisingly, many Americans failed to see the logic of giving away valuable private property and actually paying the recipient to take it. Such logic is simply alien to the world view of the average American.

THE DEBATE OVER ETHICS

While many of the disputes over America's involvement in Panama involved legal interpretations, many others are best described as moral clashes. Treaty opponents could not comprehend how America's record in Panama could be condemned as immoral by Panamanians, by other nations, and especially by patriotic Americans. Hanson Baldwin indignantly dismissed claims that "the great big United States has exploited poor little Panama" as a "guilt trauma" that seemed particularly "to infect intellectuals."[31]

Indeed, treaty opponents were not content just to refute charges that the United States had exploited Panama. They portrayed American actions as greatly beneficial to that nation. They suggested that the United States had unselfishly rescued Panama from obscurity, poverty, and chaos, and they angrily criticized the Panamanians for failing to express their gratitude.

The ethical debate, like the debate over sovereignty, began with the treaty of 1903. Treaty opponents raged against suggestions that the United States had "stolen" the canal with an unfair agreement. Philip Crane blamed the Carter administration and the major news media for painting "America as the villain in Panama." Crane assailed those who portrayed the "story of the canal" as "a legacy of national shame" or who claimed that "our presence in the Canal Zone was secured through an immoral use of force." Judge Crowe, in the ACU television program, called it "a slap at America to say or imply that we stole the zone to build the canal, . . . and to give away the canal and zone for any reason, especially one of phony guilt, would be a stain on our history and our honor."[32]

The antitreaty version of history revealed no such wrongdoing by the United States in 1903. In Charles Maechling's words, the 1903 treaty was not "imposed upon a supine Panama." Rather, "the independence of Panama—then a mere geographic expression—was engineered by a small group of prominent conspirators headed by the French engineer-adventurer of Suez fame, Philippe-Jean Bunau-Varilla." Despite Theodore Roosevelt's boast that he "took Panama," said Maechling, "all authoritative European and American histories" agreed "that Panamanian independence was brought about by a handful of conspirators drawn from the local oligarchy who were working in concert with a few international financiers, rather than through conscious U.S. government manipulation." Treaty opponents admitted that American troops were present at the time of the revolt. But according to Crane, "the only official American 'intervention' consisted of a landing party of forty-two marines" who never fired a shot.[33] Treaty opponents emphasized that U.S. troops landed in "dress whites" only after the revolution was "almost complete," and "then only for the purpose of protecting the women and children of American citizens and the security of transit."[34]

Opponents of the treaties also dismissed the allegation that the Hay-Bunau-Varilla treaty was tainted because a Frenchman rather than a Panamanian drafted and signed the agreement. In his televised debate with William F. Buckley (later reprinted in the *National Review*), Ronald Reagan noted that Jimmy Carter, Sol Linowitz, and the Panamanian "dictator" Torrijos had "made much of the fact that no Panamanian signed the 1903 treaty," implying "some kind of skulduggery on our part." Calling this "pure, unadulterated nonsense," Reagan presented a version of events revealing no ethical violations on the part of the United States:

> On November 8, the provisional government of the new Republic of Panama named a Frenchman, Bunau-Varilla, as minister plenipotentiary to negotiate the canal treaty with the United States. They knew what they were doing. He was a representative for the bankrupt French company, as avid to get that $40 million for his clients as the Panamanians were to get the canal. Bunau-Varilla nego-

tiated the treaty with our Secretary of State, Hay. It was immediately and unanimously ratified by the provisional government of
Panama, and subsequently by the permanent government.[35]

John McGarret sounded the same theme in his antitreaty
pamphlet: "It is true that Panama's representative, Bunau-
Varilla, who signed the treaty, was a Frenchman. It is also true
that he was fully commissioned as the official representative by
Panama. The treaty he drafted and signed was later ratified by
the provisional and constitutional governments of Panama
which were composed of only Panamanians."[36]

Debate over the morality of America's historical presence in
Panama ultimately focused on the broader issue of whether the
1903 treaty, regardless of how it was obtained, established "colonialism" in Panama. Treaty opponents objected to use of the
word "colonialism," arguing that it had been "misapplied" in
describing the situation. John McGarret, noting that the word
"connotes the subjugation of a weaker people by a stronger
people or nation, by force, for the purpose of exploiting resources," pointed out that the independence movement in Panama in 1903 was "for the express purpose of negotiating a treaty
directly with the United States for construction of a waterway
across the Isthmus." The Canal Zone had not been "wrested
from Panama by force," he noted, nor had Panama "been sub-
jugated or exploited by the United States." Similarly, Ronald
Reagan objected to the term "colonialism" in his debate with
William F. Buckley: "The Canal is not a natural resource of Panama that has been exploited by the United States. We haven't
taken minerals out of the Canal Zone. We haven't lumbered it.
We've gone in for one purpose and one only, the one the Treaty
called for: to build and operate a canal." Reagan also dismissed
the charge of "colonialism" in his nationally televised address
on the treaties, proclaiming in an indignant tone: "The Canal
Zone is not a last vestige of colonialism. It has never been a
colony."[37]

Advocates opposing the treaties ultimately took the offensive on the issue of "colonialism" by arguing that the United
States actually had bestowed great benefits upon Panama.

147

Ronald Reagan noted that the United States "helped Panama achieve independence" and "reach one of the highest per capita income levels in Latin America." Philip Crane noted still more favors the United States had done for Panama, concluding that Panama owed its very existence to American benevolence:

> The United States did for Panama what the Spanish, Simon Bolivar, the French company, and the Colombians had all failed to do: built and operated a magnificent interoceanic canal that pumped commercial vitality and opportunity into the stagnant economic bloodstream of Panama. We also rid the country of the scourges of malaria and yellow fever, brought good jobs and opportunity to thousands of needy Panamanians, and promptly paid increasingly large subsidies to the Panamanian government—all after helping Panama to win independence in the first place. To the extent that Panama exists and is a viable state today, it is because a strong America, which could have taken what it wanted without giving anything in return, has been a generous friend of Panama from the moment of ratification of the 1903 treaty.

Thus, treaty opponents maintained that the United States had transformed an "impoverished tropical backwater into a thriving commercial center and one of the healthiest and wealthiest countries in Latin America."[38] They concluded that economic statistics alone exploded the "myth of exploitation" created by those favoring the treaties.[39]

Publicists opposing the Panama Canal treaties never denied that the 1903 treaty benefited the United States; it was, in Crane's words, "a shrewd bargain."[40] But the Panamanians had duly ratified it, and they had benefited greatly from the presence of the canal. Antitreaty advocates rejected characterizations of U.S. policy as "colonial"; they emphasized how America helped Panama achieve its independence and its prosperity. The history of U.S.-Panamanian relations, as told by opponents of new Panama Canal treaties, revealed absolutely no wrongdoing by the United States. On the contrary, it displayed America's generosity toward an infant nation struggling for its identity and its material prosperity.

Treaty opponents contrasted their "true" version of America's history in Panama with the "revisionism" of "dishonest

and incompetent historians and . . . corrupted news media."
Among the "revisionists" the "worst offenders" were those
"with the highest responsibility to deal candidly with the American people: the White House and the State Department."[41] But
advocates on the other side were not about to admit that they
were "revisionists." They indeed told a very different history of
U.S.-Panamanian relations, but they too claimed to tell the
"true" story. Moreover, they claimed a morally superior philosophy of international relations—a belief that "fairness" should
be the measure of America's foreign policies. What seemed a
"shrewd bargain" to Philip Crane seemed an unfair advantage
to advocates favoring the treaties. They believed the 1903 treaty
pained the national conscience, and they offered the new Panama Canal treaties as medicine for America's soul.

Protreaty advocates did not merely echo the Panamanian
version of the Canal Zone's history. That undoubtedly would
have seemed overly radical to many Americans. They instead
occupied a middle ground, mixing moral indictment of U.S.
policy with veneration for Theodore Roosevelt and the glorious
canal-building project. For example, they implied that the
United States engineered the Panamanian revolution, but they
stopped short of saying the United States "stole" the canal. According to Sol Linowitz, the Panamanian revolution "occurred
. . . with the knowledge, if not the acquiescence of the United
States."[42] After the revolution, the United States hurriedly negotiated and signed a treaty, not with the Panamanians, but
with the Frenchman Bunau-Varilla.[43] But President Carter refused to "condemn my predecessors for having signed" the
1903 treaty. In his fireside chat, Carter even speculated that
Theodore Roosevelt—a "true conservative"—would have endorsed the new treaties:

> Theodore Roosevelt, who was President when America built
> the canal, saw history itself as a force, and the history of our own
> time and the changes it has brought would not be lost on him. He
> knew that change was inevitable and necessary. Change is growth.
> The true conservative, he once remarked, keeps his face to the
> future.
>
> But if Theodore Roosevelt were to endorse the treaties, as I'm

149

quite sure he would, it would be mainly because he could see the decision as one by which we are demonstrating the kind of great power we wish to be. . . .

In this historic decision, he would join us in our pride for being a great and generous people, with the national strength and wisdom to do what is right for us and what is fair to others.[44]

In a similar vein, treaty proponents walked a thin line between expressing guilt over American policy and actually charging America with "colonialism." They evoked guilt by asking Americans to imagine how they would feel if the French had retained a five-mile zone along the Mississippi River following the Louisiana Purchase.[45] Yet COACT and other pro-treaty advocates refused to call the situation "colonialism," arguing only that it came "close enough" to colonialism to justify Panamanian resentment. COACT acknowledged that the Canal Zone was not "a classic example of 'mother' country control," but offering reasons of expediency rather than morality, the group suggested that it still tarnished America's image as a "world leader in bringing an end to colonialism." Similarly, the State Department, while not directly admitting that America was a colonial power, observed that the Canal Zone was "regarded by many in Latin America and elsewhere as a colonial enclave, in which the U.S. imposes its will only because Panama lacks the power to alter the situation." The danger in such a perception, Sol Linowitz told the Council on Foreign Relations, was that it caused "substantial resentment" which "the Communists and other enemies" could "exploit . . . to their own ends." According to COACT, destroying the *perception* of colonialism "alone would be sufficient argument in favor of the documents."[46]

By refusing to contest their opponents fully on the morality of America's historical involvement in Panama, the administration hoped to avoid alienating citizens who took great pride in the canal and in American history generally. At the same time, the administration hoped to be sufficiently critical of the status quo to justify new treaties and to please the special interest groups that led the way in calling for change in U.S. policy. Yet by trying to persuade middle Americans to embrace the treaties with reasons of expediency, the administration alienated many of the ideologues who had been early support- ers. The administration's indictment of America's involvement in Panama did not go far enough to please many supporters on the left-wing of the protreaty coalition, while it was sufficiently "anti-American" to upset many conservative supporters.

Many religious leaders reconsidered their early support for the treaties precisely because of the administration's refusal to indict the United States on charges of "colonialism." Objecting to the emphasis in administration rhetoric on expediency and U.S. interests rather than morality, James Wall chided the ad- ministration in *Christian Century* for failing to make the word "justice" part of its "diplomatic vocabulary." Wall ultimately en- dorsed the new treaties only half-heartedly as "the best option available for justice in this particular moment of history." Simi- larly, Wes Michaelson of *Sojourners*, though a supporter of the treaties, wrote critically of the administration's lack of morally based rhetoric and its refusal to condemn American history. According to Michaelson, "the only way for an American to . . . avoid any sense of shame over the Panama Canal [was] to avoid reading the history of the canal." [47]

Other religious advocates flatly retracted their earlier sup- port for a new treaty in protest against the administration's "selling" of the pacts. The Ecumenical Program for Inter-Ameri- can Communication and Action (EPICA)—the lobbying and "educational" group sponsored by American churches—with- drew its long-standing support because of the lack of concern for justice in "official U.S. government propaganda and the me- dia." In *Treaty for Us, Treaty for Them*, EPICA claimed that the treaties were being "sold to the American public" because they were "good *for us*, which is precisely the problem with the Treaty of 1903 and the colonial environment of the Panama Ca- nal Zone: good for some Americans but extremely prejudicial to the Panamanian people." In *Panama: Sovereignty for a Land Di- vided*, EPICA described the "true" history of American moral abominations in Panama as seemingly planned by "satan and his imposters." EPICA's "revolutionary" poetry and revisionist historiography accused the "gringos" of everything from "the slaughter and exploitation of [Panama's] people" to crossing "the sidewalk of the nearby zone line to take [its] women."[48] Clearly, EPICA concluded, the new treaties did not go far enough to atone for such sins.

Although the administration's rhetoric did not condemn America's history sufficiently to please the leftists, it went far enough to cause an uprising on the right-wing of the protreaty coalition. One of the administration's most cherished allies, William F. Buckley, Jr., refused to remain silent amid suggestions that the United States "stole" the canal and exploited Panama. According to Buckley, the U.S. title to the canal was "morally and historically secure," and he refused "to renounce the foreign policy of Theodore Roosevelt." He was especially critical of guilt over "colonialism," proclaiming that colonialism was "far preferable to much that now goes on." In his debate with Ronald Reagan, he outflanked even his opponent on the right by announcing: "I for one am singularly unmoved by lachrymose appeals to pull out of Panama on the grounds that our presence there is 'the last vestige of colonialism.' My instinctive response to assertions put to me in those accents is: Maybe we should have a little *more* colonialism, not less of it."[49]

THE APPEAL OF THE ANTITREATY CASE

Despite their objections to the administration's historical case, many religious and political elites on both the left and the right continued to support the Panama Canal treaties, perhaps because they considered other issues more important. Because they worried more about America's economic and defense interests in the future, many treaty supporters seemed unconcerned that the administration downplayed historical controversies or offered unclear, seemingly contradictory responses to antitreaty arguments.

Public opinion polls, however, told a different story about the objections of the American people to the Panama Canal treaties. In October 1977 the Gallup poll asked those who had heard or read about the treaties, "What do you think are the best arguments against the treaties?" As William Schneider has observed, "one answer stood out: 'We built it and paid for it— we should keep it.'" Likewise, a Roper poll in January 1977 asked those who opposed the treaties about the most compelling arguments. From a list of arguments heard frequently in the debate, about half the respondents chose historical arguments: "We not only paid for the canal originally, but we have also paid a yearly fee to Panama for U.S. rights in the Canal Zone," and "When we made the Panama Canal treaty, it was supposed to last forever." In both polls, arguments concerning America's future military and economic interests in the canal were cited by far fewer citizens than were historical arguments.[50]

If it hoped to convert those who opposed new treaties for historical reasons, the administration needed to make a strong case that America had *not* "bought" the canal in 1903 and that the situation was unfair. Instead, administration advocates presented a seemingly contradictory case in an effort to please everyone. Not surprisingly, the administration alienated ideologues on both the left and the right. Moreover, the administration presented a case with very little emotional appeal. In the end, the administration's case seemed a repudiation of the accomplishments that Americans had celebrated with pride since 1903. Many Americans apparently felt uncomfortable hearing that the story of their country's actions in Panama had been wrong all along. They undoubtedly did not like hearing their country transformed from a hero into a villain.

The rhetoric of antitreaty forces solidified this emotional predisposition to reject negative "revelations" about American history. Treaty opponents told Americans that they had no reason to be ashamed of their country. They resurrected the patriotic emotions surrounding the building of the canal, emphasized America's unselfish contribution to the world in operating the canal, and shifted all blame for troubles in U.S.-Panamanian relations to the Panamanians themselves.

Recollections of the glorious canal-building project proved effective emotional appeals in antitreaty rhetoric. With rhetoric reminiscent of the celebration as the canal neared completion, antitreaty advocates rekindled patriotic memories of the triumphs and sacrifices of their fellow citizens over a half century ago. The French failure, the resistence of the jungle, the ingenuity of the dams and the locks, and the "brilliant victory" of U.S. health and sanitation forces all added up to one of the "brightest chapters" in American history. We built the "eighth wonder of the world," Ronald Reagan exclaimed in his debate with William F. Buckley. And to make keeping this "wonder of the world" and "marvel of American engineering" even more emotionally compelling, Philip Crane reminded viewers of the ACU's taped "telethon" that twenty-five thousand people had sacrificed their lives on the job.[51]

Pride was the controlling motif throughout the ACU's "telethon," as both visual images and rhetorical questions enticed Americans to contemplate the canal's patriotic symbolism. Through film and animation, the videotape treated viewers to the "thrill of taking a ship through . . . 'the Big Ditch.'" Later, Senator Jesse Helms asked: "If we cannot be proud of our engineering, commercial, medical, peacekeeping and other laudatory accomplishments in the Canal Zone, in what *can* we find pride?" Similarly, Senator Strom Thurmond stirred patriotism by imagining the excitement of some future archaeologist: "What a civilization it must have been to build this!"[52]

Treaty opponents also encouraged patriotic pride by talking of America's record in running the canal. Philip Crane noted that the United States had given the world a magnificent canal and had operated it on an inexpensive, nondiscriminatory basis: "Uncle Sam, if he had wished, could have gouged the world's shipping with heavy tolls." Instead, the United States operated the canal "on a break-even, or non-profit basis" and "saved consumers . . . in the world—especially Latin America—billions of dollars."[53] Treaty opponents spoke of "an honorable record in operating the canal as an international public utility," and they urged Americans to be proud of that record. As Reagan summarized the point in his nationwide address: "We can be proud of the way we've used [the] right [to operate the canal]. For 64 years, we've run the canal at no profit, and kept it open to all peaceful shipping of the world."[54]

Treaty opponents expunged American guilt over problems

in U.S.-Panamanian relations by making Panama the scapegoat. Despite all the sacrifices, all the favors to Panama, and all the magnificent accomplishments of the Americans, the Panamanians were ungrateful and hostile. They had not invested even "one bent dime in the canal,"[55] yet they demanded control and used threats to force their demands. According to Philip Crane, the Panamanians, prodded by "political demagogues—and the certainty that the United States [would] react with fairness, compassion, and restraint, even when provoked"—had "whipped themselves into an unthinking frenzy of jingoism and anti-Americanism." Their "specialty" was "to bite America's hand while simultaneously demanding bigger and bigger American handouts." Robert Strother called Panama's "hate-America campaign" an effort to divert attention from its own domestic ills, while Donald Dozer argued that Panamanian demands had assumed "the character of *blackmail* threats." Dozer summarized the antitreaty explanation of Panama's behavior by claiming that they simply were jealous: "The very success of the United States . . . has filled Panamanian demagogues with envy which has driven them to covet their neighbor's canal and canal zone. There would be no Canal problem today if these politicians would follow the commandment 'Thou shalt not covet thy neighbor's Canal Zone, his Canal, or anything that is thy neighbor's.'"[56]

The Carter administration denied that the opposition had a monopoly on pride in America's history in Panama. In his fireside chat, President Carter sounded as chauvinistic as his harshest critics: "The building of the canal was one of the greatest engineering feats of history. . . . We Americans are justly and deeply proud of this great achievement." Speaking to an audience in Florida in November 1977, Deputy Secretary of State Warren Christopher also sounded like many of his opponents:

Since it was built, the canal has been more to us than simply another waterway for our ships. It was built at a time when America was just emerging on the world scene. We were able to conquer this monumental engineering problem where others failed. Even today, it is impressive to see how ingenious the canal system really is. In-

deed, the canal came to symbolize the resourcefulness and ingenuity of the American people—qualities that we all believe to be
among our greatest assets as a nation.[57]

Especially before conservative audiences, administration
advocates emphasized America's historical achievements, as in
a speech by Sol Linowitz before a hostile American Legion
convention:

> And we have more than the canal's technology which we can
> point to with such pride. For 62 years we have operated the canal
> for the nations of the world more as a public service than as a busi-
> ness. The canal's tolls have been set as low as has been compatible
> with meeting costs and providing a modest return, and world com-
> merce has been a major beneficiary, not just our own domestic and
> foreign trade.[58]

But the administration's claims of pride in the canal's history rang hollow amidst its more frequent claims that the United
States had wronged Panama. Like William F. Buckley, Jr., many
Americans probably found it difficult to reconcile professions
of pride in America's past with protreaty claims about American
"colonialism" and "imperialism." Moreover, the administration's historical case lacked popular appeal in general because it
repudiated heroes like Theodore Roosevelt and an era recalled
fondly by many Americans. The era when America worked its
will on the world looked even better in the context of America's
retreat from Vietnam.

Of course, there was more to the public debate over the
Panama Canal treaties than controversies over history. Protreaty advocates may not have hoped to win the debate over history, but they thought they had a strong case for America's economic and military interests in ratification. Treaty supporters
considered issues involving the impact of the treaties on America's future international role to be more important than issues
concerning the past. But arguments about the future are by
definition more speculative, and again protreaty advocates
faced determined opposition.

7

Predicting the Future

Debates over long-range foreign policy call upon advocates to do the impossible: to predict the future. Nobody really knows what circumstances might be in ten, fifty, or a hundred years, yet policymakers must judge treaties and other agreements in the light of such long-term repercussions. When contemplating the future, policymakers frequently look for guidance in the testimony of experts or in historical analogies. But expert opinion typically is divided, and analogies to the past involve the questionable assumption that history repeats itself. More often than not, policymakers must rely on little more than their own intuition about what the future might bring.

Three sorts of issues in the debate over the Panama Canal treaties combined to create very different portraits of the future. First, economic issues, ranging from the short-term costs of implementing the treaties to their long-term impact on the American economy, produced very different predictions. In general, opponents of the treaties predicted that the agreement would have direct and indirect costs amounting to billions of dollars, while those supporting the treaties minimized their costs and predicted favorable economic impacts. Second, issues relating to American military interests led to heated controversy over the future. These issues, ranging from the immediate impact of the treaties on existing bases and operations in Panama to the canal's role in warfare in the twenty-first century, became perhaps the most important in the debate. With opponents of the treaties arguing that the treaties would jeopardize the security of the United States, predictions involving military issues assumed great importance. Finally, issues surrounding the international political competition between the United States and its adversaries led both sides to very different predictions. While opponents of the treaties predicted that the treaties would symbolize America's lost resolve and aid the cause of communism in Latin America, treaty supporters spoke of creating a new, more positive image for America, thereby preventing communism from spreading.

Both sides in the debate over Panama ultimately viewed the controversy as a contest over the basic philosophy of American foreign policy in the coming generation. As the first major foreign policy debate in the post-Vietnam era, the debate over Panama provided an opportunity for American policymakers to reflect on mistakes of the past and to restore direction and purpose to American foreign policy. Both sides in the debate agreed that American foreign policy was in disarray; both sides agreed that America had no coherent set of principles to guide specific decisions. Thus, the debate over Panama became, not just a contest over new policies in Panama, but a competition to establish the overarching framework for America's relations with the rest of the world.

The Economic Debate

Opponents of the Panama Canal treaties coined the term "payaway" to describe their most immediate economic objection to the Panama Canal treaties.[1] Ronald Reagan explained the term in his nationally televised address on the canal: "We're debating over treaties by which we not only will give away the canal. We'll also pay a considerable amount to the government of Panama for taking it off our hands." He then detailed the costs and the total economic burden: "In additionto some hundreds of millions of dollars in loans and aid, we would pay the $10 million a year I mentioned for municipal-type services, another $10 million from canal operations each year, plus thirty cents a ton on cargo going through the canal. Estimates on the total range up to . . . $80 million a year."[2]

Treaty opponents claimed that American taxpayers would pick up the tab for this forty-fold increase in payments to Panama. "Contrary to the statements of Ambassadors Linowitz and Bunker," John McGarret wrote, "the sums of money the Agreement proposes to pay Panama *cannot* be generated from increased tolls alone, due to competitive alternatives and the economic impact of diminishing returns. Additional sums will have to be provided by American taxpayers." For the total amount of payments, one also had to add the value of properties to be relinquished to Panama. Reagan estimated the total value of the canal properties "to be as high as six to ten billion dollars, depending on whose estimate you choose." Perhaps this could be justified if the Panamanian people were to benefit from the deal. But according to Reagan, the treaties proposed "an outright payment to the Panamanian government," with "no assurance that the Panamanian people would benefit."[3]

The long-term costs could be even greater, according to treaty opponents. They argued that Americans would pay indirectly through higher consumer prices, depressed farm prices, loss of jobs, and other disruptions of the U.S. economy. Part of the long-term threat of the treaties stemmed from anticipated toll increases of up to 46 percent. Reagan warned that such increases would "price some American exports . . . out of world competition," with devastating effects on American farmers and workers.[4] Opponents of the treaties also claimed that the canal would not always remain open under a Panamanian regime and predicted serious economic consequences from periodic closures. Philip Crane pointed out that the cost just of rerouting American naval vessels would run "to nearly $10 million a year in extra fuel alone." When one considered that 70 percent of all cargo transiting the canal either originated from, or headed to, an American port, it seemed clear "that dislocations in the U.S. economy could take place if the Canal were closed by accident or design." Treaty opponents predicted that if the treaties passed, the American consumer would "be hit in the wallet and forced to pay higher prices for almost everything—including our own Alaskan oil."[5]

Alaskan oil became a special topic, as treaty opponents exploited the energy crisis of the late 1970s. With oil production in Alaska, Philip Crane argued, "the canal's importance to America increases rather than decreases." Crane predicted in *Surrender in Panama* that "American consumers . . . will have to pay more at the pump for every gallon of gas flowing from Alaska to the East Coast and energy-hungry communities of the Midwest":

> If, as projected, the flow of Alaska crude creates an oil glut on our West Coast, efficient, economical shipping of vast amounts of it to the East Coast becomes imperative, and this, in turn, makes an open, low-toll canal a vital economic necessity to the United States. The companies developing the Alaska slope recognized this when they planned a building program for medium-sized tankers . . . designed for transit through the canal.
>
> But at almost the precise moment that the flow of Alaskan oil began pouring into the hulls of the tankers at Valdez, the Carter administration signed the Panama treaties, which guarantee substantial increases in the price of the oil, through higher freight costs—and could even lead to closure of the canal.
>
> Even assuming that the ultimate catastrophe of closure is prevented, we still face the problem of toll increases. Article XIII of the Panama Canal Treaty provides that the government of Panama shall receive 30 cents per ton on all cargo passing through the canal once the treaty comes into force. Thus, for each 60,000-ton oil tanker, we would have to pay additional political tribute to Torrijos of about $18,000 in increased tolls.[6]

Increased tolls or closure of the canal would affect not just oil shipments but all commercial shipping. Treaty opponents noted that 96 or 97 percent of the world's shipping could still use the canal; the few ships that could not squeeze through "were designed for specific purposes that do not include a need for passage through either the Panama or Suez Canal."[7] Furthermore, they argued that the trend in ship-building was toward smaller vessels. They argued that the canal was not becoming obsolete but was actually increasing in importance. In any case, they concluded that large ships gave cause for "enlarging and modernizing" the canal, not for getting rid of it.[8]

Those favoring the treaties, of course, painted a very different portrait of the economic impact of the treaties. Were we paying Panama to take the canal off our hands? No, said President Carter in his "fireside chat." "Under the new treaty," he said, "any payments to Panama will come from tolls paid by ships which use the canal." According to Secretary of State Cyrus Vance, this meant that the treaties would "require no payments of tax dollars from the U.S. Treasury to Panama, either now or in the future."[9] Treaty proponents admitted that there would be some increase in payments to Panama, but they claimed that the use of the territory would remain a bargain compared to payments to other countries for use of their lands.[10] Rather than "paying Panama to take the canal," they liked to describe the increases as "paying a higher rent to Panama for the use of its territory." They claimed that the treaties simply made a long-overdue adjustment in payments for use of Panama's "major national resource—its territory."[11]

Treaty supporters also disputed predictions that Panama would raise canal tolls to "unbearable" levels under the new arrangement. The Panamanians would not do this, COACT argued, because of "the marketplace." Panama's goal would be to "maximize its revenues from tolls," and if it raised tolls too high, it would "drive away its business." Similarly, President Carter dismissed the prospect that "the board of directors would go wild and set a transit fee that would be extraordinarily high." He argued that if tolls became excessive, ships would go around the Horn or "off-load on the east or west coast or the gulf coast and let rail shipment replace transit shipment."[12] Although Carter and his allies admitted there would be an increase in tolls of up to 30 percent, they insisted that such an increase would still leave fees at Panama far lower than those at Suez and considerably behind the rate of inflation.[13] In forty years, Warren Christopher observed, tolls at Panama had risen from 90 cents per ton to $1.29. "Can you think of any other product or service which has increased so little in 40 years?"[14]

Treaty supporters insisted that toll increases resulting from the treaties would affect the United States very little. Treaty negotiator Ellsworth Bunker gave some examples in his speech in Des Moines: "North Slope oil shipments would be increased in price by about a tenth of a cent a gallon; and at 70 cents a gallon this increase to the consumer would be a small fraction of one percent; transportation costs for a Toyota or Datsun would go up by only about $3." By the same token, American exports would not be adversely affected, according to treaty supporters. Secretary of State Vance claimed that even a 40 percent toll increase would increase the price of Iowa corn in Japan "by less than 1/2 cent per bushel." The overall impact of the anticipated toll increase thus would not be substantial, according to protreaty publicists. Ellsworth Bunker summarized the protreaty case on the treaties' economic impact:

> A toll increase of about 30 percent would involve a transportation cost increase of less than 1 percent. All users of the canal would pay only about $50 million more in tolls per year on cargoes that have a value in excess of roughly $50 billion, that is, one-tenth of 1 percent. But in most instances it is the buyer who is the ultimate payer of canal tolls and not the seller or the shipper. Thus, of this $50 million, it should be understood that businesses and consumers in the United States would be the ultimate payers of only about $15 million.
>
> In conclusion, it is our judgment that the overall impact of such a toll increase on a $2 trillion economy would be virtually negligible in the aggregate on either our business or the purchasing power of the consumer.[15]

Predictions of a relatively small toll increase went hand-in-hand in protreaty rhetoric with a general depreciation of the canal's value to U.S. commerce. According to treaty proponents, America's economic dependence on the Panama Canal had been "steadily declining."[16] Only about 7 percent of the "waterborne portion" of U.S. trade used the canal, they pointed out—an amount affecting only 1 percent of America's GNP.[17] In the future that value would decline further because of new trading patterns and because of new, larger cargo ships incapable of using the canal.[18] Even closing the canal would therefore have little impact on the U.S. economy. "It would be like a slight tremor," said COACT's sample speech, "felt only at the points of impact and otherwise barely noticed." Cargo shipments could simply be rechanneled "to other routes or modes of transport, resulting in some instances in somewhat higher consumer prices."[19]

Treaty supporters, of course, presented scenarios involving closure of the canal only for the sake of argument; they did not share their opponents lack of faith in the Panamanians' ability to keep the canal open. They assumed that the new treaties would result in political stability and a regime of military defense which would make the canal less vulnerable to attacks that could shut it down. Even though it had never been attacked, they insisted that the canal could be even more secure under the proposed new treaties.

Opponents of the treaties were not so optimistic. They viewed provisions governing defense of the canal as intolerably vague and weak, and they predicted all sorts of disasters if the treaties were ratified. They also wondered why the United States should ever relinquish an asset of such great military value. They wondered why the United States should abandon an arrangement with proven military utility for an uncertain future of Panamanian control.

Debate over economic issues thus led inevitably to concerns over the security of the canal. The canal obviously would be of no value economically if it could not be kept open. But beyond concern over closure of the canal, advocates on both sides debated a broad range of military issues. These issues were paramount in the debate, as each side accused the other of jeopardizing the security interests of the United States itself.

THE DEBATE OVER MILITARY INTERESTS

Debate over military issues closely paralleled debate over economic concerns. Opponents of the treaties presented the canal as an invaluable American military asset, while defenders of the treaties spoke of its diminishing value. Those against ratifying the treaties predicted military disaster under the proposed new treaties, while treaty defenders spoke of a happy "partnership" resulting in a more secure and efficient canal. As the debate touched on military issues, the advocates seemed to realize that the stakes were much higher. No longer were they concerned merely with the price of a Toyota or a bushel of corn. Now the debate concerned America's security and military interests in the post-Vietnam era.

Opponents of the treaties stressed military issues over all others in the debate. Like opponents of concessions to Panama throughout the twentieth century, they considered the Panama Canal primarily a strategic rather than a commercial asset. They theorized that U.S. security depended upon control of "the world's sea routes" and "maritime choke points," and they called the canal "an indispensable link in this network of maritime lifelines." To lose control of this "choke point," they suggested, would be to lose perhaps the greatest asset in defense of the West. It could mean, in Ronald Reagan's estimation, the loss of "our own freedom."[20]

"To seasoned observers," Captain Paul Ryan wrote, "the missing ingredient in the canal negotiations was the critical question of whether the security of the United States and the Western Hemisphere would be adversely affected by the proposed treaty." According to treaty opponents, American negotiators simply did not take strategic considerations into account. Worse yet, the State Department then misled the American people by "understating the canal's importance to U.S. strategic . . . interests." As Philip Crane put it in the ACU's television program, those who advocated "giving away" the canal were not "telling the truth" when they downgraded the canal's "military usefulness."[21]

The most obvious distortion was the claim that "many major warships" or "our largest warships" could not use the canal.[22] In truth only the thirteen largest aircraft carriers could not squeeze through the canal, while the "remaining 470 U.S. combat vessels, including nuclear submarines," posed no problem at all.[23] Treaty opponents cited statistics showing that most of the supplies bound for the wars in Korea and Vietnam had passed through the canal, and they insisted that those wars could not have been fought effectively without the waterway.[24]

Opponents of the treaties insisted that the canal would become even more important militarily in the future. First, they noted a trend in shipbuilding toward smaller ships that could use the canal. Military affairs writer Hanson Baldwin argued that "a major change in naval ship size, construction, and design" was underway and that this trend would do away with the giant aircraft carriers—the "behemoths of the seas." In their place would be a new generation of ships—"smaller, but more effective, with VSTOL aircraft, drones, missiles, or other new state-of-the-art developments like hovercrafts and hydrofoils."[25] Second, treaty opponents argued that the nature of modern warfare actually enhanced the value of the canal. Charles Maechling admitted that the canal would be relatively unimportant in all-out war but noted that "limited wars have been the rule since 1945." In limited wars, he argued, "the role of the canal is vital." Philip Crane explained that "small, swift military 'police actions'" required the "speed of response and quick logistical support" that only the canal could provide.[26]

Because they so emphasized the military value of the canal, opponents of the Panama Canal treaties faced a significant dilemma in responding to concerns that rejecting the treaties would prompt Panamanian rioting, sabotage, or even guerilla war that might close the canal. If they succeeded in defeating the pacts, would they not be to blame if angry Panamanians attacked the waterway? In their efforts to portray Torrijos as a radical and the treaties as attempted "blackmail," treaty opponents themselves publicized threats by the Panamanians. Hanson Baldwin was among those noting that General Omar Torrijos had "invoked the threat of open attack" on the Canal Zone if the treaties were rejected "on at least twenty occasions." Treaty opponents noted how Torrijos and his associates went about speaking of the "route of Ho Chi Minh" and of wars of national liberation. They reported that on one occasion Torrijos proclaimed that if angry Panamanian citizens assaulted the Canal Zone, he would have but two options: to crush them or to lead them. Torrijos, they noted, promised that he would not "crush the Panamanians."[27]

At the same time, treaty opponents urged Americans not

to take the threats too seriously. The threats proved the radicalism of the Panamanians, they suggested, but they assured their audiences that the canal would not be destroyed if they prevailed in the debate. James Lucier, for instance, ridiculed Panamanian talk of "another Vietnam" as a publicity stunt:

> Another Vietnam? An *opera bouffe* Vietnam, perhaps, staged for the TV cameras, with one detachment of the *Guardia Nacional* running behind the scenes to march in from stage left over and over again. Some shooting, some arson, some easily repaired damage to the Canal. The whole of Panama has only 1.6 million people, about the same number as Atlanta. The Vietnam talk is meant for scare headlines in the American press, with which to beat recalcitrant legislators in Congress.[28]

Other treaty opponents pointed out that in an assault on the Canal Zone the ill-prepared *Guardia Nacional* would face nearly ten thousand U.S. troops who were "very close to being the top of the U.S. military."[29] Furthermore, Torrijos realized that a successful assault on the canal would destroy Panama's chief economic resource and undermine his own power.[30] Treaty opponents dismissed the threats as political propaganda intended "to divert attention from corruption, waste, favoritism, inflation, high taxes, and other familiar ills" in Panama, where "anti-Yanqui demagoguery" was "the time-tested road to political power."[31]

Sabotage was another matter, since the canal conceivably could be disabled by enraged Panamanians beyond the control of their government. Treaty opponents dismissed this threat too, however, by pointing out that the United States had successfully prevented sabotage throughout four wars and years of Panamanian rioting. "If the Panama Canal is so vulnerable," asked Senator Helms in the ACU's telethon, "why didn't the Germans or Japanese in World War II just slip ashore a few guerillas to shut it down? Why didn't Communist sympathizers do the same during the Vietnam War, when at one point 70 percent of the shipments to the war zone in Asia were sent through the canal?" The answer, of course, was that the canal was not as vulnerable as Panamanian threats suggested. Ronald Reagan argued the point in his televised debate with William F. Buckley, Jr.: "I claim that with the United States' military force . . . it's going to take more than a single saboteur slipping in in the night with a hand grenade or an explosive charge. It's going to take a trained demolition team, with plenty of time to work and no interruption, to do something to disable the gates, the locks, and so forth."[32]

Whatever the vulnerability of the canal, treaty opponents denied that the proposed treaties would improve the political climate and reduce the likelihood of attacks on the canal. In the first place, they deemed rioting and other political disorders "endemic" in Panama. The new treaties would not change that fact, especially since the "leftist elements" historically responsible for violence in Panama seemed no more satisfied with the proposed treaties than with the status quo. As Reagan noted in an interview with *Newsweek*, dissidents in Panama already had warned that they would not be satisfied "as long as there is a single American left in the Zone." Given that the proposed treaties called for "a declining presence over 23 years," the threat of sabotage would remain whether the Senate ratified or rejected the treaties.[33]

Second, treaty opponents argued that "an American withdrawal, and the power vacuum it would leave in its wake," would "most likely . . . encourage internal disorder in Panama and terrorist or sabotage activities within the Canal Zone." They argued that only the American presence kept Panama's endemic disorder in check. John McGarret wrote that unrest resulting from rejecting the treaties would seem "but a small brush fire compared to the uncontrollable forest fire" that would ensue later without the deterrent of American forces.[34]

Finally, opponents of the treaties argued that all the talk of rioting and sabotage raised a larger issue—that of "U.S. response to terrorist threats" and attempted "blackmail."[35] If the United States ratified treaties negotiated "under duress," they argued, it would create "the picture of a United States that bows to demands" and bring demands that the United States also evacuate Guantanamo, Puerto Rico, and other important holdings. "Precisely where and when the next demand will come we cannot say," warned Ronald Reagan, "but come it will."[36] And the cost would go beyond the loss of a few strategic bases. The final cost could be a "widespread loss of respect" for the United States.[37]

As the debate progressed, general arguments concerning the military value of the canal and its vulnerability to Panamanian attack were supplanted by debate over the specific military provisions of the proposed agreement. In particular, opponents of the treaties raised concerns that the Panama Canal Treaty—the pact providing for joint defense of the canal until the year 2000—rested upon the faulty assumption that the Panamanians would be cooperative. In his debate with William F. Buckley, Jr., Ronald Reagan ridiculed the protreaty vision of American and Panamanian troops acting in harmonious partnership to defend the canal, as called for in the agreement:

> Joint defense. . . . Now, that brings to mind a picture of friendly allies going forward, shoulder to shoulder, in friendly camaraderie, the Americans voicing, probably, their customary marching chants, such as the well-known "Sound off. One, two." The Panamanian Guardia Nacional will be chanting the words that they use in their present training. They march to these words: *"Muerte al gringo! Gringo abajo! Gringo al paredon!"* Translation: "Death to the gringo! Down with the gringo! Gringo to the wall!"
>
> Now, that should reassure us gringos about the kind of cooperation we might have under the new treaties.[38]

The defense provisions of the neutrality treaty seemed even more absurd to opponents of the treaties, especially the notion that Panama could assume primary responsibility for defending the canal after the year 2000. Once American troops withdrew, Philip Crane argued, "the only thing standing between chaos and disruption in Panama and the Canal Zone will be the politicized Panamanian National Guard and police, smaller in number than our current garrison with three-fourths of their numbers lacking even basic infantry training." This "pathetic rabble would be incapable of guarding and defending the Canal Zone from attack or sabotage even if it wanted to." And there was "every reason to believe that, in a crisis, their loyalties would lie not with any abstract treaty commitments, but with whatever dictator or faction happened to be dispensing Panamanian salaries and graft at the moment." Albert Norman presented a similar (though less insulting) assessment of the capacity of Panama to defend the canal:

> With what national resources—manpower, air power, naval power, and financial power—will the Panamanian republic be able to guarantee the canal's "permanent neutrality," its non-belligerency, in time of war among the great powers of the world and resist the political and military pressures and threats that may come in time of peace? . . .
> To place so heavy a burden on so small a nation as the Republic of Panama is, from all appearances and calculated future capabilities, both unreal and unnecessary.[39]

The neutrality treaty also failed to assure America's right to use the canal to military advantage, treaty opponents argued. Indeed, they objected to the concept of neutrality itself. Neutrality "could be extremely dangerous to America, in time of war," Philip Crane contended. Major General J. Milnor Roberts (United States Army Reserve, Retired) explained to viewers of the ACU "telethon" that neutrality actually could protect Communist use of the canal in wartime:

> "Neutrality" is a word that sounds good to many ears. But when you apply it to something of strategic value, "neutrality" becomes dangerous. For example, would you want your local police to practice "neutrality" if vandals raided your home or neighborhood? The proposed neutrality treaty for our canal at the Isthmus of Panama would guarantee peaceful passage for all ships—*including* ships of any enemy and its allies in time of war. This means that communist troops and supplies could be shipped right under our nose in order to kill American troops. . . .
> Teddy Roosevelt . . . successfully fought the notion of a neutral canal. He wrote: "I do not see why we should dig the canal if we are not to fortify it so to insure its being used for ourselves and against our foes in time of war."

According to Phelps Jones, head of the VFW, the neutrality treaty created "the same neutrality monster that the U.S. Senate was wise enough to reject before it agreed to build the canal."[40]

Because they believed Panama could not defend the canal,

treaty opponents demanded that the United States retain the right to intervene militarily and to receive priority passage during military emergencies. The Carter administration claimed that the treaties would give the United States these rights. But treaty opponents remained unconvinced. Ronald Reagan proclaimed that the neutrality treaty was "so ambiguous that already the people of the United States are being told by our government that we have rights which the government of Panama is telling its people we don't have." Reagan and others pointed out that high-level Panamanian officials, especially treaty negotiator Dr. Romulo Escobar Bethancourt, refused to allow the word "guarantee" to describe America's right to intervene in defense of the canal. The Panamanians also reportedly deemed the phrase "expeditious passage" a meaningless expression designed only to help the Carter administration sell the pacts to its own Pentagon.[41]

The Carter administration moved to silence such criticism in October 1977 with the Carter-Torrijos Statement of Understanding. As noted earlier, the statement of understanding reaffirmed the right of the United States to defend the neutrality of the canal, but it added that this could not be interpreted as a right of intervention in the internal affairs of Panama. Also, the statement interpreted the right of "expeditious passage" to mean that American warships, "in case of need or emergency," could go "to the head of the line of vessels in order to transit the Canal rapidly."

But while the statement of understanding "purported to clarify the Neutrality Treaty," Philip Crane argued, it only succeeded in "further muddying the waters." The statement "was merely a personal agreement—and a vague one at that—between Jimmy Carter and Omar Torrijos, and in no way a legally binding part of the Neutrality Treaty." And even if it were part of the treaty, it would hurt rather than enhance American rights. The addition of language prohibiting "intervention" in the "internal affairs" of Panama would effectively ban American intervention in the former Canal Zone altogether, since "under the terms of the treaties, the zone would become Panamanian territory. Thus, by definition, any American intervention in the former Canal Zone would be intervention in the internal affairs of Panama."[42]

Opponents of the treaties also claimed that the statement did nothing to assure priority passage for American warships. The statement clarified the term "expeditious passage" somewhat by defining it as the right to go to the "head-of-the-line." But it failed to define what constituted "need or emergency" and it did not say who had the power to declare that an emergency existed. More important, since it was never signed or submitted to Congress the statement guaranteed nothing beyond the vague rights already in the treaty. Treaty opponents noted how Torrijos boasted to his countrymen that he had signed "not even . . . an autograph" while in Washington.[43]

The Carter administration presented a very different picture of the treaties' military aspects. In speaking of the military implications of the agreement, the administration navigated a middle course designed to satisfy a variety of audiences. As their opponents charged, protreaty advocates typically minimized the military value of the canal and mentioned the threat of violence if the treaties were rejected. But they also professed many of the same values and goals as the opposition and they responded to Panamanian threats with "tough talk" about America's resolve to defend the canal. They too claimed to be primarily concerned with protecting American military interests, and they insisted that the military provisions of the treaties assured the canal's security and continued use by the United States. They predicted that the Panama Canal treaties would protect American military interests fully while being fair and generous to a lesser military power.

The administration's play for broad-based support was evident in its arguments concerning the military value of the canal. On the one hand, administration advocates minimized the value of the canal by speaking of the "larger warships" that could not use it. "Clearly," Sol Linowitz declared, the canal was "no longer as useful as it once was for the shifting of combat forces." President Carter even claimed that "only four or five Navy Warships" had used the canal in the previous twelve months.[44] On the other hand, treaty proponents insisted that

American negotiators had operated on the premise that the canal remained important to the U.S. military.[45] Ellsworth Bunker told the Rainer Club in Seattle that the negotiators considered the canal to be "of continuing importance" because it enabled the United States to "shorten our supply lines to some areas." Bunker admitted that the canal's "contributions during the Second World War, Korean war, and Viet-nam war" had been "amply documented." But still he insisted that the canal's military value was "probably not as great relatively speaking as in earlier years."[46]

Protreaty strategists chose one theme to emphasize over all others: the argument that the new treaties would best assure America's continued "use" of the canal. Since the United States legally had this right under the 1903 treaty, of course, the implication of the argument was that Panamanian hostility might explode into an assault or sabotage of the canal, and treaty proponents deemed the canal extremely vulnerable to closure. The COACT sample speech explained: "The Panama Canal is not just a ditch between two seas, like the Suez Canal. Its locks are small and fragile, and each one—like links in a chain—indispensable. Its reservoir system is filled by rainfall, and, if emptied by a sudden break in a dam or the lock system, would take up to two years to refill. Enough explosives to cause that damage could be carried by one person in a lunchpail." President Carter insisted that it would be "almost impossible to prevent the disruption or closing of the Panama Canal by sabotage" if the new treaties were rejected.[47]

Approving the treaties, on the other hand, would reduce the chances of sabotage by giving the Panamanians a "stake" in the canal. The "greatest asset in defending the canal," Ellsworth Bunker argued, was not American power but the "absence of hostility and the active and harmonious support of the Panamanian population." By making it "overwhelmingly unlikely that a violent confrontation would find the Americans and the Panamanians on opposite sides," according to COACT's sample speech, the new treaties would render "the problem of the canal's extreme vulnerability largely moot—somewhat like the problem of how we would defend our borders against an attack from Canada or Mexico." Administration spokesmen admitted that the threat of sabotage could not be eliminated entirely. As Elliot Richardson told the Kansas City Lawyers Association, "with or without the new treaties, no one can promise you a foolproof defense against sabotage." But the new treaties would "give the Panamanian Government an increasing role in its operation and defense." Because of their greater economic, political, and psychological stake in the canal under the new agreement, he concluded, "the incentive for sabotage by individual Panamanians would be diminished; the capability and the motivation of the Panamanian Government to deter sabotage would be increased." [48]

Perhaps because they were stung by charges of Panamanian "blackmail," protreaty advocates sometimes denied that Panama had made threats.[49] More often, however, they simply balanced their talk of sabotage with "tough talk." While the administration told some audiences that it would be impossible to defend the canal against sabotage, it told others that America could and would repel any attack on the canal. President Carter, for instance, told a group of editors and news directors that "our nation would have the military capability to defend [the canal] in spite of a threat of sabotage or other similar threats." He also promised a group of citizens in Denver that he would not hesitate to use that military capability: "It would be a mistake for anyone to say that our country couldn't defend [the canal] if it were attacked by insurgents, by terrorists, or by well-meaning patriots of Panama in opposition to the stance of the Panama Government. We could defend the Panama Canal, and if it is attacked by any means, I will defend it, and our country will be able to defend the canal." The administration claimed to agree that threats from Panama did not provide good reason to support the treaties. As Sol Linowitz put it, "we're not stressing that aspect because we don't want people to feel that the reason to vote for the treaties is to avoid guerilla warfare." [50]

The administration's pledge to prevent sabotage did not answer questions concerning the defense of the canal once American troops were removed. Would the Panamanians be capable of defending the canal against sabotage once they took over?

More important, would the Panamanians be able to defend the canal against an all-out attack by an outside military power? Despite the vigor with which treaty opponents raised these questions, treaty proponents provided few answers. Even COACT admitted that the Panamanian National Guard would require "an expansion of . . . current strength and capabilities" just to provide assistance with "routine security for Canal installations" in the short-term. As to what might happen after the Americans left in the year 2000, COACT could offer only "hope that Panama could assume major responsibility for Canal defense" as stipulated in the neutrality treaty. COACT admitted that Panama would always "require considerable assistance in the event of an all-out attack by a major power."[51]

Similarly, supporters of the treaties provided only perfunctory responses to criticism of the neutrality called for in the new treaties. COACT provided virtually the only response to the charge that enemy ships could use the canal against the United States in wartime. According to COACT, the United States "never had the right to exclude the shipping of other countries even when we were at war with them." COACT pointed out that "even German and Japanese ships were technically permitted to use the Canal during World War II, though they did not use that right."[52] America's enemies declined to use the canal, of course, because technicalities mean little in wartime, and the United States had troops and installations in Panama which could have attacked enemy ships in the waters approaching the canal. COACT did not address the question of whether enemies would continue to shy away from the canal once the American military presence in Panama ended.

Treaty supporters had more to say about specific defense provisions, especially the controversial matters of defense rights and "expeditious passage" after the year 2000. With the news media and members of Congress complaining about the vagueness of these provisions,[53] the administration was forced to respond. Early in the debate administration spokesmen stuck to the standard response articulated by President Carter in an interview with editors and news directors:

174

Following the year 2000, the Panamanians will take operating control of the canal. We will retain the right, unilaterally, to decide what is necessary on our part to guarantee the neutrality of the canal. . . . In case of an emergency, we and the Panamanians have so-called rights of expeditious passage, which means that we get priority use of the canal for our warships and for strategic cargo to be passed through the canal.[54]

But this response soon proved inadequate. Many audiences apparently wanted to hear that the United States would retain the right to "intervene" in defense of the canal, while the word "intervene" outraged the Panamanians. Official spokesmen like Sol Linowitz thus sought to deflect the issue by saying: "I don't like the word intervene. . . . I think the answer to the question is let's wait and see. We are trying not to get into those situations in the future." Similarly, administration spokesmen seemed evasive when responding to questions concerning the meaning of "expeditious passage," as in this curious exchange between Linowitz and a reporter on whether "expeditious" meant "priority" passage:

Q: What is meant by expeditious passage? That seems to be sort of an arcane word that is subject to several interpretations. How do you interpret it?

Ambassador Linowitz: Get through with it as soon as you reasonably can. . . .

Q: I want to know whether it means priority for U.S. vessels over those of other flags.

Linowitz: The United States and Panama alone will have the right to expeditious passage.

Q: Which means priority over other flags. Is that correct?

Linowitz: We have not used the word priority.

Q: Is that a correct interpretation?

Linowitz: It means they will be in the position where two ships are coming at the same time, one being the U.S.-Panamanian and another ship, the U.S.-Panamanian could be accorded expeditious passage.[55]

According to Linowitz, "expeditious passage" thus meant "expeditious passage." Not surprisingly, such responses failed to satisfy those demanding that U.S. ships have the right to go to the "head of the line."

Treaty supporters did not seem very certain about the impact of the statement of understanding issued by Carter and Torrijos in October 1977. While proclaiming the original language of the neutrality treaty "adequate," President Carter agreed to issue the statement "to make sure that we have a common agreement on what the treaty means." After the statement, some treaty supporters suggested that it changed nothing in the treaties while others seemed to admit that there had been ambiguity in the original language. Sol Linowitz declared in an interview with *U.S. News:* "What this statement of understanding . . . did was say again what we have always understood the treaties said. There was nothing added." Ellsworth Bunker, on the other hand, told an audience in Des Moines that the statement "laid to rest" earlier doubts "about whether the new treaties insure our security interests."[56]

The Battle for Hearts and Minds

The military concerns of those opposing the Panama Canal treaties raised several broader questions of international politics and the balance of power in Latin America. Treaty opponents disputed contentions that relinquishing the canal would improve America's image and reduce world tensions. On the contrary, they argued that the treaties would promote communism in America's backyard and increase the likelihood of conflict. Also, they argued that the treaties would prop up a dictatorial government and make a mockery of America's professed ideals and its commitment to human rights. This, they concluded, was the "larger significance" of the debate over Panama; America's leadership of the free world was ultimately at stake.

Treaty opponents acknowledged that Latin American leaders publicly supported the treaties, but they dismissed such pronouncements as "ritualistic support" arising "largely out of an imperative of 'Latin American solidarity.'" Privately, they argued, Latin Americans were "reluctant to see the benefits of orderly U.S. administration transferred to an uncertain fate in the hands of an unstable Panama."[57] They claimed that Latin American leaders recognized that Panamanian control over the canal would not be in their commercial or military interests. Ronald Reagan even claimed to have made "personal contact with representatives of governments" in Latin America who expressed such views.[58] Furthermore, they argued that Latin Americans held in highest contempt the sort of weakness demonstrated by the treaties. In Latin America, they argued, "the national qualities that win respect are strength and decisiveness." In this area where "firmness is respected and cowardice is held in contempt," the treaties would only make the United States a "laughingstock." According to Donald Dozer, the notion that the new treaties would improve the image of the United States in Latin America was, "at best, mere wishful thinking."[59]

Treaty opponents also called it wishful thinking to assume that nations outside of Latin America would admire America for ratifying the new canal treaties. Allies and enemies alike would lose respect for America, they argued, because of its "humiliating retreat in the face of blustering threats from the corrupt dictator of a backward banana republic."[60] The United States could ill-afford to send such signals to the world, particularly at this moment in history. Hanson Baldwin argued that because the retreat from Panama followed a string of defeats for U.S. foreign policy it would further encourage "even second- and third-rate powers" to "tweak Uncle Sam's nose." If the Panama treaties passed, "the world would again ask as it did after the *Pueblo*, Vietnam, Angola: 'Is the United States a paper tiger? Are its will and resolution to be depended on? Where would Washington draw the line if not at its own back door?'" Ronald Reagan predicted that the world would consider America's "retreat from the role of global leader and responsible ally" a "proven fact" if the Senate ratified the treaties. This was "the bottom-line cost of surrender in Panama," Philip Crane concluded, and "even the construction of a new, two-ocean fleet would not be enough to restore our credibility in the eyes of the world."[61]

Above all, treaty opponents talked of how the treaties would help the Communists "gain influence, if not full control, of this vital international waterway."[62] According to Captain Paul Ryan, Soviet naval strategists eagerly awaited the opportunity to fill the void left by American withdrawal. They understood the military value of the canal, and in particular they had learned the lesson of World War II:

> Following the canal negotiations with fascinated interest are the Kremlin's Americanologists, including those Soviet leaders who determine the frequency of naval cruises into the Caribbean. . . .
>
> There is little doubt that Moscow understands the strategic importance of the Caribbean-Panama area. . . .
>
> It may be assumed without question that astute Soviet strategists have assigned as a principal mission of the Soviet Navy in war the interdiction of the maritime highways connecting the United States with its allies and its sources of strategic raw materials. . . . Soviet submarine commanders cruising in the Caribbean and South Atlantic are training their crews to operate in this prime hunting area against the same type of fat targets which drew the German U-boats in World War II. Significantly, the Soviets—with some 200 attack and 140 missile submarines and the Cuban bases—enjoy advantages not available to the Germans. The latter began World War II with only 57 U-boats, yet sank some 2.3 million tons of shipping in the area.[63]

Thus, the canal issue was "not a local problem between the United States and Panama, but one of global significance." Control of the canal was "the prime objective in the struggle by the U.S.S.R. for conquest of the Gulf-Caribbean area," and the new treaties would create "an inviting vacuum" which would allow the Soviets to achieve that objective.[64]

The presence of Communists in Panama itself furthered the cause of the Soviets, according to opponents of the treaties. Anti-treaty spokesmen stopped short of accusing Torrijos himself of being a Communist. Some described him only as "chummy" with Fidel Castro, while others admitted that evidence of his

Communist leanings was only "circumstantial."[65] But as Hanson Baldwin observed, it mattered little whether Torrijos carried Communist credentials; Castro, he noted, "was not a self-proclaimed Communist until he seized power." The important point was that Torrijos, like Castro, was surrounded by Communists and susceptible to their influence. As Philip Crane wrote in *Surrender in Panama*, the list of Torrijos' Communist associates began with his family and the leaders of his army:

> [There is a] long list of Torrijos relatives and cronies with direct communist ties, including his brother, Moises Torrijos, described by the Panamanian Committee for Human Rights as "a Marxist since his youth," and a member of the Panamanian Communist Party's Central Committee. Also cited as a member of the Central Committee is Torrijos' brother-in-law, Marcelino Jaen, who played an instrumental role in the 1968 coup and, under Torrijos, became president of the leftist-dominated National Legislative Commission. . . .
>
> Key officers of Torrijos' National Guard, especially the notorious Manuel Antonio Noriega, Commander of the G-2 security police, maintain close ties with Cuba's C–2 secret police.

John McGarret claimed that Torrijos' Communist associates also included people in "high cabinet and advisory positions in the Panamanian Government," as well as some who held "senior positions on the Panamanian Treaty Negotiating Team."[66] In short, a pro-Communist bureaucracy was already in place in Panama, as Hanson Baldwin noted in the *AEI Defense Review:* "A kind of neo-Marxist establishment rules the country, even though there is no proof that Torrijos himself is a Communist. . . . Known and open Communists occupy high positions in the Torrijos regime."[67]

Treaty opponents claimed that the results of all the Communist influence in Panama could be seen in Torrijos' "triumphal five-day tour of Cuba" in January 1976 and in the unusually large Cuban Embassy in Panama.[68] Treaty opponents also pointed out that the Communist party operated freely in Panama, despite a ban on organized political activity, and they contended that Torrijos had "introduced Marxist teachings into Panama's educational system."[69] Philip Crane reported on student exchanges with Cuba, on Cuban "advisors" in Panama, on

Russian planes at Panama's Rio Hato airstrip, and on Russian business dealings with Panama. According to Crane, these signs suggested a "pattern of communist subversion and influence" in Panama. More excitable treaty opponents even reported that "Soviet made machine guns in large trunks" had arrived on the isthmus, presumably for use against American soldiers.[70]

Finally, treaty opponents exploited President Carter's own political trademark: the rhetoric of human rights. While there may have been doubt over whether Torrijos was a card-carrying Communist, there was no doubt among treaty opponents that he was a corrupt dictator notorious for violating the human rights of his fellow citizens. Treaty opponents told of "the murder, the massive human rights violations, the drug smuggling, and the financial corruption of the Panamanian dictatorship." They noted that Freedom House, the international watchdog on human rights, called Panama's human rights record "one of the worst in Latin America."[71] They wondered how the Carter administration, in light of its human rights rhetoric, could seek to enhance the position of a regime that exiled political opponents, controlled the press, prohibited elections, and participated in the heroin traffic that destroyed American youth.[72] According to treaty opponents, the same administration that promised a new era in human rights "consistently ignored or minimized evidence of Torrijos' abuses."[73] They wondered how support for such a dictator could enhance America's image as a champion of human rights.

Those favoring the treaties had answers for all these questions. Indeed, the impact of the treaties on America's image was perhaps their favorite topic. They had little trouble finding evidence that a new Panama treaty had become a "rallying point for all Latin American nations."[74] Ellsworth Bunker reviewed just a few of the early public endorsements of new treaties to come out of Latin America:

When the Latin American Foreign Ministers met in Bogota, Colombia, in November 1973 they voted to put the Panama question on the agenda of the "New Dialogue" proposed by Secretary Kissinger. In March of this year the Presidents of Colombia, Costa

Rica, and Venezuela publicly expressed their support for Panama's cause. More recently, the General Assembly of the Organization of American States, meeting in Washington in the last 2 weeks, approved unanimously a resolution reaffirming their interest in the negotiation.[75]

Other treaty supporters cited the presence of leaders from all Latin American nations except Cuba at the signing of the treaties in Washington as proof of their support. President Carter praised the Latin leaders for taking "the time to leave their own jobs" and coming to Washington "to express publicly their support for the treaty terms."[76]

President Carter also responded to claims that Latin American leaders privately opposed the treaties by reporting on his own private contacts. He claimed to have met privately with representatives of "almost all the Latin American countries" and concluded: "I believe they're unanimously supportive of the treaty itself." He also claimed that "eight different heads of state in Latin America" had sent private messages urging him "to put as our number one foreign policy matter the completion of a new Panama Canal treaty."[77] Finally, he noted that he had met individually with nineteen heads of state attending the signing ceremony, and he claimed that all considered the treaties "a crucial demonstration of our willingness to be fair."[78]

The administration's reading of Latin American sentiment, like that of the opposition, rested upon certain assumptions about the Latin American mind. While treaty opponents claimed that Latin American *machismo* would bring disrespect for a retreating America, treaty supporters argued that Latin Americans considered U.S. strength a function of its ideals of fairness, equality, and self-determination. Latin Americans, Sol Linowitz argued, viewed the issue primarily as a "test of our intention to put aside relationships based on our superior strength and to begin to deal with them cooperatively, as equals."[79] Good relations with Latin America depended upon reducing "mistrust and disagreement" rather than upon respect for American military power. In a sense, the treaties would demonstrate American strength—the strength derived from America's "reputation for fairness and justice." The treaties would demonstrate that

181

America remained strong enough "to be fair in its dealings with smaller and poorer nations."[80]

The same logic underlay protreaty claims that the treaties would improve America's image in the world as a whole. Treaty supporters challenged suggestions that the treaties would signal further isolationism and weakness. On the contrary, President Carter called the treaties symbolic of strength as well as fairness before an audience in Denver:

> I look on the ratification of the Panama Canal treaties as a show of strength and as a show of national will and as a show of fairness and as a show of confidence in ourselves now and in the future to act, if necessary, but not to have to show that we are strong just because we can run over a little country. . . .
>
> We don't have to show our strength as a nation by running over a small nation, because we're stronger than they are. So, I don't see the treaties as a withdrawal.[81]

COACT sounded a similar theme in its sample speech, arguing that the United States could not lead the free world "by size, or wealth, or superior power." Rather, leadership depended on "the admiration and respect of other nations and peoples." This could be won only "by living up to our own ideals, and by treating other nations and peoples with the same respect and equity and dignity we ourselves expect of others." COACT concluded that ratifying the Panama Canal treaties would send "the signal the whole world has been waiting for." As Secretary of State Cyrus Vance summarized the argument, the treaties would "say to all the world that we will define our national interests carefully and we will protect those interests. They say to the world that disputes—even between large countries and small ones—can be resolved peacefully. And they say that we will act in the world in a way that is true to our values as a nation."[82]

These themes continued to serve treaty supporters as they responded to concerns with global communism. According to treaty supporters, the pacts would rob the Communists of "one of their favorite rhetorical rallying points" by signaling that the United States was not a "colonialist power opposed to the very forces of world freedom and development which we in fact support."[83] If the treaties were ratified, Fritz Hollings argued, communism would have "no issue upon which to take root"in Latin America. On the other hand, rejecting the treaties would give Communists "a controlling issue not only in Panama but all over South America." As Ellsworth Bunker explained, "nothing would aid the Communists more than the rejection of the new treaties." The "Communists and other radicals" liked to "fish in troubled waters, and a treaty rejection would without a doubt lead to tension and unrest which would improve their fishing possibilities."[84] It was for just this reason, treaty supporters argued, that the Communist Party in Panama had been the "most vocal and adamant opponent of Panama's ratification of these treaties!"[85]

In speaking of Communists who opposed the treaties, of course, treaty supporters admitted that Communists were politically active in Panama. COACT even acknowledged rumors that Cuba had provided arms and training for the Panamanian National Guard and had sought "to indoctrinate the Guard's members with anti-American ideas." But COACT claimed the rumors were not true "so far as we are aware," while other treaty supporters responded to fears of Communist influence by pointing out that the treaties prohibited "any nation other than Panama from either operating the canal, or maintaining a military presence in their country."[86]

Most of the debate over communism focused on the political leanings of General Torrijos and his associates. Treaty supporters defended Torrijos by calling him a "nationalist" who had "made it clear that he wants Panama to develop in accordance with its own needs and traditions and not in accord with any foreign model."[87] Keenly aware of opposition portraits of Torrijos as an iron-fisted dictator as well as an incipient Communist, administration spokesmen portrayed Torrijos as a man "fully supported by the people in his country" and "sensitive to public opinion."[88] Torrijos' agitation for new treaties revealed, not his radicalism, but his traditionalism. He merely followed "in the footsteps of every Panamanian head of state since 1903, irrespective of any ideological differences."[89] President Carter celebrated Torrijos as the head of "a stable government which has encouraged the development of free enterprise in Panama," while COACT made the dictator sound vaguely "democratic." In COACT's rhetoric the nation that Freedom House saddled with its lowest human rights rating began to sound like an open constitutional system with a Bill of Rights and only temporary restrictions on political freedom:

> It is not a democracy as we understand that term. Its legal basis is the Constitution of 1972, drafted by a national commission composed of 25 Panamanians from all sectors of national society, approved by the National Assembly of Municipal Representatives. The Constitution guarantees common, basic rights and freedoms. The Constitution also authorized General Torrijos to perform certain functions during a six-year term, due to expire in 1978. Popular representation in Government is effected through the 505 directly elected members of the National Assembly of Municipal Representatives, primarily a consultative body, which has limited powers but which elects the President and Vice-President.[90]

Some treaty supporters admitted that Torrijos' "certain functions" had included exiling political opponents and that his human rights record was "less than perfect." But they insisted that "incidents of brutality for political purposes had not come to light" and that Panama's human rights record was "better than that of many other regimes in the Western Hemisphere."[91] Still others shifted the discussion of human rights from principle to expediency. Senator Fritz Hollings argued that rejecting the treaties would not further the cause of human rights by toppling Torrijos. Instead, it would only "make him a hero."[92]

Treaty supporters capped off their case on the military and international political repercussions of the treaties by citing the endorsement of the Joint Chiefs of Staff. As the experts with "initial responsibility for our military defense," the Joint Chiefs provided the "first place to look" for advice on all issues affecting American security.[93] And according to treaty supporters, the Joint Chiefs had been "a party to the negotiations," had "specifically approved" all provisions "affecting national defense and security," and had "unanimously endorsed" the final

184

product.[94] Sol Linowitz claimed that the Joint Chiefs viewed the treaties as "not only preserving but enhancing our national security."[95]

Opponents of the treaties challenged the credibility of the Joint Chiefs and claimed the backing of better military experts. They suggested that the Joint Chiefs had withheld their "best military judgment" because they were compelled to echo the administration line or resign their posts.[96] They frequently cited a "poll" of retired military officers that showed a 278 to 4 count against the new pacts. "That's 99% against the treaties," exclaimed Major General J. Milnor Roberts in the ACU telethon.[97] Treaty opponents also publicized a strongly antitreaty letter sent to President Carter by four American admirals who were retired and therefore free to speak their minds.[98]

Those favoring the treaties disputed suggestions that the Joint Chiefs were "under the thumb of political leaders." Sol Linowitz called such charges "inaccurate, unfair and an insult," while President Carter insisted that the Joint Chiefs endorsed the treaties "on their own initiative, without any orders or encouragement from me."[99] But those favoring the treaties could not really dispute the fact that military experts outside the administration overwhelmingly opposed the new treaties. They could only suggest that those currently in service better understood America's future military needs.

The questionable support for the treaties among military experts detracted further from the persuasiveness of a protreaty case already hurt by confusion and controversy over military provisions. The administration's case was perhaps most damaged by disagreements with Panama over the defense and transit provisions of the neutrality treaty. But more generally, the protreaty vision of a military "partnership" with Panama probably seemed unrealistic to Americans familiar with the history of threats and anti-American rhetoric by Panamanian leaders.

Polling during the early stages of the debate also suggested that the administration faced considerable skepticism when it tried to minimize the military value of the canal. A Field Institute poll taken in September and October of 1977 revealed that respondents rejected the statement that the "Panama Canal is no longer vital to the U.S." by a margin of 62 to 27 percent, and 43 percent disagreed strongly with the statement. Even those who already supported the treaties split evenly on the question: 47 percent agreed that the canal was no longer "vital," while 47 percent disagreed. Columnist George Will seemed correct in deeming it "folly for advocates of the treaty to denigrate the canal's importance." [100]

The administration tempered its downgrading of the canal's military value by insisting that its negotiators, above all, sought to guard America's military interests. The administration also tried to transcend specific questions about the value of the canal and about the military provisions of the treaties and to stress instead the impact of the treaties on America's "image" in Latin America. They made a reasonable case for the notion that the treaties would lessen tensions in the area and thereby reduce the threat of attacks on the canal. And their argument that the treaties would rob Communists of one of their greatest anti-American issues in Latin America seemed confirmed by the opposition of Panamanian Communists to the treaties.

As the Senate debate over the treaties was about to begin, however, it was obvious that the strategy of transcending specific issues did little to assuage concerns over the treaties' military provisions. Public controversy over the neutrality treaty's military provisions escalated on the eve of the Senate debate, and the controversy rose quickly to the top of the Senate's agenda. Yet as the Senate debate progressed, arguments about the merits of the treaties, including those about military provisions, increasingly gave way to arguments about public opinion. In the end, both sides in the Senate debate talked less about the national interest and more about "the people." And in the end, both sides claimed to represent "the will of the people" on the Panama Canal treaties.

8

Public Opinion and the Senate Debate

Americans have a "moral conception" of public opinion that deems it "mandatory that the will of the people prevail."[1] Yet on occasion we also uphold the Hamiltonian notion that policies, especially in foreign affairs, should be insulated from the "prejudices," the "intemperate passions," and the "fluctuations" of the popular will.[2] In one of those curious contradictions of American politics, we at once want our foreign policies dependent upon, and protected from, the "will of the people." But which impulse actually prevails in American politics?

For many years diplomatic historians simply assumed that public opinion did in fact determine American foreign policy. For instance, Thomas Bailey concluded in 1940 that "the American people, exercising their democratic privilege and enjoying freedom of speech and press, have shaped their own foreign policies."[3] In the 1960s and 1970s, however, other diplomatic historians challenged this assumption. According to revisionists, such as Gabriel Kolko, "the close and serious student of modern American foreign relations" could "rarely, if ever, find an instance of an important decision made with any reference to the alleged general public desires or opinions." The revisionists held that American policymakers since the turn of the century have promoted the economic interests of an elite, while an indifferent public has been duped into quiescence with appeals to "a broader social welfare and erstwhile consensus."[4]

The first generation of survey research, in the 1950s, seemed to confirm that the general public was too uninformed, disinterested, and easily manipulated to play a significant role in the conduct of American foreign policy.[5] But empirical research in the 1960s and 1970s indicated that Americans were more aware, concerned, and politically active than they had been in previous years.[6] These findings led political scientists to develop situational theories of public opinion. As the research accumulated, it became clear that the role of public opinion could be described only in particular historical contexts, or in regard to the changing national agenda and political dialogue.[7]

Policy-making does not always reflect public opinion—especially on foreign affairs—because our political philosophy is ambivalent, allowing policymakers to justify the "national interest" taking precedence over "the will of the people" in certain situations. Furthermore, the empirical problems of "knowing" public opinion may bedevil even policymakers intent on obeying its dictates. As Bernard Cohen has written, accurate characterizations of public opinion are not "absorbed, by osmosis, into the political bloodstream."[8] Rather, policymakers must evaluate often conflicting evidence, and frequently they choose to believe portraits of public opinion that are based on faulty evidence or misinterpretations of the evidence. American policymakers routinely assume that "the will of the people" may be discerned through "scientific" polling, yet the conceptual and technical limitations of polls call this assumption into question. Polls typically fail to distinguish between strong and weak opinions, between rational and irrational opinions, or among shades of opinion on particular issues. Even slight differences in methodology—differing methods of sampling and data collection or slightly differing questions—can make enormous differences in findings. And once statistics are gathered they still may be interpreted in very different ways, especially by politicians with partisan concerns.[9]

188

The Senate debate over the Panama Canal treaties revealed both the reality of the public's influence on American foreign policy and some of the problems caused by our political philosophy and by our imperfect methods for assessing public opinion. As characterized in the rhetoric of the debate, public opinion played a major role in the decision to ratify the treaties. Senate proponents of the treaties used claims of a "turnabout" in public opinion to entice recalcitrant senators to support ratification. Early in the debate, those favoring the treaties conceded that the public overwhelmingly opposed them and argued that the Senate should not be guided by public opinion grounded in emotionalism and ignorance. Later, however, treaty proponents began to speak of a shift in public opinion—a shift in which the public allegedly came to support the treaties with certain pivotal amendments.

In retrospect, however, the turnabout proved illusory—the product of wishful thinking and poorly worded and misinterpreted polls. Senators who wished to support the treaties accepted uncritically claims that the public also would support them if they were amended to "guarantee America's right to defend the canal." Numerous polls supported these claims. But most of the pollsters' questions failed to distinguish between the amendments actually adopted by the Senate and much stronger language unsuccessfully advocated by conservative senators. As a result, people who supported the treaties *only* with stronger defense guarantees apparently were counted as treaty supporters. This became evident as polls following the debate—polls assessing public opinion on the treaties as *actually* amended—revealed that opposition had "returned" to the level found at the start of the debate.

THE SENATE DEBATE

The long public debate over the Panama Canal treaties set the stage for Senate consideration of the agreement. In the fall of 1977, a number of congressional committees began hearings on the treaties, but most attention focused on the Senate For-

eign Relations Committee. As the committee with primary responsibility for the treaties, the Foreign Relations Committee
conducted exhaustive hearings, featuring testimony from virtually every major advocate in the public debate. In addition to
administration officials and other politicians claiming special
knowledge of the issue, the committee heard from a long list of
prominent leaders from the military, religious, business, professional, and academic communities.

Next came the historic debate on the floor of the Senate in
February, March, and April 1978, the second longest treaty debate in American history. For the first time, radio carried deliberations of the Senate to the American people. For the first time
in fifty years, the Senate considered a treaty article-by-article as
a Committee of the Whole. And also for the first time in half a
century, the Senate amended a treaty against the public wishes
of the president.[10]

But while the Senate debate was historically momentous, it
did little to enhance the Senate's reputation as the world's greatest deliberative body. Marquis Childs called the debate "an in-
tolerable charade . . . since all the arguments pro and con have
been rehearsed a dozen times." Senator Patrick Leahy of Vermont agreed, saying the proceedings resembled "the plot line
of a television soap opera. You could listen to the debate for several days, leave for a week or two, and come back to it having
missed very little."[11]

The repetitiousness of the debate reflected the relatively
settled state of Senate opinion on the treaties' merits. Arguments about the merits of the treaties, especially the historical
and economic arguments so prominent in public debate, had
become old news by the time the Senate began considering the
treaties.[12] But to say that most senators already had judged the
treaties is not to say that the debate was superfluous. Although
prospects for ratification were dim at the outset,[13] the Senate ultimately did ratify the treaties, announcing the end of nearly
eighty years of American control over the legendary waterway.
On March 16, the Senate ratified the neutrality treaty by a vote
of sixty-eight to thirty-two—a two-thirds majority with one

vote to spare. After an additional month of debate, the Senate ratified the Panama Canal Treaty by exactly the same vote.[14] How does one explain this outcome? How could such a static, repetitious debate produce such a dramatic turnaround in Senate opinion?

Participants and observers alike agree that two amendments to the neutrality treaty account for the shift from opposition to support for the treaties. The amendments, known as the "leadership" amendments, presumably clarified America's right to defend the canal and to have priority passage in military emergencies after the year 2000. A number of senators who had opposed the treaties became active supporters of the amended version. Charles Percy, for instance, demanded that the military guarantees be made a "formal and binding part of the treaties" and declared: "I could not support the treaties otherwise. With these changes, however, I believe our interests would be well protected." Similarly, Robert Stafford of Vermont stated on February 27 that he opposed the treaties without the amendments but would support them with the changes:

> The treaties signed by President Carter and General Torrijos . . . do not serve the best interest of the United States.
>
> I will not vote for ratification of either treaty as submitted.
>
> They do not adequately and clearly protect the right of the United States to have expedited, head of the line passage for our warships in time of need or emergency. They do not clearly establish the right of the United States to defend the neutrality of the canal militarily after the year 1999.
>
> Fortunately, it is clear at this point that at a minimum the Senate will insist on amending both treaties to insure our rights of passage and defense.
>
> With these two amendments specifically added to the treaties, I shall support ratification.[15]

Similar public statements by Senators Baker, Brooke, Heinz, and Sparkman,[16] along with the fact that only two votes could have changed the outcome, testify to the importance of the leadership amendments. Over three-quarters of the lawmakers actually co-sponsored the changes. Clearly, the leadership

191

amendments proved crucial to ratification of the treaties. Seldom does a single factor play such an important role in the resolution of a major Senate debate.

THE DEBATE OVER MILITARY PROVISIONS

The neutrality treaty and its military provisions took center stage almost as soon as the Foreign Relations Committee began its hearings. Amid reports that Panamanian officials interpreted America's rights of defense and military transit differently from the administration, committee members qualified opening statements supportive of the treaties to demand that these rights be clarified.[17] Appearances before the committee by treaty negotiators Sol Linowitz and Ellsworth Bunker did little to reassure its doubtful members. Linowitz told the committee that the original language of the treaty left the United States "in a position to assume that the canal's permanent neutrality is maintained" and set no limitation "on our ability to take such action as we may deem necessary in the event the canal's neutrality is threatened or violated from any source." He also claimed that a "special provision" authorizing "expeditious passage" of American warships in an emergency constituted "a preferential right to expeditious transit of our naval vessels whenever we consider this necessary."[18]

But continued complaining by committee members eventually forced President Carter and General Torrijos of Panama to issue their "clarifying statement" on October 14, 1977. As noted earlier, the statement of understanding reaffirmed the right of the United States to defend the neutrality of the canal but explicitly denied that this could be interpreted as a right of intervention in the internal affairs of Panama. The statement also interpreted the right of "expeditious passage" to mean that American warships, "in case of need or emergency," could go "to the head of the line of vessels in order to transit the Canal rapidly."[19]

Although members of the Foreign Relations Committee praised the administration for the statement of understanding,

192

they remained skeptical because it was not a legally binding addition to the neutrality treaty.[20] Skepticism increased after committee members visited Panama for talks with Panamanian officials.[21] Thereafter, debate in the Foreign Relations Committee focused not on whether to add language to the treaties but on the exact form the addition should take.[22] Majority Leader Robert Byrd and Minority Leader Howard Baker eventually settled the matter by announcing that they would support the treaties only if they included the language of the statement of understanding. The Senate leaders then set about fashioning amendments incorporating the exact language of the statement. Once it became clear that both the Panamanians and the administration would tolerate the leadership amendments, the Foreign Relations Committee voted fourteen to one to approve the Panama Canal treaties.[23]

When debate commenced on the floor of the Senate in February, Majority Leader Byrd defended the first of the two leadership amendments by arguing that it would guarantee the right of the United States to defend the canal against "not just some threats, not just certain threats—but any threat; not just any threat emanating from a certain source, but any threat no matter from whence it may come." Byrd argued that the amendment would make it "as clear as the sun in a cloudless sky" that the United States had "the right to take whatever action is necessary against any aggressor." Senator Frank Church led the defense of the second amendment, claiming that it would allow U.S. ships to go to the "head of the line" in a military emergency. Church concluded: "It provides that our naval ships and auxiliary vessels will not have only priority passage, but the right to go to the head of the line. We determine it; what more do we want?"[24]

Treaty opponents obviously wanted more. They wondered *how* the United States would exercise its right to defend the canal, since the treaties provided for removing all U.S. troops and bases by the year 2000.[25] They also argued that the amendment would give Panama a "veto" over *any* U.S. action in the Canal Zone once it became Panamanian territory, since it prohibited interference in the "internal affairs" of Panama.[26] Finally, they

193

pointed out that the amendment merely incorporated the statement of understanding, which had not silenced Panama's differing interpretations of key provisions. Most important, it remained unclear whether the United States would need Panama's permission to defend the canal.[27]

Treaty opponents argued that the second leadership amendment, while theoretically guaranteeing the right of priority passage during emergencies, neither described nor defined "emergency"; nor did it specify who would decide whether an emergency existed. "What might be an emergency to us in our country," Senator Allen argued, "might not be an emergency to Panama." Since Panama would control the canal's operation, the practical effect would be that "Panama would determine whether there was an emergency." Allen dramatized his point by asking, "What will we do, radio to Panama and say, 'Look, we have an emergency here and we want to move our ships to the head of the line,' with the Panamanians replying, 'Well, we don't feel that there is an emergency. What are you talking about, an emergency? You stay where you are, at the rear of the line, and wait your turn.'"[28]

The Senate rejected attempts by conservative senators to modify the first leadership amendment with language more clearly asserting America's right to defend the canal unilaterally with or without the blessings of Panama. The Senate then adopted the first leadership amendment on March 9 by a vote of eighty-four to five; the second was adopted by a vote of eighty-five to three. But these votes did not end controversy over the leadership amendments. Indeed, the amendments remained at the top of the agenda during a full month of additional debate because of a reservation proposed by Senator Dennis DeConcini of Arizona and adopted at the last minute.

The DeConcini reservation aimed to clarify the Senate's understanding of the first leadership amendment. It merely attached nonbinding language to the neutrality treaty affirming America's right to take unilateral action in Panama to restore operations of the canal if it were closed for any reason after the year 2000.[29] If one accepted the administration's rhetoric un-

194

critically, of course, the reservation was unnecessary. The administration insisted all along that the neutrality treaty guaranteed the right stipulated by the reservation, and the first leadership amendment presumably reiterated that guarantee. So why did General Torrijos write to 115 heads-of-state suggesting that Panama would reject the treaties with the DeConcini reservation? Why did Panama's representative in the United Nations claim that the reservation violated the charters of the U.N. and the OAS, along with the Inter-American Treaty of Reciprocal Assistance? Why did Panamanians take to the streets to burn Carter in effigy and to destroy American flags? And why did some Panamanians refer to the reservation as "the DeConcini corollary to the Brezhnev doctrine?"[30] The answer would seem obvious: treaty opponents had been correct all along that the Panamanians interpreted the neutrality treaty and the leadership amendments differently than the administration did.[31]

Eventually the Panamanians calmed down when the Senate leadership redecorated the Panama Canal Treaty with language designed to both "preserve DeConcini's language and nullify it."[32] This "verbal mirage," fashioned in private consultations including State Department officials, Senators Byrd and Church, and representatives of the Panamanian government, affirmed that "any action taken by the U.S." would be "only for the purpose of assuring that the Canal shall remain open, . . . and shall not have as its purpose nor be interpreted as a right of intervention . . . or interference with [Panama's] political independence or sovereign integrity."[33]

Despite the fact that this language merely echoed the administration's interpretation of the leadership amendments, it seemed to satisfy all concerned. But the controversy over the DeConcini reservation raised an interesting question about the motivations behind support for the leadership amendments. Why did the leadership amendments, despite their obvious failure to resolve ambiguity over American military rights, motivate so many senators to support the treaties? The answer lies more in perceptions of public opinion than in any supposed merits of the amendments. An examination of how protreaty senators popularized the notion that the amendments assuaged a hostile public reveals perhaps the decisive factor in the Senate's ratification of the treaties.

Public Opinion and Political Philosophy

Both philosophical and empirical questions concerning public opinion played important roles in the debate over Panama, as senators debated both the propriety of "the people" deciding the matter and the state of public opinion and its discernible trends. The first major national poll on the issue came as early as June 1975, and for the next two years pollsters charted every response of the public to the progression of events. Eventually no fewer than forty national public opinion polls showed everything from a nearly ten-to-one majority against the treaties to a majority in favor of the pacts.[34]

In the early stages of the controversy, treaty opponents cited polls showing overwhelming opposition to relinquishing the canal.[35] They also noted a remarkable flood of mail to Senate offices confirming the message of the polls. A compilation of Senate mail by the American Conservative Union showed that some senators received as many as four thousand communications on Panama in a single week, with opposition running from 90 to 100 percent. Senator Orrin Hatch alone had received three thousand communications as of August 1977, only three of which expressed support for the treaties.[36]

It was little wonder, then, that protreaty senators initially took argumentative refuge in the philosophical rationale for acting contrary to "the will of the people." Senator Joseph Biden of Delaware argued that "we spend too much time on what the public opinion polls say." He urged his colleagues on the Foreign Relations Committee to "decide what is good and what is not good" and to "stop listening so much to the polls and talk about the issues." On the floor of the Senate, Robert Byrd expanded the argument, insisting that courageous public servants must sometimes risk political fortune in the best interest of a mistaken constituency:

> There is no question but that the majority of West Virginians today oppose the treaties. The easy vote for me, would be to vote against the treaties.
>
> There is no political mileage to be gained in voting for these treaties.
>
> I know what my constituents are saying. However, I have a responsibility not only to follow them and to represent them but also to inform them and to lead them when, in my judgment, based on the facts as I have carefully weighed them, it is in the best interests of the United States that the treaties be approved. That is my responsibility to the people of West Virginia—to act in the best interests of the United States as my lights allow me to see the facts and to understand what is in the best interests of the United States—because what is in the best interests of the United States is in the best interests of West Virginia and West Virginians.[37]

Byrd added that "a computer and a set of scales" could replace elected representatives if decisions were to be "based only on the number of names on a petition or upon the weight of the mail." Senators owed constituents more than deference, he concluded. They owed them "a judgment, an honest judgment, a sincere judgment, a considered judgment." Byrd and other protreaty senators quoted Edmund Burke's letter to the electors of Bristol on the proper philosophy of representation: "Your representative owes you not only his industry but also his judgment, and he betrays rather than serving you if he sacrifices it to your opinion."[38]

The philosophical rationale for ignoring public opinion went hand-in-hand in protreaty rhetoric with claims that the public was too ignorant and emotional about the Panama Canal treaties to exercise good judgment. Byrd again led the way by wondering aloud on February 9: "How many of those who urge us to oppose the treaties have actually read the content of these treaties?" Senator Pell argued on February 28 that public opposition to the treaties could only be based on "false impressions about the basis of our current presence in the Canal Zone, about what America's interests in the canal are, how those interests are protected in the proposed new treaties, and what our realistic choices are in considering these treaties." On March 10, Senator Paul Sarbanes cited a Gallup poll showing that most Americans did not know when Panama would assume control over the canal under the new treaties, what military rights America would have after the Panamanians took over, or how many American aircraft carriers and supertankers were capable of using the canal.[39] According to treaty proponents, ignorance of such details proved the irrationality of opposition. It proved that "offended sensitivities and ruffled chauvinism" caused hostility toward the treaties.[40] And they blamed this emotionalism on the demagogic, misleading campaign by the radicals of the New Right.[41]

Treaty opponents had plenty of ammunition to fight the philosophical battle over public opinion. While protreaty senators quoted Burke, Senator William Scott quoted a fellow Virginian on "the type of government we have in the United States and the part the people of the country should play in the decision-making process":

> Mr. President, in 1820 when Thomas Jefferson wrote from Monticello to a friend regarding some constitutional question, he said:
>
> "I know no safe depository of the ultimate powers of the society but the people themselves; and if we think them not enlightened enough to exercise their control with a wholesome discretion, the remedy is not to take it from them, but to inform their discretion by education."
>
> Since 1820, of course, the general level of education throughout our country has risen considerably. I believe that with the ultimate sovereignty residing in the people of the country, we cannot, in making a decision, decline to be swayed at least in part by the overwhelming desire of the American people that these treaties be rejected.

Scott subsequently marshalled testimony from a long list of American political heroes, including John Adams, John Marshall, Daniel Webster, and Abraham Lincoln, all reminding his colleagues that "sovereignty resides in the people." He asked his colleagues to "remember that we are here in a representative capacity as servants and not masters of the people." Scott and other treaty opponents professed faith in the seemingly mystical corporate wisdom of "the people." As Senator Curtis expressed it: "The American people sometimes have a notion and an intuition that is right. They have been endowed with that. They can sense when something is wrong, and the vast majority of them know that this canal treaty is wrong."[42]

Other treaty opponents agreed in principle that an ignorant or overly emotional public should not guide the actions of the Senate, particularly on a matter of foreign policy.[43] But in opposition to treaty supporters, they argued that the public was concerned and informed about the Panama Canal treaties. Orrin Hatch first challenged characterizations of the public as ignorant about the treaties on February 9: "I think the people of this country are not as foolish as many of our leaders think they are." Later, he added that "the vast majority" of the people had "more knowledge about these treaties than any of my protreaty colleagues have been willing to admit." Paul Laxalt went further, arguing that he had "never seen more knowledge exhibited by the public generally throughout this country [on] an issue." Senator J. Bennett Johnston of Louisiana provided the most elaborate defense of the public's capacity to guide the Senate on the treaties:

> This is not an issue which is mysterious to the people of my State or this country. It is not an issue which the average citizen can fail to comprehend or have an understanding of.
>
> I would guess that almost everybody in this country knows what the Panama Canal is and knows its general history. . . . They may not have attended the hearings. But it does not take a huge amount of study, it does not take years of training, it does not take a doctor's degree to understand basically what we are doing in these canal treaties.
>
> I think my people understand it fairly well. . . . I think there is something to be said for the collective judgment of the people of this country. I think we can tend to trust the collective judgment on an issue of this kind. . . .
>
> This is not an issue of a complicated weapons system where the American people are to decide whether the AWACS control airplane should be sold to Iran, whether we ought to have cruise mis-

199

siles or B-1 bombers. Those are technical questions which need great study.

This is a very simple, straightforward issue, and people of the country, I believe, understand the issue.

I am frank to say that I have no special knowledge that this is of such an esoteric nature, of such a difficult or technical nature, that my constituency cannot understand it.[44]

Thus the philosophical controversy over public opinion was not simply a contest between champions and opponents of deference to "the people." Both sides in the debate agreed that public opinion should not shape policy-making when an issue is too complex, too technical, or too shrouded in secrecy to be understood by the average citizen, and both sides disavowed deference to a misinformed or emotional public. The debate over public opinion on the Panama Canal treaties ultimately boiled down not to a dispute over the ideology of popular sovereignty in America, but to questions about the nature of the issue and the competence of the public.

Public Opinion as an Empirical Issue

As the debate over the Panama Canal treaties progressed, protreaty senators began to sound more sanguine arguments about public opinion. Instead of evoking the ideological rationale for ignoring the people, they set out to prove that the public had changed its mind. They argued that an "education process" had begun to "gradually turn around this public opinion."[45] As administration spokesmen appeared before the Foreign Relations Committee to speak of their "very extensive program of explanation,"[46] protreaty senators began to speak of an emerging "trend" toward public support for the treaties. By November 1977, Majority Leader Byrd was telling the press about a national "shift of opinion" on the treaties, and in January Charles Percy claimed that the shift had begun to show up in congressional mail—a sure indication that people were "really beginning to think."[47] In January 1978 protreaty senators noted that the Gallup poll showed for the first time a plurality of Ameri-

cans favoring the treaties. Now 45 percent of the public reportedly favored the treaties, while 42 percent remained opposed.[48]
Senator Church noted a similar trend in Patrick Caddell's polls
and attributed the shift to education about the treaties:

National surveys by Pat Caddell's Cambridge Research Organization show that when the treaties were first announced in August,
they were opposed by a margin of 61 percent against to 25 percent
for. In December, however, as the public came to understand the
treaties better, the results had shifted. By then, 49 percent—less
than a majority—opposed the treaties, while those declaring their
support had increased to 35 percent, up from one-fourth to better
than one-third. By February, Caddell's surveys showed a drop to 46
percent in the numbers of those opposed, and a continuing rise in
the number of those in support, to 37 percent.[49]

Protreaty senators attributed this turnabout in public opinion to more than just "education," however. They principally
credited the leadership amendments. George McGovern provided one of the earliest explanations of the connection between public opinion and the amendments during the hearings
of the Foreign Relations Committee:

Two or three recent public opinion polls . . . indicate that when the
American people were asked if they support the Panama Canal
Treaties, most of them were inclined to say no, but when they were
asked if the treaties were modified to include the two provisions
that are in the Carter-Torrijos Memorandum, and which are in the
amendments that you are suggesting, the overwhelming majority—I think a 2-to-1 majority—favor the treaties. . . . I think it is
important to show that even in the absence of very much education
and information on this subject, by margins of 2 to 1 the American
public supports these two treaties as we now propose to modify
them.[50]

Other protreaty senators elaborated on the turnabout on
the floor of the Senate, citing still more polls showing the positive impact of "information" and of the leadership amendments. Senator Sarbanes discussed a study by Professor William Schneider which suggested that polls would have shown
the public evenly split all along if "information" about the dis-

puted military provisions had been included in the questions.[51] Other senators cited polls which presumably provided such information and testified to the "turnabout." Senator Dick Clark, for instance, cited a *New York Times*/CBS News poll which presumably described the first leadership amendment in a follow-up question:

> A poll conducted by the *New York Times* and the Columbia Broadcasting System last fall found that 49 percent of those polled opposed the treaties, and 29 percent approved. But when asked, "Suppose you felt that the treaties provided that the United States could always send in troops to keep the canal open to ships of all nations. Would you then approve of the treaties?" Sixty-three percent approved and only 24 disapproved. The "no opinion" category had dropped from 22 percent to only 13 percent.[52]

Protreaty senators concluded from such data that the public had been "overwhelmingly opposed to these treaties as they were submitted," but would "support [them] as . . . the Senate may amend them." Senator Byrd even conceded that the amendments may have added little or nothing to the original treaties, but he urged their adoption anyway because they went "a long way toward alleviating the concerns of the American people."[53]

In developing these arguments, protreaty senators created an image of an attentive and dynamic public. They suggested that an initially hostile public had followed the debate closely and rather suddenly came to favor the treaties because of "education" and because of the leadership amendments. Ultimately they claimed that their decision was not only "right" but also supported by "the people."

Antitreaty senators, of course, were not about to concede that any turnabout had taken place. They could not let claims of a trend toward public support for the treaties go unanswered, for they had been championing the doctrine of deference to "the people." Hence, they too changed their strategy and began attacking the evidence of a "turnabout." They denied claims by Senator Percy and others that congressional mail had begun to reflect a change in public opinion. They insisted that the "overwhelming majority" of letters continued to oppose the treaties, citing figures ranging from "95 percent" to "1,000 to 1" against the pacts.[54] Senator Scott admitted that there had been some change in the mail; he reported that his mail had become heavier, but he insisted that there had been "little, if any, change in the ratio of those for and against the treaties."[55]

The major battle, however, focused on the public opinion polls, and treaty opponents cited both state and national polls to show that no turnabout had occurred despite administration "propaganda" and a protreaty bias in the "major news media."[56] State-wide polls provided the most startling figures. Senator Hatch cited a poll in Utah showing a persistent margin of nearly four-to-one against the treaties, while Senator Scott reported that his own poll in Virginia revealed that 87 percent of the people opposed the agreement.[57] National polls cited by treaty opponents also showed persistent and overwhelming opposition to the treaties. After protreaty senators began talking of a "turnabout," treaty opponents spoke mostly of figures from the Opinion Research Corporation (ORC)—a "very distinguished and reliable polling organization"—because it had asked "fair" questions on Panama for the preceding four years.[58] As the "most comprehensive survey ever taken on the question of the Panama Canal," the ORC's four-year survey certainly would show any trend toward public support for the treaties. But instead, the ORC survey showed the opposite; opposition to giving up "ownership and control" of the canal actually had *risen* from 66 percent in 1975 to 72 percent in February 1978.[59]

More important, the ORC data exposed the fallacy in protreaty arguments about the impact of the leadership amendments on public opinion. Treaty opponents admitted that the findings shifted "dramatically to nearly 50–50" when pollsters asked the question: "What if the treaties are amended to allow for continued U.S. defense of the canal after the year 2000?"[60] But only the ORC had taken into account the controversy over whether the leadership amendments provided such a guarantee. The ORC recognized that antitreaty senators had tried to substitute stronger language for the leadership amendments— language asserting America's right to act unilaterally in defense of the canal. Rather than ask respondents only if they supported treaties amended to "guarantee America's right to defend the canal," the ORC questioned respondents specifically about the leadership amendments versus the stronger language. The results showed that only 18 percent of the public favored the leadership amendments, while 68 percent favored the stronger language. "When given a fair choice of alternatives," Senator Laxalt said in summarizing the findings, the "overwhelming sentiment of the American public . . . was for an amendment . . . which gives the United States the right to act 'by itself' in defense of the canal." [61]

THE ILLUSORY TURNABOUT

Treaty opponents persuaded few of their colleagues with the ORC data. Instead, the protreaty portrait of public opinion prevailed, influencing the procedures and the outcome of the Senate debate. Belief in a turnabout first influenced the Foreign Relations Committee, where a protreaty majority dictated procedures for the floor debate which promoted ratification. While arguing that senators could assuage hostile constituencies by co-sponsoring the leadership amendments, the committee reported a "clean" resolution of ratification for the neutrality treaty; the committee left the amending process up to the full Senate acting as a Committee of the Whole. [62] The unusual procedure allowed treaty supporters to argue to "skeptical constituents that they had refused to rubber-stamp the treaties, insisting instead on strengthening the protection of American interests." [63] The Carter administration actually promoted this strategy by refusing to endorse the leadership amendments. One White House aide called Carter's public opposition to the amendments a tactical move designed to allow senators to "go back home and say they made us do something we didn't want to. . . . Now they can vote for the treaties." [64] And in the end, the strategy worked. More than seventy-five senators co-sponsored the leadership amendments, with many of them stating publicly that they would have opposed the agreement without the changes. Obviously, the amendments proved the key to the outcome. If only two supporters of the treaties had voted differently, of course, the treaties would have been defeated.

The protreaty portrait of public opinion also prevailed outside the Senate. Senator Helms correctly predicted that the American media would not report the ORC survey.[65] Instead, major media reported that public hostility toward the treaties had been overcome by "education" and by the leadership amendments. On January 13, 1978, *NBC Nightly News* reported that while "most Americans" still opposed the "treaties as they now stand," 65 percent of the public would approve ratification if the United States reserved the right to intervene militarily in emergencies.[66] On February 1, *The New York Times* reported that the treaties had "yet to win the approval of a majority of Americans" but that a "change in opinion since last summer [had] created a political climate" more favorable to ratification. Going a bit further, *Time* reported in February that public opinion had shifted from "2-to-1 opposition" to a "majority" in favor of the pacts, and later *Time* noted that Gallup's poll had shifted from 39 percent to 45 percent in favor of the treaties. "Few times in recent history has a President mounted such a strenuous campaign to influence public opinion," *Time* commented, and the administration could "claim substantial credit" for the "turnabout."[67] Similarly, *Newsweek* claimed that the "remarkable turnabout" revealed by Gallup would boost Carter's image and make the Panama campaign "the model on which the Administration will base its future campaigns for passage of other key legislation."[68]

President Carter gave the myth of a turnabout in public opinion its ultimate expression in a victory address following Senate ratification of the treaties. The Panama Canal treaties, he proclaimed, now had a "firm base in the will of the American people."[69] Over the next several months, however, Carter's statement, along with the entire protreaty case on public opinion, was belied by numerous polls. Rather than revealing that the Panama Canal treaties had a "firm base in the will of the people," later polls—polls assessing attitudes toward the treaties as actually modified by the leadership amendments—revealed "the public's fundamental distaste for what had been wrought." The Harris poll of April 1978 showed that only 37 percent of the public believed ratification of the amended treaties was a "good thing for the United States," while 44 percent did not "feel that way." A better question by Harris in June ("All in all, do you favor or oppose the treaties on the Panama Canal passed by the U.S. Senate?") produced even higher figures in opposition: 35 percent in favor and 49 percent opposed. Also in June, the Roper poll asked Americans whether the Senate should have approved the Panama Canal treaties, and only 30 percent said yes, while 52 percent said no. Finally, NBC News polled Americans in September and found the greatest opposition yet. In NBC's poll, only 34 percent of the respondents said they approved of the Senate's action, while 56 percent said they did not approve.[70]

How does one explain these findings? Perhaps there had been another turnabout in public opinion. Perhaps many Americans came to favor the treaties during the debate only to change their minds again and oppose them. But there is another, more likely, explanation: that there had not been a turnabout in the first place. In retrospect, it appears that the antitreaty portrait of public opinion had been correct all along. Protreaty forces apparently misinterpreted polls showing support for treaties amended to "guarantee America's right to defend the canal" as support for the Carter-Torrijos treaties with the leadership amendments. The data from the ORC, of course, would explain such a misinterpretation. They suggest that Americans who actually favored the treaties *only* with the sort of amendments rejected by the Senate were mistakenly counted as treaty supporters by pollsters who failed to discriminate between the leadership amendments and the stronger amendments proposed by conservatives. Many people might have answered "yes" to a pollster who asked only if they would favor the treaties if they were amended to "guarantee America's right to defend the canal." Many senators who opposed the treaties also claimed they would have supported them if there had been real guarantees of America's right to defend the canal. Some protreaty senators even cited polls assessing support for an amendment allowing the United States to "intervene" in Panama as support for the leadership amendments. This constituted an even more blatant misinterpretation, of course, for the leadership amendments explicitly renounced any right of American "intervention."[71]

Once the Senate ratified the treaties with the leadership amendments the illusion of a turnabout in public opinion could not be sustained. When respondents were asked to judge the final product of the debate, those favoring stronger guarantees of military rights "returned" to the antitreaty column, and opposition to the treaties "returned" to almost exactly the same level found by pollsters at the beginning of the debate.[72] Undoubtedly many protreaty senators honestly believed in the turnabout in public opinion on the Panama Canal treaties. Nonetheless, the fact that the turnabout was illusory raises some troubling questions, both about the Panama Canal treaties, and about the role of public opinion in American foreign policy generally.

Adoption of the leadership amendments as a palliative for hostile public opinion raises serious questions about the integrity of the Panama Canal treaties. The administration insisted all along that the leadership amendments merely reiterated America's right to act unilaterally in defense of the canal, while the Panamanian reaction to the DeConcini reservation revealed that they did not agree. Since the amendments so obviously failed to clear up confusion over this matter, one must wonder if the Senate sacrificed the clarity of the agreement for political reasons. Will the new relationship between the United States and Panama—a relationship that depends heavily upon good will and cooperation—be jeopardized by renewed bickering over the meaning of the treaties in the future? More important, will Panamanian and American diplomats someday be called upon in the midst of a military emergency to resolve the confusion left by the Senate?

The role of public opinion in the Senate debate over Panama also raises larger, more timeless issues about the conduct of foreign affairs in a democratic society. The episode could be cited as evidence that policy-making elites rhetorically create fictional publics in order to justify a priori decisions. Most of the political, business, and religious "establishment" in America—indeed, most of the educated elite—favored the treaties,[73] and the treaties were negotiated and submitted to the Senate despite polls showing overwhelming public opposition. During the Senate debate, public opinion was, in effect, reconstructed rhetorically to favor the treaties despite the fact that the polls, at best, were inconclusive. One might argue that the conception of public opinion that most influenced the Senate's decision was indeed a "fiction" created by those favoring the treaties.

But this does not mean that the Senate "lied" about public opinion. There *were* empirical bases for believing in the turnabout in public opinion. Senators who cited the turnabout to justify their protreaty votes may have been guilty of nothing more than wishful thinking, ignorance about the mechanics of polling, or befuddlement in the face of voluminous and conflicting evidence. The proliferation of polling in recent years has not eliminated uncertainty in policymakers' judgments about public opinion. Public opinion remains an elusive phenomenon; the most accurate portrait of public opinion still may be lost among numerous inaccurate portraits. The debate over Panama reveals how subtle differences in questions asked by pollsters can lead to very different conclusions. It also shows how a major issue can prompt so many polls with such widely varying findings that virtually any characterization of "the people" can be justified with "scientific" data.

The debate over Panama does not give cause for handwringing over the plight of representative democracy in America. The "will of the people" may have been thwarted. But the debate actually reaffirmed the extraordinary sensitivity of American policymakers to public opinion, for even senators who considered the public misguided remained reluctant to support the treaties until there were signs that "education" and changes in the treaties produced public support. The episode testifies more to the empirical difficulties of "knowing" public opinion than to philosophical objections to popular sovereignty. It suggests that policymakers might better understand how differing methods of sampling, data collection, and interpretation make some polls better than others. And it suggests that policymakers should be skeptical than any poll reveals accurately the state of American public opinion.

CONCLUSION

Panama disappeared from the headlines following ratification of the Carter-Torrijos treaties. Attempts by conservatives to defeat legislation to implement the treaties made news in 1979, as did General Torrijos' death in a plane crash in 1984.[1] But even Ronald Reagan's election to the presidency did little to rekindle controversy over U.S.-Panamanian relations. The former antitreaty crusader has presided quietly over the early phases of the transition to a Panamanian regime. With no real crisis in Panama, both Reagan and the news media have shifted their attention to more dramatic situations elsewhere. Discussion of U.S.-Panamanian relations has once again become the province of political, academic, business, and religious elites with special interest in Panamanian affairs.

Jimmy Carter will be remembered within some quarters as a courageous president who risked political popularity to do what was "right" in Panama. And if U.S.-Panamanian relations prove cordial under the new arrangement, historians may judge Carter more favorably than did many of his contemporaries. At the same time, however, other Americans will remember Carter as the man who "gave away" an invaluable commercial and military asset. More than that, they will remember him as one who repudiated the "good-old-days" in American foreign policy.

Conclusion

The fact that Carter will be extolled by some and excoriated by others reflects the basic philosophical divisions behind controversy over Panama throughout the twentieth century. The Panama Canal historically has been a diverse political symbol; it divided Americans long before Jimmy Carter arrived on the scene. For some Americans, the canal has always served as an endorsement of American globalism; it has represented the political, economic, and even spiritual benefits to be realized from the sort of aggressive international adventurism championed by Theodore Roosevelt. For other Americans, the Panama Canal has been a very different symbol; it has represented a shameful history of "imperialism" and "colonialism" in American foreign policy. For critics of American internationalism, the Panama Canal has symbolized the arrogance of gun-boat diplomacy, an approach to foreign policy that they deem both morally wrong and counterproductive.

Virtually every article and book written about the Panama Canal in the twentieth century reflects one of these two basic points of view. Commentators on the Panama Canal almost inevitably proclaim certain points of view truthful, while dismissing opposing views as revisionism, emotionalism, or partisan posturing. But the history of controversy over Panama has been not so much a contest between truth and falsehood as a competition for *persuasiveness*. Certain beliefs and attitudes have prevailed over others because they have been more effectively promoted. And those who have most effectively shaped the domestic political climate have exerted the greatest influence over the evolution of American policy in Panama.

The Heritage of Panama and Domestic Politics

The impact of domestic politics on U.S. canal policy has been evident constantly since 1903. More than any other factor, the deference of American policymakers to public opinion—at least as they have perceived it—explains why American policy in Panama has evolved in such a gradual, tentative fashion. One can only speculate about how public opinion on the issue

210

actually evolved over the years, and one suspects that many Americans never considered the issue particularly important. But whatever the reality of public opinion, generations of American policymakers have *perceived* the canal as a cherished national monument. They have resisted relaxation of American control over the canal, above all, because they believed that "the people" would not stand for it.

Vigorous campaigning by Theodore Roosevelt and his "internationalist" political allies began to shape this possessive, intransigent political climate. In the context of the historic battles between expansionists and isolationists around the turn of the century, the vision of a magnificent waterway between the seas came to symbolize the rewards of "looking outward." In making the Panama Canal a central component in his philosophy of foreign relations, TR spoke of a "great work" that would inspire American nationalism, provide the United States with naval superiority, and signal the rest of the world that America had arrived as a great world power. Regardless of whether Americans actually embraced the Rooseveltian philosophy in all its detail, TR so dominated the national dialogue over the Panama Canal that he appeared to articulate a national consensus.

The glorious story of the canal-building project solidified this climate of support for Roosevelt's aggressive internationalism. With a campaign to portray the project as a grand, military-like venture, Roosevelt led scores of popular storytellers celebrating American power, ingenuity, and perseverance in Panama. The Rooseveltian version was perhaps no more truthful than earlier stories critical of the project. Nevertheless, it silenced the critics and elevated the canal to almost mythical status. As one of America's great heroic legends, it transformed the canal into a national monument and a symbol of America's rise to international leadership. Americans eagerly consumed the inspirational tale of America's involvement in Panama, and they called upon their political representatives to heed its "lessons." Again, Roosevelt and his allies so dominated the national dialogue over Panama that they created the impression of a national consensus.

The critical version of America's history in Panama emerged

as early as the Rooseveltian version. But as the product of foreign critics, the story of American "imperialism" and "colonialism" in Panama received little attention and had little influence on American policy prior to World War II. In the context of the Cold War, the "revisionist" story of Panama gained status. The architects of American foreign policy increasingly viewed the Canal Zone as a vestige of colonialism that hurt America's image in an era of competition for support among the developing nations. The Eisenhower, Kennedy, and Johnson administrations all acceded to some of Panama's demands. But their economic and symbolic concessions failed to satisfy Panama and still generated strong opposition at home. In the absence of a concerted presidential effort to "sell" the "new look" in thinking about Panama prior to the mid-1970s, the Rooseveltian story of the canal remained so emotionally compelling, so inextricably linked to national pride, that few politicians risked championing the alternative viewpoint.

THE "GREAT DEBATE" AND PUBLIC OPINION

Promising a new era of "human rights" and "fairness" in American foreign policy, Jimmy Carter led the first serious challenge to the Rooseveltian perspective on the Panama Canal. Carter committed the full resources of the executive branch to reshaping congressional and public opinion on new Panama Canal treaties, and he actively recruited help from the political, business, and religious establishment. In the end, he secured Senate ratification of the new agreement, but he apparently did little to change public attitudes about America's role in Panama.

The New Right's campaign against the treaties posed one major obstacle to Carter's success. Hoping to exploit the issue to broaden its political base, the New Right crusaded against the treaties with state-of-the-art campaign techniques and old-fashioned emotional zeal. With unprecedented organizational strength, new communicative technologies, and a more mature attitude toward the established news media, the New Right effectively countered the superior resources of protreaty campaigners. While it lacked the money, manpower, and political "favors" at the disposal of the White House, the New Right had an excess of sheer determination.

The Carter administration's troubles also stemmed from deficiencies in its own case for the treaties. At bottom, the administration failed to reshape public opinion because its arguments for the Panama Canal treaties were intellectually untenable and emotionally unappealing. The historical revisionism of protreaty advocates was incomplete, confused, and disparaging toward America. Treaty supporters often simply dismissed important historical controversies, while at other times they presented weak or even contradictory arguments. In contrast to their opponents' reiteration of familiar historical arguments, protreaty advocates tried to popularize attacks on America's presence in Panama originated by foreign critics. In contrast to their opponents' rekindling of national pride in the Panama Canal, the protreaty case called upon Americans to feel ashamed and guilty about their nation's past.

Protreaty arguments about the future economic and military utility of the canal were also unpersuasive; they were insufficiently elaborated, confused, and an affront to the "common sense" of many Americans. While treaty opponents offered elaborately documented arguments on economic and military issues, protreaty advocates offered only perfunctory and ambiguous answers to critical questions, particularly regarding the military provisions of the neutrality treaty. In the end, they left a troubling ambiguity concerning America's right to defend the canal. And while opponents of the treaties talked about the need to stand fast against the spread of communism in Latin America, treaty supporters offered the counterintuitive argument that communism was most effectively resisted by American withdrawal.

The Carter administration asked the American people to endorse a philosophy of American foreign policy associated with the decline of American preeminence in world affairs and with the unpleasant tensions of the Cold War. There seemed little in the history recalled by the debate or in protreaty predictions of the future to recommend further retreat, international equality, and "partnerships" with third-rate powers. The philosophy of foreign affairs articulated by protreaty forces seemed destined to produce further international humiliation and further advances for America's adversaries. It was a philosophy at odds with America's popular historical consciousness.

By contrast, the historical myths evoked by those on the other side of the issue arose out of an era of American greatness—an age of seemingly unmitigated success in American foreign policy. Treaty opponents recalled the glorious tale of America's triumph in Panama, and they touted the philosophy of foreign policy that had carried America to global leadership. Their vision of the future suggested that the United States could again be strong and lead the free world. Opponents of the treaties promised a return to the "good-old-days" of national pride and purpose—an attractive prospect indeed in the wake of Vietnam.

The Carter administration assumed a heavy burden of proof in the debate over Panama, not just in showing the advantages of the treaties, but in justifying a new blueprint for American foreign policy. On ideological grounds one might say that the administration shouldered that burden; more than one elite commentator has disparaged the public for not recognizing that Carter was "right."[2] But by standards of everyday argument, the public had sound reasons for not buying the protreaty case. Proponents of the treaties offered neither a convincing intellectual case nor a powerful emotional plea for "giving away" the Panama Canal. The public may have been nostalgic in rejecting the "expert" opinion that times had changed. But in an era when America looked more and more like a helpless giant, it seemed understandable that some Americans longed for the "good old days."

THE HIGH PRICE OF SENATE RATIFICATION

From the start of Senate deliberations over the Panama Canal treaties in February 1978, debate returned again and again to the military provisions of the neutrality treaty. With senators on both sides arguing that America's rights of defense and transit needed to be clarified, the Senate overwhelmingly adopted the so-called leadership amendments. These amendments proved crucial to ratification of the treaties, but the reason for their impact was not so obvious. Perhaps some senators genuinely believed that the amendments clarified American military rights after the year 2000. But there was another, more important reason for their influence on the Senate: the belief that they produced a "turnabout" in public opinion.

At the start of the Senate debate, a number of senators voiced support for the treaties but remained reluctant to endorse them because of hostile constituencies. The leadership amendments appeared to solve their dilemma. Polls showing support for the treaties if they were amended to guarantee America's right to defend the canal suggested that the public could be appeased by rather simple changes in the agreement. Citing other polling data, opponents of the treaties countered that the public overwhelmingly preferred much stronger guarantees: language asserting America's right to act unilaterally in defense of the canal. But in the end, the protreaty argument carried the day; belief in a turnabout in public opinion became perhaps the decisive factor in the Senate's decision.

When the debate was all over, a number of polls, all assessing attitudes toward the treaties as actually amended, exposed the fallacy in protreaty claims of a turnabout in public opinion. By failing to distinguish between the leadership amendments and stronger guarantees of defense rights rejected by the Senate, pollsters apparently counted people favoring the treaties only with the stronger language as treaty supporters. Additional evidence that the Senate misread public opinion came later as the New Right exploited the issue to build its organizational strength, to add hundreds of thousands of names to its mailing lists, to increase its fund-raising revenues dramatically, and to "punish" liberal senators at the polls in 1978 and 1980.[3] Although these developments cannot be attributed solely to the Panama issue, observers from Jimmy Carter to Richard Viguerie agree that the debate was a key factor in the conservative renaissance of the late 1970s.[4]

Americans obviously disagree over whether conservative advances are good for the nation. But there may be other, more subtle, ramifications of the debate over Panama that should concern Americans of all ideological stripes. Senator Edward Brooke articulated one of these concerns on the floor of the Senate: the possibility that ratification of the treaties might contribute to the alienation of Americans from their government. Although Brooke spoke forcefully in favor of the new agreement, he remained fearful that such unpopular treaties might produce "the long-term debilitating effect" of deepening "the disillusion felt by many with their Government."[5]

Brooke's concern with public opinion involved more than the problem of alienation. In articulating one of the many "lessons" of Vietnam heard during the debate, he suggested that continued public opposition might also impede successful implementation of the treaties. The Panama Canal treaties come into force gradually, and Brooke feared that public hostility could prompt renewed political bickering disruptive of the process. Brooke thus urged his fellow treaty supporters to listen to their constituents. Instead of patronizing constituents with talk of their ignorance and emotionalism, he urged treaty supporters to respond sincerely to their "legitimate concerns": "In a democracy, the success of any long-term undertaking . . . is based on the sustained support or, at a minimum, the tolerance of the overwhelming majority of its citizens. This is a fundamental reality that has been painfully brought home to the people of this country in the last decade and a half. . . . Modernization of our relationship with Panama must be achieved in such a way as to elicit the necessary sustained level of support from the American people."[6]

Beyond any repercussions of public hostility, there remained one last problem with the Panama Canal treaties. By ultimately failing to resolve confusion over American military rights, the Senate laid the groundwork for conflict in U.S.-Panamanian relations after the turn of the century. By failing to clearly define America's rights to defend the canal and to use the canal in military emergencies, the Senate virtually assured that hurried negotiations will become necessary in the event of a military emergency.

As rhetorical strategy, the ambiguity in American military

rights unquestionably proved useful. The ambiguity is perhaps best viewed as an attempt to resolve a dilemma created by conflicting demands from Panamanian and American audiences. In selling the treaties to the American public, protreaty advocates promised that the United States would always be able to defend the canal, both against outside threats and against threats from within Panama. Americans wanted to hear that the United States could act "by itself" or even "intervene" to defend the canal if the Panamanians proved unwilling or unable to repel some threat. Yet such claims offended the Panamanians. The Panamanians considered any assertion of America's right to act unilaterally or to intervene in Panama an infringement on their sovereignty, and they were willing to scrap the entire agreement if the Senate adopted amendments containing such language. In effect, as controversy over the DeConcini reservation revealed, the Senate ultimately both claimed and denied America's right to intervene in Panama. The fact that the final agreement satisfied both Panamanians and Americans testifies to the rhetorical value of this ambiguity.

But while ambiguity may have served the administration politically in the short-term, it may manifest itself later in serious international conflict. What happens on some future day if the canal is actually threatened? Will confusion over American military rights reemerge and preclude effective action? How is the United States to defend the canal against a domestic Panamanian threat—a new government hostile to the United States or internal political chaos? Indeed, how is the United States to defend the canal against *any* threat if Panama withholds its permission? And how will the United States enjoy its right to "expeditious passage" in a military emergency if it must first debate the definition of "emergency" with Panamanian officials?

Perhaps American and Panamanian diplomats will never be called upon to clarify the military provisions of the Panama Canal treaties. Perhaps, as the Carter administration predicted, the treaties will produce a harmonious partnership between the United States and Panama and the canal will operate smoothly for many years to come. If disagreements do arise, however,

217

they will come at the most inopportune moment—in the midst of a military emergency. Diplomats will then have the unenviable task of looking to the voluminous and inconclusive record of the Great Debate over Panama for clarification of the disputed rights.

Notes

Bibliography

Index

NOTES

Introduction

1. Angus Deming, et al., "A Panama Production," *Newsweek*, 19 September 1977, 46.

2. "Squaring Off on the Canal," *Time*, 30 January 1978, 31.

3. "Carter Wins on Panama," *Time*, 27 March 1978, 10.

4. Walter LaFeber, *The Panama Canal: The Crisis in Historical Perspective*, rev. ed. (New York: Oxford Univ. Press, 1979), 249.

5. Senate, Committee on Foreign Relations, *Senate Debate on the Panama Canal Treaties: A Compendium of Major Statements, Documents, Record Votes and Relevant Events*, 96th Cong., 1st sess., 1979, Committee Print, 10–11.

6. The debate was broadcast over National Public Radio (NPR). NPR's coverage extended for 37 days, totaled 297 broadcast hours, and was carried by 170 affiliates in 48 states, Puerto Rico, and the District of Columbia. NPR also broadcast nightly summaries of each day's debate.

The Roper poll reported that 21 percent of Americans surveyed tuned in to some portion of the debate, and that these listeners were four times more likely than nonlisteners to have written or phoned their senators or representatives regarding the treaties. A survey by Market Facts Inc. revealed that the audience for the debate was disproportionately male and well-educated. Among listeners, one in four said that listening to the debate had affected their opinion on the treaties.

See "Roper: High Audience for the Canal Debate," *CPB Report*, 19 June 1978, 3; National Public Radio, "Estimated Audience for Broadcasts of Panama Canal Treaties Debate," Washington, 1978, provided for the writer by NPR.

7. Committee on Foreign Relations, *Senate Debate on the Panama Canal Treaties*, 11. On the general increase in congressional assertiveness in foreign affairs see I. M. Destler, "Treaty Troubles: Versailles in Reverse," *Foreign Policy*, Winter 1978–1979, especially 52–57.

8. Angus Deming, et al., "The Canal: Time to Go?" *Newsweek*, 22 August 1977, 29–30; William J. Lanouette, "The Panama Canal Treaties: Playing in Peoria and in the Senate," *National Journal*, 8 October 1977, 1562.

221

Notes

9. Richard Steele and Hal Bruno, "Stand Up and Be Counted," *Newsweek*, 12 September 1977, 27; Ken Bode, "The Hero of Panama," *New Republic*, 21 January 1978, 13; Lanouette, "The Panama Canal Treaties," 1560.

10. Thomas M. Franck and Edward Weisband, *Word Politics: Verbal Strategy among the Superpowers* (New York: Oxford Univ. Press, 1972), 117.

11. Murray Edelman, *Political Language: Words that Succeed and Policies that Fail* (New York: Academic Press, 1977), 3; Murray Edelman, *Politics as Symbolic Action: Mass Arousal and Quiescence* (Chicago: Markham, 1971), 66; Edelman, *Political Language*, 3; Stephen E. Lucas, *Portents of Rebellion: Rhetoric and Revolution in Philadelphia, 1765–1776* (Philadelphia: Temple Univ. Press, 1976), xi.

1. THE INTERNATIONALIST VISION AND THE PANAMA CANAL

1. See Reuben E. Bakenhus, Harry S. Knapp, and Emory R. Johnson, *The Panama Canal: Comprising Its History and Construction, and Its Relation to the Navy, International Law and Commerce* (New York: John Wiley and Sons, 1915), 11; "Secretary of State Clay's Instructions to United States Representatives to the Panama Congress, May 1, 1826," in Senate, Committee on Foreign Relations, *Background Documents Relating to the Panama Canal*, 95th Cong., 1st sess., 1977, Committee Print, 3.

For major nineteenth-century canal treaties see "Article 35 of a General Treaty Of Peace, Amity, Navigation, and Commerce between the United States of America and the Republic of New Granada (Colombia), December 12, 1846"; "Convention Negotiated between the United States and Nicaragua, June 21, 1849"; and "Convention between the United States and Great Britain Concerning a Ship Canal Connecting the Atlantic and Pacific Oceans, April 19, 1850 (Clayton-Bulwer Treaty)," in Committee on Foreign Relations, *Background Documents*, 7–10, 16–21, 27–30.

Major proclamations of canal policy include "Resolution of the U.S. Senate Adopted March 3, 1835" and "Resolution of House of Representatives, 1839," in Committee on Foreign Relations, *Background Documents*, 4, 5; Ulysses S. Grant, "First Annual Message," in *A Compilation of the Messages and Papers of the Presidents*, 11 vols., ed. James D. Richardson (1897; reprint, Washington: GPO, 1914), 6:3987; and President Hayes' insistence that the United States maintain "supervision and authority" over any canal built by another nation in "President Hayes' Message of March 8, 1880," in Committee on Foreign Relations, *Background Documents*, 51.

For studies of canal routes see Philippe Bunau-Varilla, *Panama: The Creation, Destruction and Resurrection* (New York: McBride, Nast, 1914), 23. Also see "An Act of June 4, 1897, Constituting the Nicaragua Canal Commission, and the Commission's Conclusions of May 9, 1899"; "An Act of March 3, 1899 Authorizing the President to Make an Investigation of the Panama and

Nicaragua Routes, . . . and the Membership of the Isthmian Canal Commission"; "Conclusions of the Isthmian Canal Commission, 1899–1901, November 16, 1901"; and "Supplementary Report of the Isthmian Canal Commission, January 18, 1902," in Committee on Foreign Relations, *Background Documents*, 103–5, 106, 133–39, 143–52.

2. See "The Collapse of the Maritime Canal Company of Nicaragua, 1893," in Committee on Foreign Relations, *Background Documents*, 96.

3. See "Contracts between Colombia and Lucien N. B. Wyse, . . . for the Construction of an Interoceanic Canal, 1876 and 1878 (Wyse Concession)"; and "Secretary of State Evarts' Instructions to Mr. Dichman, Minister to Colombia, Regarding the French Interoceanic Canal Enterprise, April 19, 1880," in Committee on Foreign Relations, *Background Documents*, 40–45, 46–47. Also see LaFeber, *The Panama Canal*, 13–14.

4. Walter LaFeber, *The New Empire: An Interpretation of American Expansion, 1860–1898* (Ithaca: Cornell Univ. Press, 1963), 150.

5. William L. Merry, *The Nicaragua Canal: The Gateway between the Oceans* (San Francisco: Commercial Publishing,1895), 7.

6. Howard K. Beale, *Theodore Roosevelt and the Rise of America to World Power* (1956; reprint, New York: Collier Books, 1967), 52. Also see Beale's discussion of Roosevelt's circle on 36–38. Of the internationalists other than Roosevelt, Alfred T. Mahan is of most interest for studies of the Panama Canal and related issues. Roosevelt, also a naval historian of some repute in the 1880s, established contact with Mahan when TR spoke at the Naval War College. Both Roosevelt and Henry Cabot Lodge eagerly read Mahan's *The Influence of Sea Power upon History* in 1890. Later, Mahan wrote a series of articles emphasizing the need for an American canal on the isthmus and the necessity of a powerful navy to protect the canal and to enforce the Monroe Doctrine. After Roosevelt became president, Mahan wrote articles defending TR's actions in obtaining the canal rights and his program of naval expansion. See Walter Millis, *Arms and Men: A Study of American Military History* (New York: Mentor Books, 1956), 139–46; LaFeber, *The New Empire*, 232.

7. Brooks Adams, *The Law of Civilization and Decay: An Essay on History* (1896; reprint, New York: Alfred A. Knopf, 1943).

8. For a time, Adams apparently supported economic solutions to thwart his "law." But eventually he came to agree with Roosevelt that the martial spirit could be infused into an economically advanced state without returning the people to a condition of barbarism (see LaFeber, *The New Empire*, 82–84). For the initial points of disagreement between Adams and Roosevelt, see TR's review of *The Law of Civilization and Decay* in Theodore Roosevelt, *The Works of Theodore Roosevelt*, Memorial Edition, ed. Joseph B. Bishop, 24 vols. (New York: Charles Scribner's Sons, 1923–1926), 14:129–50.

9. LaFeber, *The New Empire*, 98. For Mahan's views on the need for the martial spirit see Alfred T. Mahan, "Possibilities of an Anglo-American Reunion," in *The Interest of America in Sea Power, Present and Future* (Boston: Little, Brown, 1898), 118–22.

Notes

10. Theodore Roosevelt, "The Strenuous Life," in *The Strenuous Life: Essays and Addresses* (New York: Century, 1902), 3–4; Theodore Roosevelt, "National Duties," in *The Strenuous Life*, 286.

11. Theodore Roosevelt, *The Naval War of 1812: A History of the United States Navy during the Last War with Great Britain*, 4th ed. (New York: G. P. Putnam's Sons, 1889; reprint in *The Works of Theodore Roosevelt*). In the first edition of his biography of Roosevelt, Pringle calls this work a "first-class study . . . so technical as to be quite unintelligible, in certain parts, to the layman." The book, published in 1882, received favorable reviews in the New York press. See Henry F. Pringle, *Theodore Roosevelt: A Biography* (New York: Harcourt, Brace, 1931), 62.

12. Theodore Roosevelt, *The Winning of the West: An Account of the Exploration and Settlement of Our Country from the Alleghanies to the Pacific*, 4 vols. (New York: G. P. Putnam's Sons, 1889–1896; reprint in *The Works of Theodore Roosevelt*), 9:115; Henry Cabot Lodge and Theodore Roosevelt, *Hero Tales From American History* (New York: Century, 1895; reprint in *The Works of Theodore Roosevelt*); Theodore Roosevelt, *Oliver Cromwell* (New York: Charles Scribner's Sons, 1900; reprint in *The Works of Theodore Roosevelt*).

13. Theodore Roosevelt, "Washington's Forgotten Maxim," in Theodore Roosevelt, *American Ideals and Other Essays, Social and Political*, rev. ed. (New York: Knickerbocker Press, 1903), 258; Roosevelt, "The Strenuous Life," 6, 8. Also see Roosevelt's attack on the economic spirit in "American Ideals," in Roosevelt, *American Ideals*, 10–11.

14. See LaFeber, *The New Empire*, 191–96.

15. Fiske, whom LaFeber calls "perhaps the most popular public lecturer in American history," championed a doctrine of Anglo-Americanism premised on the ultimate triumph of American commercialism. He foresaw a glorious future of American industrial advances that would force European states to forego militaristic pursuits in order to remain economically competitive. He envisioned the ultimate victory of the economic spirit; he sought the elimination of martial pursuits and envisioned an economic alliance with England led by superior American industrialists. In "Manifest Destiny," a lecture he delivered 4 times in England and some 46 times in America, he argued that even the character of individuals would change to less martial states: "Manifestly the development of industry is largely dependent upon the cessation or restriction of warfare; and furthermore, as the industrial phase of civilization slowly supplants the military phase, men's characters undergo, though very slowly, a corresponding change." See LaFeber, *The New Empire*, 99; John Fiske, "Manifest Destiny," in *American Political Ideas Viewed from the Standpoint of Universal History* (New York: Harper and Brothers, 1885), 106–7.

16. Fiske, "Manifest Destiny," 150.

17. Alfred T. Mahan, "Hawaii and Our Future Sea Power," in *The Interest of America in Sea Power*, 34; Mahan, "Possibilities of an Anglo-American Reunion," 107–126.

18. Mahan, "Possibilities of an Anglo-American Reunion," 114; Alfred T. Mahan, "Application of the Monroe Doctrine: Anglo-American Community of Interest," in *Mahan on Naval Warfare: Selections From the Writings of Rear Admiral Alfred T. Mahan*, ed. Allan Westcott (Boston: Little, Brown, 1941), 295.

19. Theodore Roosevelt, "The Monroe Doctrine," in *American Ideals*, 221; Roosevelt, *The Winning of the West*, 3; Roosevelt, "The Monroe Doctrine," 226–27. As Beale has noted, Roosevelt shared Mahan's view that *formal* alliance was neither possible nor necessary. Instead, he envisioned only a "mutual understanding of common interests and common traditions." See Beale, *Roosevelt and the Rise of America*, 142.

20. Roosevelt, "Washington's Forgotten Maxim," 243–44.

21. Quoted in Beale, *Roosevelt and the Rise of America*, 142, n. 26.

22. Alfred T. Mahan, *The Influence of Sea Power upon History, 1660–1783* (1890; reprint, New York: Hill and Wang, 1957), 29–30; Alfred T. Mahan, "The United States Looking Outward," *Atlantic Monthly*, December 1890, 819.

23. Henry F. Pringle, *Theodore Roosevelt: A Biography*, rev. ed. (New York: Harvest Books, 1956), 211–12.

24. William R. Thayer, *The Life and Letters of John Hay*, 2 vols. (Boston: Houghton Mifflin, 1915), 2:341.

25. Mahan, "The United States Looking Outward," 818; Alfred T. Mahan, "The Battle of Trafalgar," in *Mahan on Naval Warfare*, 227; Alfred T. Mahan, "The Future in Relation to American Naval Power," in *The Interest of America in Sea Power*, 152–54.

26. Roosevelt, "The Monroe Doctrine," 222, 226.

27. Mahan, "The United States Looking Outward," 819; Mahan, "The Future in Relation to American Naval Power," 152, 157.

28. Alfred T. Mahan, "Preparedness for Naval War," in *The Interest of America in Sea Power*, 193, 198.

29. Mahan, *The Influence of Sea Power*, 30; Mahan, "Preparedness for Naval War," 214.

30. Theodore Roosevelt, "The Influence of Sea Power upon History," *Atlantic Monthly*, October 1890, 563, 567.

31. Roosevelt, "Washington's Forgotten Maxim," 254–55.

32. Roosevelt, "Washington's Forgotten Maxim," 256–58.

33. Mahan, "Hawaii and Our Future Sea Power," 52–53.

34. Theodore Roosevelt, "Expansion and Peace," in *The Writings of Theodore Roosevelt*, ed. William H. Harbaugh (Indianapolis: Bobbs-Merrill, 1967), 31–32, 35.

35. David McCullough, *The Path between the Seas: The Creation of the Panama Canal, 1870–1914* (New York: Simon and Schuster, 1977), 247. Also see Beale, *Roosevelt and the Rise of America*, 72.

36. See Addison C. Thomas, *Roosevelt Among the People: Being an Account of the Fourteen Thousand Mile Journey from Ocean to Ocean of Theodore Roose-*

velt . . . Together with the Public Speeches Made by Him During the Journey (Chicago: L. W. Walter, 1910), 313; and McCullough, *Path between the Seas,* 248.

37. See Harbaugh's commentary in Roosevelt, *The Writings of Theodore Roosevelt,* 83–84.

38. Theodore Roosevelt, speech at Chicago, 2 April 1903, in *Addresses and Presidential Messages of Theodore Roosevelt, 1902–1904* (New York: G. P. Putnam's Sons, 1904), 116; Theodore Roosevelt, "First Annual Message," in *The Works of Theodore Roosevelt* 17:132; Theodore Roosevelt, "Second Annual Message," in *The Works of Theodore Roosevelt* 17:176; Roosevelt, "First Annual Message," 17:132.

39. Roosevelt, "Second Annual Message," 17:177.

40. Roosevelt, speech at Chicago, 2 April 1903, 115–16.

41. Theodore Roosevelt, speech at Haverhill, Mass., 26 August 1902, in *Addresses and Presidential Messages,* 28; Theodore Roosevelt, speech at the unveiling of the Sherman Statue, Washington, 15 October 1903, in *Addresses and Presidential Messages,* 253; Roosevelt, speech at Chicago, 2 April 1903, 121.

42. Pringle, *Theodore Roosevelt,* 1931 ed., 244.

43. "The Spooner Act of June 28, 1902" and "Hay-Herran Treaty with Colombia, January 22, 1903," in Committee on Foreign Relations, *Background Documents,* 178–80, 202–13. The most complete account of events surrounding the Spooner Act and the Hay-Herran treaty is Dwight C. Miner, *The Fight for the Panama Route: The Story of the Spooner Act and the Hay-Herran Treaty* (New York: Columbia Univ. Press, 1940).

44. See "Correspondence of 1903 During the Period of Colombian Consideration of the Hay-Herran Treaty (Excerpts)," in Committee on Foreign Relations, *Background Documents,* 214–45.

45. See Miles DuVal, Jr., *Cadiz to Cathay: The Story of the Long Diplomatic Struggle for the Panama Canal,* rev. ed. (Stanford: Stanford Univ. Press, 1947), 273–355.

46. Senator Morgan, 23 November 1903, *Congressional Record,* 58th Cong., 1st sess., 37:429; DuVal, *Cadiz to Cathay,* 379–86.

47. Theodore Roosevelt, "Message Communicated to the Two Houses of Congress at the Beginning of the Second Session of the Fifty-Eighth Congress" and "Message Communicated to the Two Houses of Congress on January 4, 1904," in *Addresses and Presidential Messages,* 423, 452.

48. Morgan chaired the Senate Committee on Interoceanic Canals—often called the "Morgan Committee"—and was a strong advocate of a canal in Nicaragua rather than in Panama. He made his national reputation by promoting the Nicaraguan canal and he "became almost vicious toward anyone who opposed him." Before the debate over the Hay-Bunau-Varilla treaty he was among Roosevelt's closest Democratic allies. He shared Roosevelt's expansionist sentiment and Roosevelt had been known as a "Nicaragua man." But when Roosevelt came out in favor of building the canal in Panama, Morgan became his harshest Senate critic. See McCullough, *Path between the Seas,*

259–61; Shelby Moore Cullom, *Fifty Years of Public Service* (Chicago: A. C. Mc-Clurg, 1911), 348–51.

49. See Morgan's remarks, 23 November 1903, *Congressional Record,* 58th Cong., 1st sess., 37:425–29; 9 December 1903, *Congressional Record,* 58th Cong., 2d sess., 38:79–81; 25 January 1904, *Congressional Record,* 58th Cong., 2d sess., 38:1121.

50. Roosevelt, "Message Communicated to the Two Houses of Congress at the Beginning of the Second Session of the Fifty-Eighth Congress," 425; Roosevelt, "Message Communicated to the Two Houses of Congress on January 4, 1904," 461, 463.

51. 27 January 1904, *Congressional Record,* 58th Cong., 2d sess., 38: 1245;23 February 1904, *Congressional Record,* 58th Cong., 2d sess., 38:2246.

52. 23 February 1904, *Congressional Record,* 58th Cong., 2d sess., 38:2245; 23 February 1904, *Congressional Record,* 58th Cong., 2d sess., 38:2246; 20 February 1904, *Congressional Record,* 58th Cong., 2d sess., 38:2133; 5 February 1904, *Congressional Record,* 58th Cong., 2d sess., 38:1667.

53. Quoted in Phillip C. Jessup, *Elihu Root,* 2 vols. (New York: Dodd, Mead, 1938), 1:405.

2. THEODORE ROOSEVELT AND THE HEROES OF PANAMA

1. See Alfred C. Richard, "The Panama Canal in American National Consciousness, 1870–1922" (Ph.D. diss. Boston University, 1969), 211–13.

2. McCullough, *Path between the Seas,* 438–39.

3. John F. Stevens, "The Truth of History," in *History of the Panama Canal: Its Construction and Builders,* ed. Ira E. Bennett (Washington: Historical Publishing, 1915), 210; Stevens quoted in McCullough, *Path between the Seas,* 463; Stevens quoted in Farnham Bishop, *Panama Past and Present* (New York: Century, 1913), 159.

4. See Theodore Shonts, *Speech . . . Before the Knife-and-Fork Club, Kansas City, . . . January 24, 1907* (Washington: GPO, 1907).

5. Donald G. Payne [Ian Cameron], *The Impossible Dream: The Building of the Panama Canal* (New York: William Morrow, 1972), 122; Farnham Bishop, *Panama Past and Present,* 159.

6. Joseph B. Bishop, *Theodore Roosevelt and His Time Shown in His Own Letters,* 2 vols. (New York: Charles Scribner's Sons, 1920), 1:455; W. Leon Pepperman, *Who Built the Panama Canal?* (New York: E. P. Dutton, 1915), 245, 293–94.

7. Miles DuVal, Jr., *And the Mountains Will Move: The Story of the Building of the Panama Canal* (Stanford: Stanford Univ. Press, 1947), 201–2.

8. Poultney Bigelow, "Our Mismanagement at Panama," *The Independent,* 4 January 1906, 13.

Notes

9. Bigelow, "Our Mismanagement at Panama," 12, 17–20.

10. See Senate, Committee on Interoceanic Canals, *Hearings . . . on the Senate Resolution Providing for an Investigation of Matters Relating to the Panama Canal,* 59th Cong., 2d sess., 1907, S. Doc. 401, 1:97–115; William Howard Taft, "The Panama Canal: Why the Lock System was Chosen," *Century Magazine,* December 1906, 312; Pepperman, *Who Built the Panama Canal?* 263–67.

11. Poultney Bigelow, "Panama: The Human Side," *Cosmopolitan Magazine,* September 1906, 461–62.

12. Roosevelt, "Special Message," in *Messages and Papers of the Presidents,* ed. James D. Richardson, 10:7661.

13. See DuVal, *And the Mountains Will Move,* 228–42; Joseph B. Bishop, *The Panama Gateway* (New York: Charles Scribner's Sons, 1913), 169–71.

14. DuVal, *And the Mountains Will Move,* 237.

15. The most famous photograph showed Roosevelt perched at the controls of a ninety-five-ton Bucyrus steamshovel—the "mainstay of the work." As "an expression of a man and his era," there are "few [photographs] that can surpass it," and it quickly became "part of American folklore." McCullough, *Path between the Seas,* 430, 496. For other pictures of Roosevelt in Panama see Joseph B. Bishop, *The Panama Gateway,* facing 170; Hugh C. Weir, *The Conquest of the Isthmus: The Men Who are Building the Panama Canal—Their Daily Lives, Perils, and Adventures* (New York: G. P. Putnam's Sons, 1909), facing 80, 84.

16. Theodore Roosevelt, "Speech Made by President Roosevelt to the Employees of the Isthmian Canal Commission in the Administration Building, Culebra, Canal Zone, November 16, 1906" and "Address of President Roosevelt to the Employees of the Isthmian Canal Commission, at Colon, Panama, November 17, 1906," in Society of the Chagres, *Society of the Chagres 1911 Year Book,* 15–16, 17–18, 20.

17. Theodore Roosevelt, *Special Message of the President of the United States Concerning the Panama Canal,* 59th Cong., 2d sess., 1906, S. Doc. 144.

18. Joseph B. Bishop, *Theodore Roosevelt and His Time,* 454–55.

19. Roosevelt, *Special Message Concerning the Panama Canal,* 26–29.

20. DuVal, *And the Mountains Will Move,* 242.

21. The "Roosevelt Medals" were designed by artist Francis D. Millet and 6000 had been delivered by 1913. According to Bishop they were "very highly prized by their owners," and they "contributed materially to the patriotic pride in their work which is so universal in the canal force, and which has been the chief cause of its remarkable efficiency." See Joseph B. Bishop, *The Panama Gateway,* 171–72. For a picture of the medal see John Barrett, *Panama Canal: What It Is; What It Means* (Washington: Pan American Union, 1913), 8.

22. See Richard, "The Panama Canal in American National Consciousness," 219–21.

23. Joseph Pennell, *Joseph Pennell's Pictures of the Panama Canal: Reproductions of a Series of Lithographs Made by Him on the Isthmus of Panama, January-*

March 1912, Together with Impressions and Notes by the Artist (1912; reprint, Philadelphia: J. B. Lippincott, 1913).

24. See Richard, "The Panama Canal in American National Consciousness," 220–21.

25. See Pepperman, *Who Built the Panama Canal?* 245–94; C. H. Forbes-Lindsay, *Panama: The Isthmus and the Canal* (Philadelphia: John C. Winston, 1906), 266–67, 289–93; William R. Scott, *The Americans in Panama* (New York: Statler, 1912), 95–96.

26. Willis J. Abbot, *Panama and the Canal in Picture and Prose: A Complete Story of Panama, as Well as the History, Purpose and Promise of its World-Famous Canal—the Most Gigantic Engineering Undertaking Since the Dawn of Time* (New York: Syndicate, 1913); Frederic J. Haskin, *The Panama Canal* (Garden City: Doubleday, Page, 1913), 1; Ralph E. Avery, *The Greatest Engineering Feat in the World at Panama: The Authentic and Complete Story of the Building and Operation of the Great Waterway—the Eighth Wonder of the World*, rev. ed. (New York: Leslie-Judge, 1915), 3. Also see Barrett, *Panama Canal*, 6; Pepperman, *Who Built the Panama Canal?* v; Forbes-Lindsay, *Panama*, 3; C. H. Forbes-Lindsay, *The Story of Panama and the Canal: A Complete History . . . and a Detailed Description of the American Enterprise* (N.p., [1913?]), 5.

27. McCullough, *Path between the Seas*, 556.

28. Charles Francis Adams, *The Panama Canal Zone: An Epochal Event in Sanitation* (Boston: Massachusetts Historical Society, 1911), 14–15; William J. Showalter, "The Panama Canal," *National Geographic*, February 1912, 202. Also see C. H. Forbes-Lindsay, *Panama and the Canal Today: An Historical Account of the Canal Project . . . and the First Comprehensive Account of its Physical Features and Natural Resources*, rev. ed. (Boston: L. C. Page, 1912), 69–70.

29. Showalter, "The Panama Canal," 202. The truth, as British writers were quick to point out, was that the British discovered the connection of the mosquito to tropical diseases in India, and the theory had been well-proven in Cuba before the effort in Panama. See John Foster Fraser, *Panama and What It Means* (London: Cassell, 1913), 111–12; John Saxon Mills, *The Panama Canal: A History and Description of the Enterprise* (London: Thomas Nelson and Sons, 1913), 129–40; Charles Markham, "The Making of the Panama Canal," *Blackwood's Magazine*, August 1912, 263. Also see Gerstle Mack, *The Land Divided: A History of the Panama Canal and Other Isthmian Canal Projects* (New York: Alfred A. Knopf, 1944), 520–36.

30. Scott, *The Americans in Panama*, 43; Barrett, *Panama Canal*, 102.

31. Frank A. Gause and Charles C. Carr, *The Story of Panama: The New Route to India* (1912; reprint, New York: Arno Press, 1970), 72–75; Barrett, *Panama Canal*, 100.

32. See Abbot, *Panama and the Canal in Picture and Prose*, 178–81; Scott, *The Americans in Panama*, 166–68.

33. The reports, including wild stories that it had already collapsed, prompted President Roosevelt to appoint a commission to investigate. According to Abbot, the commission concluded that the builders had gone "far

beyond the necessary point in making the dam ponderous and safe." See Abbot, *Panama and the Canal in Picture and Prose*, 178–79; George W. Goethals, *The Isthmian Canal* (Washington: GPO, 1909), 8; Haskin, *The Panama Canal*, 32–33; George W. Goethals, ed., *The Panama Canal: An Engineering Treatise*, 2 vols. (New York: McGraw-Hill, 1916), 1 : 23–24.

34. Showalter, "The Panama Canal," 199. Also see Abbot, *Panama and the Canal in Picture and Prose*, 178; Haskin, *The Panama Canal*, 25.

35. Barrett, *Panama Canal*, 59; Fraser, *Panama and What It Means*, 32–33; Farnham Bishop, *Panama Past and Present*, 184–87.

36. Barrett, *Panama Canal*, 51; Joseph B. Bishop, "Panama's Bridge of Water," *Scribner's Magazine*, July 1913, 15; Barrett, *Panama Canal*, 51.

37. Barrett, *Panama Canal*, 55; Farnham Bishop, *Panama Past and Present*, 174; Haskin, *The Panama Canal*, 45. Also see [Joseph B. Bishop], compiler, *Official Handbook of the Panama Canal*, 3d ed. (Ancon, C.Z.: [I.C.C. Press], 1913), 16.

38. Scott, *The Americans in Panama*, 157; Abbot, *Panama and the Canal in Picture and Prose*, 185; Barrett, *Panama Canal*, 54.

39. Abbot, *Panama and the Canal in Picture and Prose*, 137, 182; Fraser, *Panama and What It Means*, 37; Barrett, *Panama Canal*, 55. For other discussions of the locks see [Bishop], compiler, *Official Handbook of the Panama Canal*, 21–26; Logan Marshall, *The Story of the Panama Canal: The Wonderful Account of the Gigantic Undertaking Commenced by the French, and Brought to Triumphant Completion by the United States* (N.p., [1913]), 168–78; Haskin, *The Panama Canal*, 57–69; Gause and Carr, *The Story of Panama*, 58–62.

40. Abbot, *Panama and the Canal in Picture and Prose*, 134; Barrett, *Panama Canal*, 47.

41. Haskin, *The Panama Canal*, 25; Abbot, *Panama and the Canal in Picture and Prose*, 135.

42. Fraser, *Panama and What It Means*, 39; Abbot, *Panama and the Canal in Picture and Prose*, 201, 204–5.

43. Haskin, *The Panama Canal*, 70; Harry A. Franck, *Zone Policeman 88: A Close Range Study of the Panama Canal and Its Workers* (New York: Century, 1913), 18; Abbot, *Panama and the Canal in Picture and Prose*, 205, 213; Haskin, *The Panama Canal*, 70.

44. Farnham Bishop, *Panama Past and Present*, 189; Arthur Bullard [Albert Edwards], *Panama: The Canal, the Country, and the People* (New York: MacMillan, 1911), 550.

45. McCullough, *Path between the Seas*, 570–71; John O. Collins, *The Panama Guide* (Mt. Hope, C.Z.: I.C.C. Press, 1912), 4.

46. See Bullard, *Panama*, 500–505.

47. Franck, *Zone Policeman 88*, 205, 117; George W. Goethals, "Colonel Goethal's Speech at Corozal as Reported in the Star and Herald of March 19, 1907," in Society of the Chagres, *Society of the Chagres 1911 Year Book*, 29; Theodore Roosevelt, *An Autobiography* (1913; reprint, New York: Charles Scribner's Sons, 1924), 528. Also see Theodore Roosevelt, "The Monroe Doctrine and the

Panama Canal," *Outlook*, 6 December 1913, 754; Abbot, *Panama and the Canal in Picture and Prose*, 330.

48. Scott, *The Americans in Panama*, 190.

49. Gause and Carr, *The Story of Panama*, 251–55. Also see Farnham Bishop, *Panama Past and Present*, 195–200; Fraser, *Panama and What It Means*, 89–91; Collins, *The Panama Guide*, 53–55. For the portrayal of the corrupt French lifestyle see George W. Crichfield, "The Panama Canal From a Contractor's Viewpoint," *North American Review*, January 1905, 86; Abbot, *Panama and the Canal in Picture and Prose*, 120–21; Forbes-Lindsay, *Panama and the Canal Today*, 69.

50. Bullard, *Panama*, 44; Charles Francis Adams, *Panama Canal Zone*, 15.

51. Gause and Carr, *The Story of Panama*, 255.

52. William L. Nida, *The Story of Panama and the Canal* (Chicago: Hall and McCreary, 1913), 20; Walter B. Stevens, *A Trip to Panama: The Narrative of a Tour . . . by the Commercial Clubs of Boston, Chicago, Cincinnati, and St. Louis, February 18th–March 14th, 1907* (St. Louis: Lesani-Gould, 1907), 232; Abbot, *Panama and the Canal in Picture and Prose*, 203; Franck, *Zone Policeman 88*, 127.

53. Bullard, *Panama*, 501; Scott, *The Americans in Panama*, 154; Joseph B. Bishop, *The Panama Gateway*, 197; Henry L. Stimson, *Some Problems of the Panama Canal* (Washington: GPO, 1911), 3.

54. Frank Trumbell, *The Panama Canal: Some Impressions and Comments* (New York: self-published, 1913), 4; Joseph B. Bishop, *The Panama Gateway*, 196; Pennell, *Pictures of the Panama Canal*, 14.

55. Haskin, *The Panama Canal*, 23.

56. See Farnham Bishop, *Panama Past and Present*, 230.

57. Fraser, *Panama and What It Means*, 29; Haskin, *The Panama Canal*, 368. Also see Elmer Grey, "The Panama-Pacific International Exposition of 1915," *Scribner's Magazine*, July 1913, 44–57.

58. Joseph B. Bishop and Robert E. Peary, *Uncle Sam's Panama Canal and World History: Its Achievement an Honor to the United States and a Blessing to the World* (New York: World Syndicate, 1913), 32; McCullough, *Path between the Seas*, 557.

59. See DuVal, *Cadiz to Cathay*, 273–450.

60. "Panama's Ambassador to the United States, Jose de Obaldia, Protests the Establishment of Ports, Custom-Houses and Post Offices in the Canal Zone, August 11, 1904," in Committee on Foreign Relations, *Background Documents*, 431.

61. See William D. McCain, *The United States and the Republic of Panama* (Durham: Duke Univ. Press, 1937), 48–189.

62. Haskin, *The Panama Canal*, 254–55.

63. McCullough, *Path between the Seas*, 408.

64. Theodore Roosevelt, "How the United States Acquired the Right to Dig the Panama Canal," in Senate, *The Panama Canal and Our Relations with Colombia: Papers Relating to the Acquisition of the Canal Zone*, 63d Cong., 2d

Notes

sess., 1914, S. Doc. 471, 59. Also see "Colombia's Protest of March 28, 1911 Against Former President Roosevelt's Statement That He 'Took the Canal Zone and Let Congress Debate,'" in Committee on Foreign Relations, *Background Documents*, 590.

3. THE "NEW LOOK" IN U.S. CANAL POLICY

1. See Arthur S. Link and William B. Catton, *The Era of the Cold War, 1946–1973*, vol. 1 of *American Epoch: A History of the United States since 1900*, 4th ed. (New York: Alfred A. Knopf, 1974), 200–249; Sheldon B. Liss, *The Canal: Aspects of United States–Panamanian Relations* (Notre Dame: Univ. of Notre Dame Press, 1967), 188–89.

2. Edwin C. Hoyt, *National Policy and International Law: Case Studies From American Canal Policy* (Denver: Social Science Foundation and Graduate School of International Studies, Univ. of Denver, 1967), 3.

3. 23 November 1903, *Congressional Record*, 58th Cong., 1st sess., 37: 425–28; 9 December 1903, *Congressional Record*, 58th Cong., 2d sess., 38:79–81.

4. Roosevelt, "Message Communicated to the Two Houses of Congress at the Beginning of the Second Session of the Fifty-Eighth Congress," 414, 422.

5. See Senator Morgan, 9 December 1903, *Congressional Record*, 58th Cong., 2d sess., 38:81.

6. Henry F. Pringle, *Theodore Roosevelt*, rev. ed., 232.

7. Theodore Roosevelt, *Presidential Addresses and State Papers of Theodore Roosevelt*, 4 vols. (New York: P. F. Collier and Son, n.d.; reprint, New York: Kraus Reprint, 1970), 3:51.

8. See McCullough, *Path between the Seas*, 408.

9. Roosevelt, *Presidential Addresses and State Papers*, 3:359.

10. See "Colombia's Protest of March 28, 1911 Against Former President Roosevelt's Statement," 590.

11. McCullough, *Path between the Seas*, 384.

12. "Colombia's Protest of March 28, 1911 Against Former President Roosevelt's Statement," 590; Joseph B. Bishop, *Theodore Roosevelt and His Time* 1:308.

13. House, Committee on Foreign Affairs, *The Story of Panama: Hearings on the Rainey Resolution*, 62d Cong., 2d sess., 1912, 47.

14. Roosevelt, "How the United States Acquired the Right to Dig the Panama Canal," 55, 60.

15. See Committee on Foreign Affairs, *The Story of Panama*, 103–521.

16. Philippe Bunau-Varilla, "Statement on Behalf of Historical Truth," in Committee on Foreign Affairs, *The Story of Panama*, 10–43.

17. "The Original Version of a Treaty between the United States and Colombia for the Settlement of Differences Arising Out of the 1903 Events Which Took Place on the Isthmus of Panama, April 6, 1914 (The Thomson-

Urrutia Treaty)," in Committee on Foreign Relations, *Background Documents*, 668–71.

18. Pringle, *Theodore Roosevelt*, rev. ed., 406.

19. Theodore Roosevelt, "The Panama Blackmail Treaty," in *The Works of Theodore Roosevelt* 20:508–9; "Amendments to Thomson-Urrutia Treaty Suggested by U.S. Senate Foreign Relations Committee, Withdrawal from Senate Consideration, and Referral to Committee in 1919," in Committee on Foreign Relations, *Background Documents*, 672–80.

20. "The Treaty of April 6, 1914 between the United States and Colombia for the Settlement of Differences Arising Out of the 1903 Events on the Isthmus of Panama, Ratified in 1922," in Committee on Foreign Relations, *Background Documents*, 694–97.

21. See, for instance, Elihu Root, "The Ethics of the Panama Question," speech before the Union League Club of Chicago, 22 February 1904, in Senate, *The Panama Canal and Our Relations with Colombia*, esp. 44–50.

22. "Establishment of United States Ports, Tariffs, Custom-Houses, and Post Offices in the Canal Zone, June 24, 1904" and "Panama's Ambassador to the United States, Jose de Obaldia, Protests the Establishment of Ports, Tariffs, Custom-Houses and Post Offices in the Canal Zone, August 11, 1904," in Committee on Foreign Relations, *Background Documents*, 420–22, 430–32.

23. Roosevelt's remarks came in a published letter to William Howard Taft dated October 18 (see "Secretary of War Taft's Visit to Panama to Negotiate a Modus Vivendi, November-December 1904," in Committee on Foreign Relations, *Background Documents*, 460); "Secretary Hay's Reply to Ambassador Obaldia, August 18 and October 24, 1904," in Committee on Foreign Relations, *Background Documents*, 444.

24. Department of State, *Foreign Relations of the United States, 1904* (Washington: GPO, 1905), 632–33.

25. "The 'Taft Agreement' with Panama Concerning Tariffs, Ports, Post Offices, etc., December 3, 6, and 28, 1904; and January 7, 1905," in Committee on Foreign Relations, *Background Documents*, 467–75; McCain, *The United States and the Republic of Panama*, 43; Willis F. Johnson, *Four Centuries of the Panama Canal* (New York: Henry Holt, 1906), 264–66.

26. "Secretary of War Taft's Visit to to Panama to Negotiate a Modus Vivendi, November-December 1904," 465; "The Statement of Secretary of War Taft before the Senate Committee on Interoceanic Canals Regarding the Government of the Canal Zone, the 'Taft Agreement' with Panama, and the Proposal to Build a Lock Canal, April 18, 1906 (Excerpts)," in Committee on Foreign Relations, *Background Documents*, 513.

27. "The Visits in Panama of Secretary of State Root and President Theodore Roosevelt, September and November 1906," in Committee on Foreign Relations, *Background Documents*, 711–12. Also see Taft's similar warning in Department of State, *Foreign Relations of the United States, 1904*, 633–34.

28. See McCain, *The United States and the Republic of Panama*, 48–96; LaFeber, *The Panama Canal*, 48–52.

29. "The Panamanian Executive Decree of August 29, 1914 Ceding

Notes

Control of Radiotelegraphic Communications in Panama to the United States" and "United States Insistence in 1921 that Panama Accept the Loubet and White Arbital Awards in the Boundary Dispute with Costa Rica," in Committee on Foreign Relations, *Background Documents*, 735, 744–51; McCain, *The United States and the Republic of Panama*, 97–189; R. L. Buell, "Panama and the United States," *Foreign Policy Reports*, 20 January 1932, 410–24; George W. Baker, Jr., "The Wilson Administration and Panama, 1913–1931," *Journal of Inter-American Studies* 8 (April 1966): 279–93.

30. Scott, *The Americans in Panama*, 99.

31. "Panamanian Proposals for the Negotiation of a New Treaty; Minister Alfaro to the Secretary of State, April 2, 1921" and "Minister Alfaro's Memorandum of January 3, 1923 Presenting Panama's Grievances and Proposals for a New Treaty" in Committee on Foreign Relations, *Background Documents*, 752–61, 764–74.

32. "Secretary of State Hughes' Reply of October 15, 1923 Reasserting American Rights" and "Notification Given to Panama in 1923 of United States Intention to Abrogate the 1904 Taft Agreement, Followed by Panamanian Protests," in Committee on Foreign Relations, *Background Documents*, 775–802, 803–9.

33. Mack, *The Land Divided*, 566. Also see "Final Negotiations and the Text of a Treaty between the United States and Panama, Signed at Washington, July 28, 1926," in Committee on Foreign Relations, *Background Documents*, 817–42.

34. Mack, *The Land Divided*, 566; "Representations by Panama Respecting a Statement by President Coolidge Classifying the Panama Canal as a Possession of the United States, and the U.S. Reply, November 1928," in Committee on Foreign Relations, *Background Documents*, 859–60.

35. "The Visit of President Arias of Panama to the United States in October 1933 for Consultations with President Franklin Roosevelt and the Agreement on General Principles Forming the Bases for Relations between the Countries," in Committee on Foreign Relations, *Background Documents*, 864, 869.

36. "A Treaty of Friendship and Cooperation between Panama and the United States, March 2, 1936 (The Hull-Alfaro Treaty)," in Committee on Foreign Relations, *Background Documents*, 871–906.

37. Mack, *The Land Divided*, 566.

38. See LaFeber, *The Panama Canal*, 89.

39. "The Report of the Senate Foreign Relations Committee on the 1936 Treaty, June 21, 1939," in Committee on Foreign Relations, *Background Documents*, 913. Also see "An Overview of the Defense Sites Negotiations between the United States and Panama, 1936–1942," in Committee on Foreign Relations, *Background Documents*, 919–20.

40. Mack, *The Land Divided*, 567.

41. LaFeber, *The Panama Canal*, 101.

42. See "Agreement for the Lease by the United States of Defense Sites in the Republic of Panama, May 18, 1942" and "The Defense Sites Agree-

234

ment of December 10, 1947, and Rejection of the Agreement by the National Assembly of Panama," in Committee on Foreign Relations, *Background Documents*, 926–33, 956–71; Almon R. Wright, "Defense Sites Negotiations between the United States and Panama, 1936–1948," in Department of State, *Bulletin*, 11 August 1952, 212–19; Lester D. Langley, "U.S.-Panamanian Relations since 1941," *Journal of Inter-American Studies* 12 (July 1970): 340–43.

43. LaFeber, *The Panama Canal*, 101.

44. See "The Defense Sites Agreement of December 10, 1947, and Rejection of the Agreement by the National Assembly of Panama," 967; "A Report by Representative Mike Mansfield on the Panamanian National Assembly's Rejection of the 1947 Agreement to Extend U.S. Occupancy of Defense Sites in Panama," in Committee on Foreign Relations, *Background Documents*, 978.

45. Hoyt, *National Policy and International Law*, 45–46.

46. Paul B. Ryan, *The Panama Canal Controversy: U.S. Diplomacy and Defense Interests* (Stanford: Hoover Institution Press, 1977), 34.

47. Department of State, *Bulletin*, 12 October 1953, 488; "A Treaty of Mutual Understanding and Cooperation between Panama and the United States, and Memorandum of Understandings Reached (The Eisenhower-Remon Treaty), January 25, 1955," in Committee on Foreign Relations, *Background Documents*, 986–1006. The chief economic concession was an increase in the annuity paid to Panama from $430,000 to $1,930,000. In return the United States received, among other concessions, a fifteen-year renewable lease for 19,000 acres in Rio Hato for use by American military forces. For an analysis of the treaty see Langley, "U.S.-Panamanian Relations since 1941," 345–47.

48. Senate, Committee on Foreign Relations, *The Panama Treaty: Hearings on Executive F*, 84th Cong., 1st sess., 1955, 79, 82.

49. 29 July 1955, *Congressional Record*, 84th Cong., 1st sess., 101:12009, 12015.

50. Committee on Foreign Relations, *The Panama Treaty: Hearings on Executive F*, 45, 164; Senate, Committee on Foreign Relations, *Executive Sessions of the Senate Foreign Relations Committee*, (Historical Series), 84th Cong., 1st sess., 1955 (Washington: GPO, 1978), 7:713. In executive session, Holland emphasized the treaty's value as a symbol of confidence in the Panamanian government.

51. "The Report of the Senate Foreign Relations Committee on the 1955 Treaty, July 26, 1955," in Committee on Foreign Relations, *Background Documents*, 1030; 29 July 1955, *Congressional Record*, 84th Cong., 1st sess., 101:12009.

52. Jules DuBois, *Danger Over Panama* (Indianapolis: Bobbs-Merrill, 1964), 197.

53. Dwight D. Eisenhower, *Public Papers of the Presidents of the United States: Dwight D. Eisenhower, 1956* (Washington: GPO, 1958), 627, 661; Department of State, *Bulletin*, 10 September 1956, 411.

54. Department of State, *Bulletin*, 11 August 1958, 238.

Notes

55. DuBois, *Danger Over Panama*, 198.

56. Milton S. Eisenhower, *The Wine is Bitter: The United States and Latin America* (Garden City: Doubleday, 1963), 216, 221–22.

57. LaFeber, *The Panama Canal*, 128, 146.

58. "Panama Canal Zone: Constitutional Domain of the United States," 26 March 1958, *Congressional Record*, 85th Cong., 2d sess., 104:5498–5505; "Panama Canal Zone: Constitutional Domain of the United States—Further Supplementary," 2 April 1958, *Congressional Record*, 85th Cong., 2d sess., 104:6152–57; "Panama: Storm Center of Hostile Propaganda Against the United States," 15 July 1958, *Congressional Record*, 85th Cong., 2d sess., 104:13866; "Panama Canal—Latest Developments,"9 June 1958, *Congressional Record*, 85th Cong., 2d sess., 104:10582; "Panama Invasion Significance," 20 May 1959, *Congressional Record*, 86th Cong., 1st sess., 105:8706; "Canal Zone Protection," 29 July 1959, *Congressional Record*, 86th Cong., 1st sess., 105:14648.

59. See Liss, *The Canal*, 59–61.

60. See "Charges and Counter-Charges Regarding the Flag Incidents of November 3, 1959," in Committee on Foreign Relations, *Background Documents*, 1043–45; "The Panama Canal: Symbol of a Fourth Front," 13 January 1960, *Congressional Record*, 86th Cong., 2d sess., 106:416–24.

61. See Milton Eisenhower, *The Wine is Bitter*, 224; "United States Nine-Point Program for Improving Relations with Panama with Respect to Operations in the Canal Zone: Statement Issued by the White House, April 19, 1960," in Committee on Foreign Relations, *Background Documents*, 1050–51.

62. Dwight D. Eisenhower, *Public Papers of the Presidents of the United States: Dwight D. Eisenhower, 1959* (Washington: GPO, 1960), 794; Department of State, *Bulletin*, 28 December 1959, 937; Department of State, *Bulletin*, 10 October 1960, 558.

63. Quoted in Lawrence O. Ealy, *Yanqui Politics and the Isthmian Canal* (University Park: Pennsylvania State Univ. Press, 1971), 113.

64. See House Concurrent Resolution 459 in "Panamanian–United States Relations," 2 February 1960, *Congressional Record*, 86th Cong., 2d sess., 106:1798.

65. Langley, "U.S.-Panamanian Relations since 1941," 353.

66. "United States Cooperation in Panama's Five-Year Development Program Within the Framework of the Alliance for Progress, Joint Statement of October 8, 1961," in Committee on Foreign Relations, *Background Documents*, 1059–60.

67. See LaFeber, *The Panama Canal*, 129, 137.

68. "President Kennedy, in Letter of November 2, 1961 to President of Panama Chiari, Affirms United States Willingness to Make a Complete Reexamination of Current and Future Needs With Respect to Isthmian Canal Facilities," in Committee on Foreign Relations, *Background Documents*, 1061.

69. Department of State, *Bulletin*, 9 July 1962, 81–82.

70. See Kennedy's remarks in John F. Kennedy, *Public Papers of the*

Presidents of the United States: John F. Kennedy, 1962 (Washington: GPO, 1963), 495.

71. LaFeber, *The Panama Canal*, 136–37.

72. DuBois, *Danger Over Panama*, 227.

73. See "Report on the Events in Panama, January 9–12, 1964, by an Investigating Committee of the International Commission of Jurists," in Committee on Foreign Relations, *Background Documents*, 1099–1142.

74. "The Flag Incidents of January 1964 and Consideration of the Incidents by the U.N. Security Council and the Inter-American Peace Committee of the OAS," in Committee on Foreign Relations, *Background Documents*, 1070.

75. Department of State, *Bulletin*, 3 February 1964, 156. For an account of President Johnson's unsuccessful attempt to resolve the controversy with a personal phone call to President Chiari of Panama see Eric F. Goldman, *The Tragedy of Lyndon Johnson* (New York: Alfred A. Knopf, 1969), 73–74.

76. Department of State, *Bulletin*, 3 February 1964, 156; "Panama's Request of January 29, 1964 that the OAS Council Take Cognizance of the Acts of Aggression Against Panama, and Meetings of the Council on January 31 and February 4, 1964," in Committee on Foreign Relations, *Background Documents*, 1081.

77. "Report on the Events in Panama, January 9–12, 1964," 1102, 1131–38.

78. Lyndon B. Johnson, *Public Papers of the Presidents of the United States: Lyndon B. Johnson, 1963–1964* (Washington: GPO, 1965), 1:220; Department of State, *Bulletin*, 27 April 1964, 655; Johnson, *Public Papers of the Presidents: Johnson, 1963–1964*, 1:440.

79. Department of State, *Bulletin*, 4 January 1965, 5–6.

80. "Panama–United States Joint Announcement of Agreement on Texts of Three New Canal Treaties, June 26, 1967," in Committee on Foreign Relations, *Background Documents*, 1148. The texts obtained by the *Tribune* were also published in *Congressional Record*, July 17, 21, and 27, 1967; and in House, Committee on Merchant Marines and Fisheries, Subcommittee on the Panama Canal, *Report on the Problems Concerning the Panama Canal*, 91st Cong., 2d sess., 1970, Appendices 4, 5, and 6: 38–81. The official texts were first published in Committee on Foreign Relations, *Background Documents*, 1149–1370.

81. Center for Strategic Studies, Georgetown Univ., *Panama: Canal Issues and Treaty Talks* (Washington: Georgetown Univ., 1967), viii.

82. See Liss, *The Canal*, 188–91.

83. See Ealy, *Yanqui Politics and the Isthmian Canal*, 136, 149.

84. Walter D. Jacobs, *The Panama Canal: Its Role in Hemispheric Security* (New York: American Emergency Committee on the Panama Canal, 1968), 1.

85. Ealy, *Yanqui Politics and the Isthmian Canal*, 133; the minority report by Donald M. Dozer and Vice Admiral T. G. N. Nettle in Center for Strategic Studies, *Panama*, 71.

86. Quoted in Ealy, *Yanqui Politics and the Isthmian Canal*, 133.

Notes

87. See Center for Strategic Studies, *Panama*, 76; "The House Subcommittee Report of 1970 on Panama Canal Problems and the 1967 Treaties," in Committee on Foreign Relations, *Background Documents*, 1381–83; Ealy, *Yanqui Politics and the Isthmian Canal*, 134.

88. Quoted in LaFeber, *The Panama Canal*, 143.

89. Department of State, *Bulletin*, 4 November 1968, 470.

90. See "The House Subcommittee Report of 1970 on Panama Canal Problems and the 1967 Treaties," 1378–85; Ealy, *Yanqui Politics and the Isthmian Canal*, 154–55.

91. "The House Subcommittee Report of 1970 on Panama Canal Problems and the 1967 Treaties," 1385; Center for Strategic Studies, *Panama*, 65.

4. Selling New Canal Treaties

1. Jimmy Carter, *A Government as Good as Its People* (New York: Simon and Schuster, 1977), 213.

2. Lloyd Bitzer and Theodore Reuter, *Carter vs. Ford: The Counterfeit Debates of 1976* (Madison: Univ. of Wisconsin Press, 1980), 316. For reviews of public opinion polls on the treaties see Bernard Roshco, "The Polls: Polling on Panama—Si; Don't Know; Hell No!" *Public Opinion Quarterly* 42 (1978); 551–62; "The Great Canal Debate," *Public Opinion*, March/April 1978, 33–34; Ted J. Smith, III, and J. Michael Hogan, "Opinion Polls and the Panama Canal Treaties of 1977: A Critical Analysis," presented to the annual meeting of the American Association for Public Opinion Research, McAfee, N.J., 1985.

3. "Ceding the Canal—Slowly," *Time*, 22 August 1977, 11.

4. LaFeber, *The Panama Canal*, 180.

5. Stephen S. Rosenfeld, "The Panama Negotiations: A Close-Run Thing," *Foreign Affairs*, October 1975, 3; "Assistant Secretary of State Hurwitch's Review for Congress of United States Relations with Panama, February 20, 1973," in Committee on Foreign Relations, *Background Documents*, 1444.

6. The United Kingdom abstained in the vote, while the U.S. was forced to cast its first veto since 1945. See "United Nations Security Council Meeting in Panama, March 15–20, 1973, Dealing with United States–Panama Relations," in Committee on Foreign Relations, *Background Documents*, 1449–54.

7. Rosenfeld, "The Panama Negotiations," 4.

8. "Joint Statement of Principles by Secretary of State Kissinger and Panamanian Foreign Minister Tack, February 7, 1974," in Committee on Foreign Relations, *Background Documents*, 1477–79. For a detailed discussion of events leading up to the principles see William J. Jorden, *Panama Odyssey* (Austin: Univ. of Texas Press, 1984), 202–23.

9. Rosenfeld, "The Panama Negotiations," 6.

10. Rosenfeld, "The Panama Negotiations," 6–10. For Kissinger's views see Henry A. Kissinger, "The United States and Latin America: The New Opportunity," speech before the Combined Service Club, Houston, Texas, 1 March 1975, in Department of State, *Bulletin*, 24 March 1975, esp. 362–63.

11. Senate, Committee on Foreign Relations, *A Chronology of Events Relating to the Panama Canal*, 95th Cong., 1st sess., 1977 Committee Print, 15–17. Also see Thomas J. McIntyre, *The Fear Brokers: Peddling the Hate Politics of the New Right* (Boston: Beacon Press, 1979), 120; "Panama Theatrics," *Time*, 26 April 1976, 16; LaFeber, *The Panama Canal*, 190–91.

12. See Committee on Foreign Relations, *A Chronology of Events Relating to the Panama Canal*, 15, 20. Also see William F. Buckley, Jr., "The Panama Canal and General Torrijos," *National Review*, 26 November 1976, 1306.

13. Bitzer and Reuter, *Carter vs. Ford*, 316.

14. Committee on Foreign Relations, *A Chronology of Events Relating to the Panama Canal*, 22.

15. See Committee on Foreign Relations, *A Chronology of Events Relating to the Panama Canal*, 24–25; Martin Mayer, "The Man from Xerox Multiplies His Roles," *New York Times Magazine*, 24 April 1976, 44.

16. Committee on Foreign Relations, *Senate Debate on the Panama Canal Treaties*, 4–5.

17. "New Deals for the Big Ditch," *Time*, 25 July 1977, 28; Committee on Foreign Relations, *Senate Debate on the Panama Canal Treaties*; 5; "President Carter's Announcement of United States–Panama Agreement in Principle on Panama Canal Treaties, August 12, 1977," in Committee on Foreign Relations, *Background Documents*, 1510.

18. "The Message of the President Transmitting the 1977 Panama Canal Treaties to the Senate, September 16, 1977," in Committee on Foreign Relations, *Background Documents*, 1524–46.

19. "The Message of the President Transmitting the 1977 Panama Canal Treaties to the Senate," 1546–53.

20. Deming, et al., "A Panama Production," 46; "Hold Everything Till Panama's Through," *Economist*, 10 September 1977, 51.

21. Committee on Foreign Relations, *Senate Debate on the Panama Canal Treaties*, 7–8.

22. LaFeber, *The Panama Canal*, 229.

23. Lanouette, "The Panama Canal Treaties," 1557.

24. Lanouette, "The Panama Canal Treaties," 1557.

25. Lanouette, "The Panama Canal Treaties," 1557; "Ceding the Canal—Slowly," 11.

26. "Carter Wins on Panama," 10.

27. "The Wooing of Senator Zorinsky," *Time*, 27 March 1978, 12–13; Susan Fraker and John J. Lindsay, "Courting Zorinsky," *Newsweek*, 27 March 1978, 45. For more on Carter's lobbying see "Carter's Panama Triumph—What It Cost," *U.S. News and World Report*, 2 March 1978, 27–28.

28. Hugh Sidey, "Does Congress Need a Nanny?" *Time*, 27 March

Notes

1978, 13; Packwood quoted in LaFeber, *The Panama Canal*, 242. Also see "Carter Wins on Panama," 10.

29. Robert Shrum, "The Narrow Passage of the Canal Treaty," *New Times*, 15 May 1978, 6–7. Abourezk eventually voted for the treaties after Carter assured him that natural gas policy would be determined by an "open democratic process." See Abourezk's remarks in Senate, Committee on the Judiciary, Subcommittee on Separation of Powers, *Panama Canal Treaties [United States Senate Debate], 1977–78*, 95th Cong., 2d sess., 1978, Committee Print, 3:5520–21.

30. "Carter's Panama Triumph," 27–28; "After Carter's Panama Victory," *U.S. News and World Report*, 1 May 1978, 25. For the president's perspective on the lobbying effort see Jimmy Carter, *Keeping Faith: Memoirs of a President* (New York: Bantam Books, 1982), 162–78.

31. Quoted in James T. Wooten, "White House Lobbying to Change Opinions on Canal," in Senate, Committee on Foreign Relations, *Panama Canal Treaties: Hearings . . . on . . . the Panama Canal Treaty and the Treaty Concerning the Permanent Neutrality and Operation of the Panama Canal*, 95th Cong. 1st and 2d sess., 1977–1978), 3:562; "Keeping the Canal Pacts Afloat," *Time*, 24 October 1977, 38.

32. Lanouette, "The Panama Canal Treaties," 1559; Karen DeYoung, "State Dept. Is 'Selling' Canal Treaties," *Washington Post*, 26 February 1978, sec. A, 1, 7.

33. DeYoung, "State Dept. Is 'Selling' Canal Treaties," sec. A, 7.

34. Richard Steele, et al., "Heading for a Win?" *Newsweek*, 13 February 1978, 18–19; Lanouette, "The Panama Canal Treaties," 1559.

35. Ken Bode, "Carter and the Canal," *New Republic*, 14 January 1978, 9. See Steele, et al., "Heading for a Win?" 18–19; Barry M. Hager, "White House Pushing for Approval of Treaties," *Congressional Quarterly*, 21 January 1978, 137.

36. Joan Peters, "Panama's Genial Despot," *Harper's*, April 1978, 61–70; Lanouette, "The Panama Canal Treaties," 1559; Hager, "White House Pushing for Approval of Treaties," 137.

37. Steele, et al., "Heading for a Win?" 19; "Squaring Off on the Canal," 31; Jimmy Carter, address to the nation, 1 February 1978, in Department of State, *Bulletin*, March 1978, 55–57.

38. "Carter Wins on Panama," 10.

39. Committee of Americans for the Canal Treaties, *COACT: The Bi-Partisan Citizens Committee of Americans for the Canal Treaties* (Washington: Committee of Americans for the Canal Treaties, [1977]), v. Also see Bill Peterson, "Notables Unite in Endorsing Canal Treaties," *Washington Post*, 16 October 1977, sec. A, 9.

40. David M. Maxfield, "Panama Canal: Groups Favoring Treaties Fight to Offset Opponents' Massive Lobbying Effort," *Congressional Quarterly*, 21 January 1978, 136. For the complete official listing of COACT's membership see Committee of Americans for the Canal Treaties, *COACT*, vii.

41. William Safire, "Panama Townhouse," *New York Times*, 2 January

1978, sec. 1, 21; Steven V. Roberts, "Panama Treaties at Stake in Bitter Propaganda War," *New York Times*, 20 January 1978, sec. A, 3.

42. DeYoung, "State Dept. Is 'Selling' Canal Treaties," sec. A, 1; Peters, "Panama's Genial Despot," 61–62.

43. Committee of Americans for the Canal Treaties, *COACT*, v.

44. Committee of Americans for the Canal Treaties, *COACT*, 35–55, 68, 73–86. Although the author of the "sample speech" is not identified, it is strikingly similar to the State Department's speeches and several passages identify it indirectly as one of the "official" speeches. Although COACT presents the speech for use by "citizens," it contains such phrases as "we in government" and "we in the Carter administration."

45. Committee of Americans for the Canal Treaties, *COACT*, 71.

46. Committee of Americans for the Canal Treaties, *COACT*, 89–135.

47. Committee of Americans for the Canal Treaties, *COACT*, 63–64, 67, 70.

48. Committee of Americans for the Canal Treaties, *COACT*, 65–66.

49. Committee of Americans for the Canal Treaties, *COACT*, 65, 87–88.

50. George D. Moffett, III, *The Limits of Victory: The Ratification of the Panama Canal Treaties* (Ithaca: Cornell Univ. Press, 1985), 84, 233–34, n. 55.

51. "A Bid for Votes on Panama," *Business Week*, 12 September 1977, 41. Also see "Panama Canal: What Happens Next?" *Nation's Business*, October 1977, 59.

52. Committee on Foreign Relations, *Panama Canal Treaties: Hearings* 3:281.

53. Penny Lernoux, "U.S. Imperialists, Old and New," *Nation*, 3 April 1976, 393; "A Bid for Votes on Panama," 41; Don Bohning, "U.S. Chamber Backs Negotiations for New Panama Canal Treaty," in Department of State, *ARA-PAF Press Clips*, 19 November 1975, 1–2.

54. See Moffett, *The Limits of Victory*, 156–62.

55. Bode, "Carter and the Canal," 9. Also see Council of the Americas, "President's Letter: The Panama Canal Treaties," New York, 22 February 1978; Council of the Americas, "Council of the Americas Announces Support for the Panama Canal Treaties," letter from Otto J. Reich, Director of Washington Operations, to the membership, Washington, n.d.; Council of the Americas, letter from Otto J. Reich to Barry Sklar, Congressional Research Service, Washington, 2 February 1977; Council of the Americas, letter from Henry G. Geyelin, President, to U.S. senators, Washington, [January 1977] (all in files of Congressional Research Service, Library of Congress, Washington, D.C.); Council of the Americas, Work Group on Panama, *United States, Panama, and the Panama Canal: A Guide to the Issues* (n.p., 1976); Don Oberdorfer, "Panama Plans Intense Publicity Effort to Push New Treaty," *Washington Post*, 24 March 1977, sec. A, 12; testimony of Henry R. Geyelin, President, Council of the Americas, in Committee on Foreign Relations, *Panama Canal Treaties: Hearings* 4:145–50.

56. David J. Kalke, "Panamanian Purpose and the U.S. Presence,"

Notes

Christian Century, 24 December 1975, 1185–86; James M. Wall, "Are the Panama Canal Treaties Just?" *Christian Century,* 15 February 1978, 147–48.

57. "The NCC and Carter," *Christian Century,* 23 November 1977, 1084.

58. James M. Wall, "Church Support for Canal Treaties," *Christian Century,* 2 November 1977, 995.

59. In Ecumenical Program for Inter-American Communication and Action, *Panama: Sovereignty for a Land Divided: A People's Primer by the EPICA Task Force* (Washington: EPICA Task Force, 1976), 95.

60. In Margaret D. Wilde, ed., *The Panama Canal and Social Justice* (Washington: Office of International Justice and Peace, United States Catholic Conference, 1976), 30–31.

61. Committee on Foreign Relations, *Panama Canal Treaties: Hearings* 3:352, 350–57.

62. In EPICA, *Panama: Sovereignty for a Land Divided,* 95.

63. See John Cardinal Krol in Committee on Foreign Relations, *Panama Canal Treaties: Hearings* 3:357–58; William F. Willoughby, "Catholic Bishops Vote Request for Lenient Treaty with Panama," *Washington Star,* 11 November 1976, sec. A, 4; "Catholic Bishops Call for a New Panama Treaty," *Washington Post,* 11 November 1976, sec. A, 3.

64. Committee on Foreign Relations, *Panama Canal Treaties: Hearings* 3:357–70.

65. Wilde, ed., *The Panama Canal and Social Justice.*

66. Washington Office on Latin America, "Special Update on Panama" (Washington, n.d.) and memorandum distributed to members of Congress (Washington, n.d.) files of Congressional Research Service, Library of Congress, Washington, D.C.; Wilde, ed., *The Panama Canal and Social Justice,* 32.

67. Ecumenical Program for Inter-American Communication and Action, publicity flyer for *Panama: Sovereignty for a Land Divided,* n.p., n.d; EPICA, *Panama: Sovereignty for a Land Divided;* Ecumenical Program for Inter-American Communication and Action, *Treaty for Us, Treaty for Them* (Washington: EPICA Task Force, 1977).

68. Washington Office on Latin America, "Action Memo on the New Canal Treaty," n.p., n.d., files of Congressional Research Service, Library of Congress, Washington, D.C.; Wilde, ed., *The Panama Canal and Social Justice,* 32.

69. EPICA, *Treaty for Us, Treaty for Them,* 1–2, 8.

70. EPICA, *Panama: Sovereignty for a Land Divided,* 6, 18, 86.

71. See especially the exchange between Morley Safer and Reverend Wheaton of EPICA in the network transcript of CBS News, "The Gospel According to Whom?" *Sixty Minutes,* 23 January 1983, 5–6.

72. See Morris Levinson in Committee on Foreign Relations, *Panama Canal Treaties: Hearings* 3:370–71.

73. The Church also sponsored a "traveling seminar in Biblical jus-

tice" that included a stop in Panama. See Professor Donald E. Miller in Committee on Foreign Relations, *Panama Canal Treaties: Hearings* 3:383–84, 391.

74. The organization's newspaper, *The Disciple*, advocated the treaties in articles on January 15 and January 29, 1978, and later published a "special resource" on the treaties. The "special resource" included the resolution of the general assembly, protreaty articles by John Wayne and Panamanian archbishop Marcos McGrath, and a boxed plea for readers to contact their senators, to sponsor forums, and to write letters to the editors of their local papers. See Christian Church (Disciples of Christ), General Assembly, "Resolution No. 7756 Concerning New Treaties with the Republic of Panama," adopted at the Kansas City, Missouri, Assembly, 21–26 October 1977; Christian Church (Disciples of Christ), Department of Latin America of the Division of Overseas Ministries and the Departments of Christian Education and Church in Society of the Division of Homeland Ministries, "The Panama Canal Treaties," Indianapolis, n.d.

75. "Gospel Disk Jockey Aids Carter in Bid for Panama Canal Treaties," *New York Times*, 18 November 1977, sec. A, 17.

76. Commission on United States–Latin American Relations, *The Americas in a Changing World: A Report of the Commission on United States–Latin American Relations* (New York: Quadrangle, 1975), esp. 3–5, 8, 11, 32, and back cover; Commission on United States-Latin American Relations, *The United States and Latin America: Next Steps. A Second Report by the Commission on United States–Latin American Relations* (New York: Center for Inter-American Relations, 1976).

77. Oberdorfer, "Panama Plans Intense Publicity Effort," sec. A, 12; LaFeber, *The Panama Canal*, 216; S. J. Ungar, "Soft-Selling the Treaties," *Atlantic*, December 1977, 16.

78. Ronald Steel, "Rough Passage," *New York Review of Books*, 23 March 1978, 10; Maxfield, "Panama Canal," 136; Roberts, "Panama Treaties at Stake," sec. A, 3; Moffett, *The Limits of Victory*, 140.

79. United States Committee for Panamanian Sovereignty, letter from E. Bradford Burns and Sheldon B. Liss to specialists in Latin American studies (Philadelphia, [1976]) and "Principles of Unity" (Philadelphia, n.d.), files of Congressional Research Service, Library of Congress, Washington, D.C.; EPICA, *Panama: Sovereignty for a Land Divided*, 121–23.

80. Committee of Americans for the Canal Treaties, *COACT*, vii, 56–57, 72; Stephen N. Burkholder, "Some Persons and Groups Lobbying For and Against the Panama Canal Treaties," Washington, n.d., files of Congressional Research Service, Library of Congress, Washington, D.C., 2; LaFeber, *The Panama Canal*, 230; "The Panama Canal Treaties," *Crisis*, December 1977, 457. For a discussion of editorial opinion on the treaties see Walter LaFeber, "Covering the Canal, Or, How the Press Missed the Boat," *More*, June 1978, 26. Also see the protreaty editorials reprinted in Committee on the Judiciary, *Panama Canal Treaties*.

Notes

5. THE NEW RIGHT'S CRUSADE

1. See Alan Crawford, *Thunder on the Right: The "New Right" and the Politics of Resentment* (New York: Pantheon, 1980), 290–310.

2. Richard A. Viguerie, *The New Right: We're Ready to Lead* (Falls Church, Va.: The Viguerie Co., 1981), 12.

3. Quoted in Viguerie, *The New Right*, 63.

4. Steele and Bruno, "Stand Up and Be Counted," 27; Viguerie quoted in Lanouette, "The Panama Canal Treaties," 1560.

5. Richard Boeth, et al., "The New Activists," *Newsweek*, 7 November 1977, 41.

6. Viguerie, *The New Right*, 15.

7. John P. Roche quoted in Crawford, *Thunder on the Right*, 4.

8. Weyrich quoted in Crawford, *Thunder on the Right*, 3; Crawford, *Thunder on the Right*, 5–6.

9. Crawford, *Thunder on the Right*, 8; "Profile: Efforts of Major Conservative Groups Opposing Ratification of the Panama Canal Treaties," *Democratic Congressional Campaign Report*, February 1978, 2–3; McIntyre, *The Fear Brokers*; 122–25.

10. Viguerie, *The New Right*, 67; "Profile: Efforts of Conservative Groups Opposing the Panama Canal Treaties," 3; Committee on Foreign Relations, *Panama Canal Treaties: Hearings* 3:392–98.

11. Viguerie, *The New Right*, 67.

12. Maxfield, "Panama Canal," 136–37; "Profile: Efforts of Conservative Groups Opposing the Panama Canal Treaties," 1.

13. Maxfield, "Panama Canal," 136.

14. Crawford, *Thunder on the Right*, 46–47.

15. Boeth, et al., "The New Activists," 41.

16. Larry J. Sabato, *The Rise of Political Consultants: New Ways of Winning Elections* (New York: Basic Books, 1981), 222.

17. Boeth, et al., "The New Activists," 41.

18. Viguerie, *The New Right*, 68–69.

19. Philip M. Crane, *Surrender in Panama: The Case Against the Treaty* (New York: Dale Books, 1978), 105–8.

20. Viguerie, *The New Right*, 4.

21. "Profile: Efforts of Conservative Groups Opposing the Panama Canal Treaties," 2. Also see McIntyre, *The Fear Brokers*, 118–19, 124.

22. Sabato, *The Rise of Political Consultants*, 240–45.

23. See Howard Phillips, ed., *The New Right at Harvard* (Vienna, Va.: Conservative Caucus, 1983), 123–24; Viguerie, *The New Right*, 21.

24. Boeth, et al., "The New Activists," 41.

25. Sabato, *The Rise of Political Consultants*, 254.

26. "Profile: Efforts of Conservative Groups Opposing the Panama Canal Treaties," 3; Lanouette, "The Panama Canal Treaties," 1560; LaFeber, "Covering the Canal," 29.

27. Sabato, *The Rise of Political Consultants,* 255–56.

28. Sabato, *The Rise of Political Consultants,* 254–55.

29. American Conservative Union, "There Is No Panama Canal; There Is an American Canal in Panama," transcript of half-hour television program, files of the Democratic Congressional Campaign Committee, Washington, D.C.

30. Adam Clymer, "TV Campaign Begun Against Panama Canal Treaty," *New York Times,* 31 October 1977, sec. 1, 20; Rudy Abramson, "Conservatives Against the Canal Treaties Planning a Multi-Media Blitz for January," *Los Angeles Times,* 7 November 1977, sec. 1, 5; John M. Goshko, "Conservatives Set TV Film Opposing Panama Treaties," *Washington Post,* 28 October 1977, sec. A, 2; "Profile: Efforts of Conservative Groups Opposing the Panama Canal Treaties," 2; Viguerie, *The New Right,* 67.

31. Sidney Blumenthal, *The Permanent Campaign* (New York: Touchstone, 1982), 239. Viguerie quoted in Phillips, *The New Right at Harvard,* 118; Blumenthal, *The Permanent Campaign,* 239.

32. "Profile: Efforts of Conservative Groups Opposing the Panama Canal Treaties," 1–3; Deming, et al., "A Panama Production," 46; "Now for the Hard Part," *Time,* 19 September 1977, 19–20; Maxfield, "Panama Canal," 135.

33. N. Thimmesch, "Panama: More Than Just a Ditch," *New York,* 23 January 1978, 6; "Profile: Efforts of Conservative Groups Opposing the Panama Canal Treaties," 4; "Squaring Off on the Canal," 31; Molly Ivins, "Treaty Foes, Led By Reagan, Crusade in Denver," *New York Times,* 20 January 1978, sec. A, 3; Viguerie, *The New Right,* 67–68.

34. Viguerie, *The New Right,* 96–97.

35. See Robert Charles Smith, National Commander of the American Legion, and Phelps Jones, Director of National Security and Foreign Affairs for the VFW, in Committee on Foreign Relations, *Panama Canal Treaties: Hearings* 3:566–78, 595–611.

36. For other groups and individuals allied with the New Right in fighting the treaties see Stephen N. Burkholder, "Some Persons and Groups Lobbying For and Against the Panama Canal Treaties."

37. William Schneider, "Behind the Passions of the Canal Debate," in Committee on the Judiciary, *Panama Canal Treaties* 2:3310.

6. INTERPRETATIONS OF HISTORY

1. Ernest R. May, *"Lessons" of the Past: The Use and Misuse of History in American Foreign Policy* (New York: Oxford Univ. Press, 1973), esp. ix–xii.

2. James L. Busey, *Political Aspects of the Panama Canal: The Problem of Location* (Tucson: Univ. of Arizona Press, 1974), 18.

3. Miles P. DuVal wrote the article in the *Encyclopaedia Britannica* in

1970. DuVal, while taking no position on a new treaty, presented the anti-treaty interpretation of history by asserting that the U.S. acquired title to all land in the Canal Zone. He also praised the framers of the 1903 treaty for their "wisdom" in insisting on sovereignty in perpetuity, and he dismissed "titular sovereignty" as "never defined." See excerpts of the article in Senate, Committee on the Judiciary, Subcommittee on Separation of Powers, *The Proposed Panama Canal Treaties: A Digest of Information*, 95th Cong., 2d sess., 1978, Committee Print, 494–506.

4. John W. McGarret, *The Key to the Panama Canal Treaty Issue* (self-published, 1978), 1–2; Crane, *Surrender in Panama*, 7; Ronald Reagan, address recorded from *The Panama Canal: An Opposition View*, A CBS News Special Report, 8 February 1978; Ronald Reagan, "The Canal as Opportunity: A New Relationship with Latin America," *Orbis* 21 (Fall 1977): 552.

5. Donald Dozer, "The Panama Canal in Danger," paper distributed by the Emergency Committee to Save the U.S. Canal Zone, March 1976, files of the Congressional Research Service, Library of Congress, Washington, D.C., 1; Robert S. Strother, "The Panama Question: An Alternative to U.S. Defeatism," *National Review*, 12 September 1975, 987.

6. American Conservative Union, "There Is No Panama Canal," 8, 9. The reference to payment of Colombia is to the Thomson-Urrutia treaty. See chapter 3 above.

7. Strother, "The Panama Question," 987. In a similar vein, military affairs writer Hanson Baldwin wrote in 1977 that the U.S. bought the canal territory "at a cost to the American taxpayer that far exceeded the cost of the Louisiana Purchase, the Mexican cession, the Florida purchase, the purchase of Alaska, or any other territorial acquisition." Hanson W. Baldwin, "The Panama Canal: Sovereignty and Security," *AEI Defense Review*, August 1977, 18.

8. Strother, "The Panama Question," 987; Reagan, address recorded from "The Panama Canal."

9. One exception was Hanson Baldwin, who argued that Panama did not have "residual, titular, or any other kind of sovereignty." Baldwin, "The Panama Canal," 18.

10. See, for example, Crane, *Surrender in Panama*, 39, 40; Strother, "The Panama Question," 987.

11. Strother, "The Panama Question," 986; McGarret, *The Key to the Panama Canal Treaty Issue*, 3; Baldwin, "The Panama Canal," 20. Charles Maechling was about the only treaty opponent to admit that the 1936 treaty "somewhat diluted the U.S. position by describing the Canal Zone as 'territory of the Republic of Panama under the jurisdiction of the United States.'" But according to Maechling, the U.S. "reverted to the earlier position that effective sovereignty remained with the United States" in negotiations for the 1955 treaty. Donald Dozer also offered a unique interpretation. According to Dozer, the reference in the 1936 treaty to "territory of the Republic of Panama" referred "only to that section of Panamanian territory in the city of

Colon formerly under the jurisdiction of the United States and known as 'New Cristobal,' which was returned to the jurisdiction of the Republic of Panama later by the treaty of 1955." See Charles Maechling, Jr., "The Panama Canal: A Fresh Start," *Orbis* 20 (Winter 1977): 1009; Dozer, "Panama Canal in Danger," 5.

12. Crane, *Surrender in Panama*, 40, 41.

13. See Dozer, "Panama Canal in Danger," 2.

14. See Crane, *Surrender in Panama*, 37.

15. Dozer, "Panama Canal in Danger," 2, 4. Also see Baldwin, "The Panama Canal," 22; Crane, *Surrender in Panama*, 37–38.

16. Maechling, "The Panama Canal," 1010–12; Crane, *Surrender in Panama*, 37.

17. See Paul Ryan, "Canal Diplomacy and United States Interests," *U.S. Naval Institute Proceedings* 103 (January 1977): 45; Judge Crowe in American Conservative Union, "There Is No Panama Canal," 8–9; Strother, "The Panama Question," 988.

18. Strother, "The Panama Question," 988; Reagan, address recorded from "The Panama Canal"; Dozer, "Panama Canal in Danger," 2.

19. Committee of Americans for the Canal Treaties, *COACT*; 75; Cyrus Vance, statement before the General Assembly, Organization of American States, St. George's, Grenada, June 15, in Department of State, *Bulletin*, 18 July 1977, 72; Ellsworth Bunker, "Panama Canal Treaties: A Negotiator's Perspective," address before the Des Moines Chamber of Commerce and Rotary Club, U.S. Department of State, *Speech*, 26 January 1978 (Washington: Department of State, 1978), 5. Also see Ellsworth Bunker, "The New Panama Canal Treaties: A Negotiator's View," in Department of State, *Bulletin*, 17 October 1977, 506.

20. Department of State, *Bulletin*, 4 April 1977, 316; 15 August 1977, 198; 4 April 1977, 316.

21. Earnest Hollings, "The Panama Canal," in Department of State, *Panama Canal Treaties Information* (Washington: Department of State, 1977), item 6, 3.

22. Department of State, "Commonly Raised Questions," in *Panama Canal Treaties Information*, item 3, 3; Committee of Americans for the Canal Treaties, *COACT*, 35. Also see the comparison between the wording of the 1903 Panama treaty and the treaties ceding sovereignty over the Louisiana Purchase and Alaska in Denison Kitchel, *The Truth about the Panama Canal* (New Rochelle: Arlington House, 1978), 71.

23. Jimmy Carter, "President Carter Discusses Panama Canal Treaties," remarks and a question-and-answer session with citizens from Arizona, Colorado, Idaho, Montana, Nevada, New Mexico, Utah, and Wyoming, Denver, October 22, in Department of State, *Bulletin*, 21 November 1977, 722 (Also see Jimmy Carter, address to the nation, 1 February 1978, in Department of State, *Bulletin*, March 1978, 56.); Department of State, "Fact Sheet: Ownership of Property in the Canal Zone," in *Panama Canal Treaties*

Notes

Information, item 2, n.p.; Jimmy Carter, "News Directors Interview President Carter," excerpts from opening remarks and a question-and-answer session in a telephone interview with members of the Radio-Television News Directors Association, San Francisco, 15 September 1977, in Department of State, *Bulletin*, 24 October 1977, 569.

24. Carter, "President Carter Discusses Panama Canal Treaties," 722. Similarly, Carter declared in his fireside chat, again with no mention of cases, that the "U.S. Supreme Court and previous American Presidents have repeatedly acknowledged the sovereignty of Panama over the Canal Zone." Carter, address to the nation, 1 February 1978, 56.

25. Sol Linowitz, "Why a New Panama Canal Treaty?" address before the American Legion Convention, Denver, 19 August 1977, in Department of State, *Bulletin*, 17 October 1977, 522. The reference is to *Vermilya-Brown Co. v. Connell*. See "*Vermilya-Brown Co. v. Connell* (1948)," in Committee on Foreign Relations, *Background Documents*, 1660.

26. See, for example, Committee of Americans for the Canal Treaties, *COACT*, 36; "President Carter Discusses Panama Canal Treaties," 722; Linowitz, "Why a New Panama Canal Treaty?" 523; Sol Linowitz, "The New Panama Canal Treaties—In Our National Interest," speech before the Council on Foreign Relations, Chicago, 18 October 1977, in Department of State, *Bulletin*, 5 December 1977, 806–7.

27. See, for example, Committee of Americans for the Canal Treaties, *COACT*, 36; Linowitz, "Why a New Panama Canal Treaty?" 523.

28. See, for example, Linowitz, "Why a New Panama Canal Treaty?" 523; Department of State, "Commonly Raised Questions," 8.

29. Carter, address to the nation, 1 February 1978, 56. Committee of Americans for the Canal Treaties, *COACT*, 35, 81.

30. See, for example, Linowitz, "The New Panama Canal Treaties," 807.

31. Baldwin, "The Panama Canal," 21.

32. Crane, *Surrender in Panama*, 2; American Conservative Union, "There Is No Panama Canal," 10.

33. Maechling, "The Panama Canal," 1012, 1019; Crane, *Surrender in Panama*, 5.

34. Maechling, "The Panama Canal," 1019; Dozer, "Panama Canal in Danger," 2. Treaty opponent Albert Norman admitted a more active role by the United States in the revolution. According to Norman, Theodore Roosevelt acted as "any great military strategist" would have acted by moving in forces which "detained and disarmed whatever troops the Colombian government had managed to land on the isthmus." For "paramount policy reasons," Norman argued, the United States could not have allowed Colombia "to suppress the new independent central American nation: the Republic of Panama." See Norman, *The Panama Canal Treaties of 1977: A Political Evaluation* (Northfield: self-published, 1978), 8, 10.

35. William F. Buckley, Jr., and Ronald Reagan, "On Voting Yes or No

on the Panama Canal Treaties," excerpts of a debate aired over PBS, 13 January 1978, *National Review*, 17 February 1978, 214–15.

36. McGarret, *The Key to the Panama Canal Treaty Issue*, 4–5.

37. McGarret, *The Key to the Panama Canal Treaty Issue*, 4; Buckley and Reagan, "On Voting Yes or No on the Panama Canal Treaties," 216; Reagan, address recorded from "The Panama Canal."

38. Ronald Reagan in Crane, *Surrender in Panama*, ix; Crane, *Surrender in Panama*, 41, 6.

39. See Baldwin, "The Panama Canal," 22–24; Maechling, "The Panama Canal," 1018; McGarret, *The Key to the Panama Canal Treaty Issue*, 9.

40. Crane, *Surrender in Panama*, 41.

41. Dozer, "Panama Canal in Danger," 2; Crane, *Surrender in Panama*, 1–2. Also see Reagan's criticism of "the rewriting of history" in Buckley and Reagan, "On Voting Yes or No on the Panama Canal Treaties," 214.

42. Linowitz, "Why a New Panama Canal Treaty?" 521.

43. For the protreaty version of the signing of the treaty see Linowitz, "The New Panama Canal Treaties," 808; Committee of Americans for the Canal Treaties, *COACT*, 36–37; Hollings, "The Panama Canal," 3.

44. Carter, "President Carter Discusses Panama Canal Treaties," 722; Carter, address to the nation, 1 February 1978, 57.

45. See, for example, Hollings, "The Panama Canal," 3; Committee of Americans for the Canal Treaties, *COACT*, 79.

46. Committee of Americans for the Canal Treaties, *COACT*, 63; Department of State, "Commonly Raised Questions," 5; Linowitz, "The New Panama Canal Treaties," 807; Committee of Americans for the Canal Treaties, *COACT*, 63.

47. Wall, "Are the Panama Canal Treaties Just?" 147–48; Wes Michaelson, "U.S. Imperial Instincts in Panama," *Sojourners*, November 1977, 8.

48. Philip E. Wheaton, "Treaty for Us," in *Treaty for Us, Treaty for Them*, 2; EPICA, *Panama: Sovereignty for a Land Divided*, 6, 18, 86.

49. William F. Buckley, Jr., "Panama—Si," *National Review*, 30 September 1977, 1132; Buckley and Reagan, "On Voting Yes or No on the Panama Canal Treaties," 210–11.

50. William Schneider, "Behind the Passions of the Canal Debate," 2:3309–10.

51. Buckley and Reagan, "On Voting Yes or No on the Panama Canal Treaties," 215; American Conservative Union, "There Is No Panama Canal," 2.

52. American Conservative Union, "There Is No Panama Canal," 2, 6, 21.

53. American Conservative Union, "There Is No Panama Canal," 3.

54. Dozer, "Panama Canal in Danger," 6; Reagan, address recorded from "The Panama Canal."

55. Strother, "The Panama Question," 987.

56. Crane, *Surrender in Panama*, 41–42; Strother, "The Panama Question," 987; Dozer, "Panama Canal in Danger," 6.

57. Carter, address to the nation, 1 February 1978, 55; Warren Christopher, "Deputy Secretary Christopher Discusses the Panama Canal Treaties," address before the Florida Council of 100 in Palm Beach, 11 November 1977, in Department of State, *Bulletin*, 12 December 1977, 835.

58. Linowitz, "Why a New Panama Canal Treaty?" 522.

7. Predicting the Future

1. See, for example, Phelps Jones in American Conservative Union, "There Is No Panama Canal," 15.

2. Reagan, address recorded from "The Panama Canal." Later in the address, Reagan talked of even more costs: "And what about the $43 million the army says it will cost to rearrange our military bases? Then there is some $16 million in interest paid to the United States Treasury annually, because we've never recovered the original cost of building the canal."

3. McGarret, *The Key to the Panama Canal Treaty Issue*, 14; Reagan, address recorded from "The Panama Canal"; Reagan, "The Canal as Opportunity," 558.

4. Reagan, address recorded from "The Panama Canal." On the probable toll increase, Reagan quoted *Industry Week* as predicting tolls between 25 percent and 46 percent above the existing level of $1.29 per ton.

5. Crane, *Surrender in Panama*, 99; James Lucier quoted in Virginia Prewett, "The Panama Canal: Past and Present in Perspective," *Sea Power*, August 1976, 30; Strom Thurmond in American Conservative Union, "There Is No Panama Canal," 20–21.

6. Crane, *Surrender in Panama*, 98–99.

7. McGarret, *The Key to the Panama Canal Treaty Issue*, 5.

8. Maechling, "The Panama Canal," 1015.

9. Carter, address to the nation, 1 February 1978, 57; Cyrus Vance, address in New Orleans, 12 January 1978, in Department of State, *Bulletin*, February 1978, 59.

10. See, for example, Buckley and Reagan, "On Voting Yes or No on the Panama Canal Treaties," 212.

11. Bunker, "Panama Canal Treaties," 5; Christopher, "Deputy Secretary Christopher Discusses the Panama Canal Treaties," 838–39.

12. Committee of Americans for the Canal Treaties, *COACT*, 43; Carter, "President Carter Discusses Panama Canal Treaties," 726.

13. Administration officials cited an uncompleted study setting the likely toll increase at 30 percent. William F. Buckley, Jr., however, dissented from fellow treaty supporters, claiming that the Panamanian government intended to "increase the toll charges perhaps as much as 200 percent." See Christopher, "Deputy Secretary Christopher Discusses the Panama Canal Treaties," 838; Vance, address in New Orleans, 12 January 1978, 58; Bunker,

"Panama Canal Treaties," 4; William F. Buckley, Jr., "And Finally on Panama," *National Review*, 12 November 1976, 1252.

14. Christopher, "Deputy Secretary Christopher Discusses the Panama Canal Treaties," 838.

15. Bunker, "Panama Canal Treaties," 4; Vance, address in New Orleans, 12 January 1978, 58; Bunker, "Panama Canal Treaties," 4.

16. Committee of Americans for the Canal Treaties, *COACT*, 43.

17. Sample speech in Committee of Americans for the Canal Treaties, *COACT*, 78.

18. Ellsworth Bunker, "Panama and the United States: Toward a New Relationship," address before the Rainer Club, Seattle, 22 May 1975, U.S. Department of State, *News Release* (Washington: Department of State, 1975), 2; Linowitz, "Why a New Panama Canal Treaty?" 523.

19. Committee of Americans for the Canal Treaties, *COACT*, 78.

20. Ryan, *The Panama Canal Controversy*, 135; Reagan, address recorded from "The Panama Canal."

21. Ryan, *The Panama Canal Controversy*, 135; Maechling, "The Panama Canal," 1013; Crane in American Conservative Union, "There Is No Panama Canal," 3–4.

22. Ryan, "Canal Diplomacy and United States Interests," 47.

23. Crane, *Surrender in Panama*, 9.

24. Maechling, "The Panama Canal," 1013; Crane, *Surrender in Panama*, 9–10; Daniel Flood, "The Challenge to the Congress over the Panama Canal," *Manion Forum*, transcript of broadcast no. 1151, 31 October 1976, 3.

25. Baldwin, "The Panama Canal," 13. Baldwin added: "The limitations of the current locks . . . have, in any case, little relevance. A third set of locks, larger than the existing ones, was long ago authorized and started, but work was suspended because of World War II; the excavations . . . still exist, and whenever the need is demonstrated the new locks could be completed" (13–14).

26. Maechling, "The Panama Canal," 1013; Crane, *Surrender in Panama*, 10.

27. Baldwin, "The Panama Canal," 29; Ryan, "Canal Diplomacy and United States Interests," 44–45. Also see Crane, *Surrender in Panama*, 15, 93; Dozer, "Panama Canal in Danger," 5; McGarret, *The Key to the Panama Canal Treaty Issue*, 18–19; Spruille Braden, "Panama and the U.S.A.: The Real Story," reprinted from a statement distributed by the Americanism Educational League, in "Should the U.S. Retain Present Jurisdiction Over the Panama Canal and Canal Zone?" *Congressional Digest*, April 1976, 126.

28. James Lucier, "Another Vietnam?" *National Review*, 12 September 1975, 990.

29. McGarret, *The Key to the Panama Canal Treaty Issue*, 15.

30. Ryan, "Canal Diplomacy and United States Interests," 51–52; Lucier, "Another Vietnam?" 990.

31. Strother, "The Panama Question," 987–88.

Notes

32. Helms in American Conservative Union, "There Is No Panama Canal," 5; Buckley and Reagan, "On Voting Yes or No on the Panama Canal Treaties," 215–16.

33. "Reagan on the Canal," *Newsweek*, 19 September 1977, 50.

34. Crane, *Surrender in Panama*, 15; McGarret, *The Key to the Panama Canal Treaty Issue*, 19.

35. Prewett, "The Panama Canal," 31.

36. Reagan, "The Canal as Opportunity," 556–57.

37. Flood, "The Challenge to the Congress over the Panama Canal," 2.

38. Buckley and Reagan, "On Voting Yes or No on the Panama Canal Treaties," 213–14.

39. Crane, *Surrender in Panama*, 14; Norman, *The Panama Canal Treaties of 1977*, 18. In addition to claiming that Panama did not have the resources to defend the canal, treaty opponents argued that Panama lacked the political stability to assure that the canal would remain open. As Representative Matthew Rinaldo of New Jersey argued: "Panama has always been as vulnerable to new political revolution stirrings in Latin America as Cuba is to the Trade Winds. Panama picks up every fresh revolutionary breeze. Indeed, it has long been identified by Latin American scholars as the Land of Endemic Revolution, endless intrigue and governmental instability. There have been 59 changes in government in Panama in 70 years." Matthew J. Rinaldo, address to the House of Representatives, 28 April 1975, in "Should the U.S. Retain Present Jurisdiction over the Panama Canal and the Canal Zone?" 116.

40. Crane, Roberts, and Jones quoted in American Conservative Union, "There Is No Panama Canal," 13, 14–15, 15.

41. Buckley and Reagan, "On Voting Yes or No on the Panama Canal Treaties," 213. Also see Crane, *Surrender in Panama*, 11; Ryan, *The Panama Canal Controversy*, 159–61.

42. Crane, *Surrender in Panama*, 84.

43. For Torrijos' remarks (as broadcast over Panamanian television) see Senator Robert Griffin in Committee on the Judiciary, *Panama Canal Treaties* 2:2800.

44. Linowitz, "Why a New Panama Canal Treaty?" 523; Jimmy Carter, "President Carter's News Conference of August 23," in Department of State, *Bulletin*, 19 September 1977, 378.

45. See, for example, Bunker, "The New Panama Canal Treaties," 507.

46. Bunker, "Panama and the United States," 2.

47. Committee of Americans for the Canal Treaties, *COACT*, 82–83; Jimmy Carter, "President Carter's Remarks at Yazoo City, Mississippi, July 21," in Department of State, *Bulletin*, 15 August 1977, 199.

48. Bunker, "The New Panama Canal Treaties," 507; Committee of Americans for the Canal Treaties, *COACT*, 83. Elliot Richardson, excerpts from an address to the Kansas City Lawyers Association, 12 January 1978, in

Department of State, *Bulletin*, February 1978, 58. Also see Committee of Americans for the Canal Treaties, *COACT*, 39–40; Terance A. Todman, "Remarks of Ambassador Terance A. Todman . . . to the Council of the Americas, September 28, 1977, New York," in Department of State, *Panama Canal Treaties Information*, item 4, 8.

49. President Carter, for instance, actually told a group of citizens in Denver that there had been "no threats, no implied statements that if you don't approve the treaty, the Panama Canal might be damaged." See Carter, "President Carter Discusses Panama Canal Treaties," 721.

50. Carter, "Editors and News Directors Interview President Carter," 26 August 1977, in Department of State, *Bulletin*, 26 September 1977, 398; Carter, "President Carter Discusses Panama Canal Treaties," 721; Sol Linowitz and Jesse Helms, "Should Senate O.K. Panama Canal Treaties?" *U.S. News and World Report*, 12 December 1977, 33.

51. Committee of Americans for the Canal Treaties, *COACT*, 50.

52. Committee of Americans for the Canal Treaties, *COACT*, 39.

53. These provisions became a major issue when the Senate Foreign Relations Committee began hearings on the pacts in September 1977. See Committee on Foreign Relations, *Senate Debate on the Panama Canal Treaties*, 7–8. Also see "Clarification Please," *Newsweek*, 17 October 1977, 61–62.

54. Carter, "Editors and News Directors Interview President Carter," 398.

55. Ellsworth Bunker and Sol Linowitz, "U.S. Negotiators Brief Press on New Panama Canal Treaties," briefing at the White House, 12 August 1977, in Department of State, *Bulletin*, 17 October 1977, 531–32, 527.

56. Jimmy Carter, "President Carter's News Conference of October 13," in Department of State, *Bulletin*, 7 November 1977, 630; Linowitz and Helms, "Should Senate O.K. Panama Treaties?" 34; Bunker, "Panama Canal Treaties," 4.

57. Ryan, "Canal Diplomacy and United States Interests," 52.

58. See, for example, Baldwin, "The Panama Canal," 24–25; Buckley and Reagan, "On Voting Yes or No on the Panama Canal Treaties," 215.

59. Admiral John S. McCain, Jr., quoted in Crane, *Surrender in Panama*, 51; McGarret, *The Key to the Panama Canal Treaty Issue*, 12; Dozer, "Panama Canal in Danger," 8.

60. Crane, *Surrender in Panama*, 103.

61. Baldwin, "The Panama Canal," 15–17; Reagan, "The Canal as Opportunity," 548; Crane, *Surrender in Panama*, 103.

62. Phelps Jones in American Conservative Union, "There Is No Panama Canal," 16.

63. Ryan, "Canal Diplomacy and United States Interests," 48–49.

64. Flood, "The Challenge to the Congress over the Panama Canal," 4; Reagan, "The Canal as Opportunity," 548.

65. Jake Garn in American Conservative Union, "There Is No Panama Canal," 11; Crane, *Surrender in Panama*, 59.

66. Baldwin, "The Panama Canal," 27; Crane, *Surrender in Panama*, 59; McGarret, *The Key to the Panama Canal Treaty Issue*, 11. Foremost among the Panamanian officials criticized by treaty opponents was Chief Treaty Negotiator Dr. Romulo Escobar Bethancourt, who was singled out for his refusal on one celebrated occasion to answer a direct question about whether he was a Communist.

67. Baldwin, "The Panama Canal," 27.

68. Ryan, "Canal Diplomacy and United States Interests," 49. On Torrijos' highly publicized tour, Ryan wrote: "He was accompanied by an elated Fidel Castro flushed with the victory of his 12,000 troops in Angola. Torrijos acclaimed Cuba as 'representing a beautiful tomorrow' and acknowledged its 'just support' for Panama." Ryan noted that the Cuban Embassy "boasted a staff of 60 people, a figure difficult to justify by the usual standards of diplomatic relations between two small countries with insignificant commercial connections." By comparison, the U.S. Embassy in Panama had "a staff of 45, plus 44 others who administer the generous aid program supported by the Agency for International Development." For more on Torrijos' trip to Cuba see Ryan, *The Panama Canal Controversy*, 74–75.

69. Senator Paul Laxalt in American Conservative Union, "There Is No Panama Canal," 17; McGarret, *The Key to the Panama Canal Treaty Issue*, 11.

70. Crane, *Surrender in Panama*, 88–89; Flood, "The Challenge to the Congress over the Panama Canal," 2. Flood also claimed that "nearly 3,000 Cubans" were in Panama "camouflaged as civilians."

71. Crane, *Surrender in Panama*, 54; McGarret, *The Key to the Panama Canal Treaty Issue*, 10.

72. Reagan, "The Canal as Opportunity," 559; Crane, *Surrender in Panama*, 53–56, 69–71.

73. Crane, *Surrender in Panama*, 55.

74. Committee of Americans for the Canal Treaties, *COACT*, 35.

75. Bunker, "Panama and the United States," 3.

76. Carter, "News Directors Interview President Carter," 568.

77. Carter, "Editors and News Directors Interview President Carter," 399; Carter, "News Directors Interview President Carter," 568.

78. Carter, "News Directors Interview President Carter," 568.

79. Linowitz, "The New Panama Canal Treaties," 807.

80. Carter, address to the nation, 1 February 1978, 57; Vance, address in New Orleans, 12 January 1978, 59; Richardson, excerpts from an address to the Kansas City Lawyers Association, 58.

81. Carter, "President Carter Discusses the Panama Canal Treaties," 725.

82. Committee of Americans for the Canal Treaties, *COACT*, 85; Vance, address in New Orleans, 12 January 1978, 59.

83. Committee of Americans for the Canal Treaties, *COACT*, 85.

84. Hollings, "The Panama Canal," 5; Bunker, "Panama Canal Treat-

ies," 5. Similarly, President Carter argued in his "fireside chat" that "nothing could strengthen our competitors and adversaries in this hemisphere more than for us to reject this agreement." Carter, address to the nation, 1 February 1978, 57.

85. Committee of Americans for the Canal Treaties, *COACT*, 85.

86. Committee of Americans for the Canal Treaties, *COACT*, 50; Bunker, "Panama Canal Treaties," 5.

87. Department of State, "Commonly Raised Questions," 1–2.

88. Linowitz, "Why a New Panama Canal Treaty?" 523; Department of State, "Commonly Raised Questions," 1.

89. Linowitz, "Why a New Panama Canal Treaty?" 523.

90. Carter, address to the nation, 1 February 1978, 57; Committee of Americans for the Canal Treaties, *COACT*, 19.

91. Department of State, "Commonly Raised Questions," 6.

92. Hollings, "The Panama Canal," 5.

93. Vance, address in New Orleans, 12 January 1978, 57.

94. Carter, "Editors and News Directors Interview President Carter," 398; Linowitz and Helms, "Should Senate O.K. Panama Treaties?" 34.

95. Linowitz and Helms, "Should Senate O.K. Panama Treaties?" 34.

96. Ronald Reagan often raised this charge, but he insisted that he did not mean to derogate the Joint Chiefs. As Reagan explained in an interview with *Newsweek*: "Our military has always respected civilian control. The Joint Chiefs either go along with the policy set by the Commander-in-Chief or they have to resign. So there's a question whether we are hearing their best military judgment on this." "Reagan on the Canal," 50.

97. American Conservative Union, "There Is No Panama Canal," 14.

98. Ryan, *The Panama Canal Controversy*, 141–44; Crane, *Surrender in Panama*, 51–52. Those signing the letter—all former chiefs of naval operations—were Admirals Robert B. Carney, Arleigh A. Burke, George W. Anderson, and Thomas H. Moorer.

99. Linowitz and Helms, "Should Senate O.K. Panama Treaties?" 34; Carter, "Editors and News Directors Interview President Carter," 398. Also see Carter, "President Carter's News Conference of August 23," 377.

100. Quoted in Schneider, "Behind the Passions of the Canal Debate," 2:3310.

8. Public Opinion and the Senate Debate

1. Robert F. Berkhofer, Jr., *A Behavioral Approach to Historical Analysis* (New York: Free Press, 1969), 162; Lee Benson, "An Approach to the Scientific Study of Past Public Opinion," *Public Opinion Quarterly* 31 (1967–1968): 522.

Notes

2. Alexander Hamilton in *The Debates in the Several State Conventions on the Adoption of the Federal Constitution*, ed. Jonathan Elliot, rev. ed., 5 vols. (1836; reprint, New York: Burt Franklin Reprints, 1974), 2:301.

3. Thomas A. Bailey, *A Diplomatic History of the American People* (New York: F. S. Crofts, 1940), 756. Even critics of foreign policies shaped by public opinion, such as Hans Morgenthau and George Kennan, assumed that American foreign policy did reflect public opinion. They suggested, as Ernest May has noted, that "this should not be so—that policies should come to a larger extent from calculation by experts." Ernest R. May, "An American Tradition in Foreign Policy: The Role of Public Opinion," in *Theory and Practice in American Politics*, ed. William H. Nelson (1964; reprint, Chicago: Phoenix Books, 1967), 102.

4. Gabriel Kolko, *The Roots of American Foreign Policy: An Analysis of Power and Purpose* (Boston: Beacon Press, 1969), 13; Joyce Kolko and Gabriel Kolko, *The Limits of Power: The World and United States Foreign Policy, 1945–1954* (New York: Harper and Row, 1972), 333–34.

5. The classic study is Angus Campbell, et al., *The American Voter* (New York: John Wiley and Sons, 1960).

6. See Norman H. Nie, Sidney Verba, and John R. Petrocik, *The Changing American Voter* (Cambridge: Harvard Univ. Press, 1976). For a summary of the changing portraits of the American public drawn by students of voting behavior see Gerald Pomper, *Voters' Choice: Varieties of American Electoral Behavior* (New York: Harper and Row, 1975), 5–12.

7. See W. Lance Bennett, *Public Opinion in American Politics* (New York: Harcourt Brace Jovanovich, 1980), esp. 12–16.

8. Bernard C. Cohen, *The Public's Impact on Foreign Policy* (Boston: Little, Brown, 1973), 11.

9. For a discussion of problems of methodology and interpretation in polling see Charles W. Roll and Albert H. Cantril, *Polls: Their Use and Misuse in Politics* (Cabin John, Md.: Seven Locks Press, 1980), 65–135. Other sorts of evidence for public opinion are, of course, even less reliable. Mail from constituents, the rhetoric of mass media, and even the size and enthusiasm of political crowds often lead to even greater misjudgments of public opinion. Nonetheless, public opinion's influence on political decision-making is sometimes a function of such judgments; it is the product of whatever characterizations of "the people" policymakers choose to believe.

10. Committee on Foreign Relations, *Senate Debate on the Panama Canal Treaties*, 10–11.

11. Marquis Childs, "McIntyre's Stand Against the Radical Right," in Committee on the Judiciary, *Panama Canal Treaties* 2:3491; Leahy quoted in Robert G. Kaiser, "What Is (and Isn't) Said in Canal Debate," in Committee on the Judiciary, *Panama Canal Treaties* 3:5249.

12. The only new economic controversy to erupt during the Senate debate concerned evidence that the treaties would cost much more to implement than the administration had predicted. Hearings before the Armed Ser-

vices Committee produced evidence that the treaties could cost as much as $2 billion to implement, and even the State Department admitted that some $350 million in appropriations would be required. Yet several senators leading the economic critique of the treaties apparently did not consider the new information sufficient reason for rejecting the agreement. Senators Brooke, Cannon, and McIntyre, for instance, all strongly supported the treaties despite serious reservations about their cost. See Senator Stennis' discussion of the hearings and the State Department's response in Committee on the Judiciary, *Panama Canal Treaties* 1:1805–1817. Also see Committee on Foreign Affairs, *Congress and Foreign Policy—1978,* 96th Cong., 1st sess., 1979, Committee Print, 193; Committee on Foreign Relations, *Senate Debate on the Panama Canal Treaties,* 522–24. For the remarks of Senators Brooke, Cannon, and McIntyre see Committee on the Judiciary, *Panama Canal Treaties* 1:1706–1709, 2:2965–71, 2286–87.

13. See Deming, et al., "The Canal," 30–31; "Now for the Hard Part," 21; "Panama: A Doomed Treaty?" *U.S. News and World Report,* 19 September 1977, 18–19; Angus Deming, et al., "Carter, Congress and the Canal," *Newsweek,* 4 July 1977, 49; Fay Willey and Scott Sullivan, "A Deal on the Canal," *Newsweek,* 15 August 1977, 29–30.

14. For a summary of votes on the neutrality treaty and proposed amendments see Committee on Foreign Relations, *Senate Debate on the Panama Canal Treaties,* 347–414. On ratification of the Panama Canal Treaty see "How the Treaty Was Saved," *Time,* 1 May 1978, 12–15; Committee on the Judiciary, *Panama Canal Treaties* 3:5584–85.

15. Senator Percy in Committee on the Judiciary, *Panama Canal Treaties* 1:850; Senator Stafford in Committee on the Judiciary, *Panama Canal Treaties* 2:2036–37.

16. Committee on the Judiciary, *Panama Canal Treaties* 1:1291–92, 1706, 2:3561–63; Committee on Foreign Relations, *Panama Canal Treaties: Hearings* 5:54. Also see Senator Brooke in Committee on the Judiciary, *Panama Canal Treaties* 2:3669–72; Senator Baker in Committee on Foreign Relations, *Panama Canal Treaties: Hearings* 5:32–33; the accounts of protreaty decisions by Senators Baker and Bentsen in Committee on Foreign Relations, *Senate Debate on the Panama Canal Treaties,* 518–19.

17. See Senators Javits, Baker, Clark, Case, and Secretary Vance, in Committee on Foreign Relations, *Panama Canal Treaties: Hearings* 1:3–4, 7–8, 30–32. On the conflicting interpretations see Senator Allen's remarks and Paul Ryan's article of September 11 in Committee on the Judiciary, *Panama Canal Treaties* 1:121–23; Senator Dole in Committee on the Judiciary, *Panama Canal Treaties* 1:226–28.

18. Committee on Foreign Relations, *Panama Canal Treaties: Hearings* 1:23.

19. Committee on Foreign Relations, *Background Documents,* 1620.

20. See Senators Church and Case in Committee on Foreign Relations, *Panama Canal Treaties: Hearings* 1:455–56, 465, 486. Also see the admin-

istration's interpretation of the statement in Committee on Foreign Relations, *Panama Canal Treaties: Hearings* 3:682–83.

21. On the trips to Panama see Committee on Foreign Affairs, *Congress and Foreign Policy—1978*, 192–93; "Squaring Off on the Canal," 31; Don Holt and Ron Moreau, "The Other Lobbyist," *Newsweek*, 13 February 1978, 20; Committee on Foreign Relations, *Senate Debate on the Panama Canal Treaties*, 516–19.

22. The committee first sought to add a new article to the neutrality treaty. But when Panamanian officials objected, the committee voted to recommend the two amendments discussed below. See Committee on Foreign Affairs, *Congress and Foreign Policy—1978*, 194.

23. See Senator Baker in Committee on the Judiciary, *Panama Canal Treaties* 1:1291–93; Senators Byrd and Baker in Committee on Foreign Relations, *Panama Canal Treaties: Hearings* 5:3–4, 23, 32; Steele, et al., "Heading for a Win?" 20.

24. Senator Byrd in Committee on the Judiciary, *Panama Canal Treaties* 1:1410, 1413; Senator Church in Committee on the Judiciary, *Panama Canal Treaties* 2:3417.

25. See, for example, Senator Hatch in Committee on the Judiciary, *Panama Canal Treaties* 1:1412.

26. Senators Allen and Griffin in Committee on the Judiciary, *Panama Canal Treaties* 1:1547, 1848, 2:3234.

27. Senator Griffin in Committee on the Judiciary, *Panama Canal Treaties* 2:2798–2840, 3237–38.

28. Committee on the Judiciary, *Panama Canal Treaties* 1:1848.

29. For the text and votes on the DeConcini reservation see Committee on Foreign Relations, *Senate Debate on the Panama Canal Treaties*, 403–5.

30. LaFeber, *The Panama Canal*, 246; "Last Test of a Battered Treaty," *Time*, 24 April 1978, 22; Richard Boeth, et al., "Canal Showdown," *Newsweek*, 24 April 1978, 28.

31. Curiously, Senate liberals also objected to the reservation, suggesting that they, too, never accepted the administration's interpretation of the neutrality treaty and the amendments. The liberals objected primarily to the symbolism of the reservation and its agitation of Panama. Senator Kennedy, for example, claimed that it stirred up "what is already an emotional issue in Panama, without adding to rights . . . already recognized by the treaty." He said it had "the ring of military interventionism—not just during this century, but for all time." Committee on the Judiciary, *Panama Canal Treaties* 2:3803. Also see Senator McGovern in Committee on the Judiciary, *Panama Canal Treaties* 3:5190–94. For President Carter's very different version of the controversy see Carter, *Keeping Faith*, 169–73.

32. Boeth, et al., "Canal Showdown," 26.

33. Richard Boeth, et al., "Victory on the Canal," *Newsweek*, 1 May 1978, 23. Also see "How the Treaty Was Saved," 12–13.

34. Smith and Hogan, "Opinion Polls and the Panama Canal Treaties," 10–18. Also see Roshco, "The Polls," 551–62; "The Great Canal Debate," 33.

35. See, for example, Senator Helms in Committee for the Judiciary, *Panama Canal Treaties* 1:62; Crane, *Surrender in Panama,* 105.

36. Crane, *Surrender in Panama,* 105–8.

37. Senator Biden in Committee on Foreign Relations, *Panama Canal Treaties: Hearings* 1:161–62; Senator Byrd in Committee on the Judiciary, *Panama Canal Treaties* 1:1252.

38. Committee on the Judiciary, *Panama Canal Treaties* 1:1252–53. Also see Committee on the Judiciary, *Panama Canal Treaties* 1:1898, 2:2062–63, 2455, 3746.

39. Senator Byrd in Committee on the Judiciary, *Panama Canal Treaties* 1:1253; Senator Pell in Committee on the Judiciary, *Panama Canal Treaties* 2:2210; Senator Sarbanes in Committee on the Judiciary, *Panama Canal Treaties* 2:3312–13.

40. Senator McIntyre in Committee on the Judiciary, *Panama Canal Treaties* 2:2286.

41. See Senators McIntyre and Hatfield in Committee on the Judiciary, *Panama Canal Treaties* 2:2287–93, 2302–3.

42. Senator Scott in Committee on the Judiciary, *Panama Canal Treaties* 1:1251, 2:3596–97; Senator Curtis in Committee on the Judiciary, *Panama Canal Treaties* 2:3346.

43. See, for example, Senators Allen and Hatch in Committee on the Judiciary, *Panama Canal Treaties* 1:1853, 2:2141, 2455.

44. Senator Hatch in Committee on the Judiciary, *Panama Canal Treaties* 1:1319, 1781; Senator Laxalt in Committee on the Judiciary, *Panama Canal Treaties* 1:1897; Senator Johnston in Committee on the Judiciary, *Panama Canal Treaties* 1:2009–10.

45. Senator Pell in Committee on Foreign Relations, *Panama Canal Treaties: Hearings* 1:5. Also see Senator Glen in Committee on Foreign Relations, *Panama Canal Treaties: Hearings* 5:24–25.

46. Ellsworth Bunker in Committee on Foreign Relations, *Panama Canal Treaties: Hearings* 1:467.

47. Committee on Foreign Relations, *Senate Debate on the Panama Canal Treaties,* 513; Committee on Foreign Relations, *Panama Canal Treaties: Hearings* 5:17.

48. Senators Byrd, Church, Sarbanes, and Riegle in Committee on the Judiciary, *Panama Canal Treaties* 1:1255–56, 2:2551, 3312–14, 3634.

49. Committee on the Judiciary, *Panama Canal Treaties* 2:2550–51. Also see the discussion of polls by Gallup and NBC News in Senator Stevenson's speech in Committee on the Judiciary, *Panama Canal Treaties* 2:3726.

50. Committee on Foreign Relations, *Panama Canal Treaties: Hearings* 5:28.

Notes

51. Committee on the Judiciary, *Panama Canal Treaties* 2:3306–12.

52. Committee on the Judiciary, *Panama Canal Treaties* 1:1504. Also see Senator Church on the leadership amendments and Caddell's poll in Committee on the Judiciary, *Panama Canal Treaties* 2:2551; Senator Byrd on polls by CBS-Time and NBC News in Committee on the Judiciary, *Panama Canal Treaties* 2:3204.

53. Senator Baker in Committee on the Judiciary, *Panama Canal Treaties* 1:1257; Senator Byrd in Committee on the Judiciary, *Panama Canal Treaties* 2:3211.

54. Senators Helms and Hatch in Committee on the Judiciary, *Panama Canal Treaties* 2:2248, 2994. Also see Senators Thurmond and Scott in Committee on the Judiciary, *Panama Canal Treaties* 2:2986, 3596.

55. Committee on the Judiciary, *Panama Canal Treaties* 1:1623.

56. Senator Helms in Committee on the Judiciary, *Panama Canal Treaties* 2:3300.

57. The Utah poll was commissioned by the *Salt Lake Tribune*. See Committee on the Judiciary, *Panama Canal Treaties* 2:2140–41. The Virginia poll was part of Scott's "annual opinion poll" conducted through his newsletter to constituents. See Committee on the Judiciary, *Panama Canal Treaties* 1:1251.

58. Senators Helms and Hatch in Committee on the Judiciary, *Panama Canal Treaties* 2:2987, 3657.

59. Senator Helms in Committee on the Judiciary, *Panama Canal Treaties* 2:3298–3306.

60. Senator Melcher in Committee on the Judiciary, *Panama Canal Treaties* 2:3736.

61. Senator Helms in Committee on the Judiciary, *Panama Canal Treaties* 2:3301; Senator Laxalt in Committee on the Judiciary, *Panama Canal Treaties* 2:3369.

62. See Committee on Foreign Affairs, *Congress and Foreign Policy—1978*, 194–95.

63. Destler, "Treaty Troubles," 50. Also see "Opening the Great Canal Debate," *Time*, 20 February 1978, 19; "Drug Debate: A Bust," *Time*, 6 March 1978, 22; Committee on Foreign Relations, *Senate Debate on the Panama Canal Treaties*, 520.

64. Steele, et al., "Heading for a Win?" 20.

65. Committee on the Judiciary, *Panama Canal Treaties* 2:2992.

66. LaFeber, "Covering the Canal," 27.

67. Terence Smith, "Carter Nears End of Long Drive for Canal Treaties," *New York Times*, 1 February 1978, sec. A, 4; "Opening the Great Canal Debate," 19; "Carter Wins on Panama," 9.

68. Steele, et al., "Heading for a Win?" 18.

69. Jimmy Carter, address to the nation, 18 April 1978, in Department of State, *Bulletin*, May 1978, 52.

70. Roshco, "Polling on Panama," 562.

71. The term "intervene" had been controversial throughout the debate, with Panama threatening to reject any agreement containing the word. Both the statement of understanding and the leadership amendments specifically renounced America's right to "intervene" in Panama. Still, Senators Church and Byrd interpreted polls showing support for treaties amended to allow the U.S. to "intervene" as support for the treaties with the leadership amendments. See Church on Caddell's poll and an Idaho poll in Committee on the Judiciary, *Panama Canal Treaties* 2:2551; Byrd on the NBC News poll in Committee on the Judiciary, *Panama Canal Treaties* 2:3204.

72. Roshco, "Polling on Panama," 562.

73. See Schneider, "Behind the Passions of the Canal Debate," 2:3310–11.

CONCLUSION

1. See Steven V. Roberts, "Administration Wins Crucial Vote in the House on Panama Canal Bill," *New York Times,* 21 June 1979, sec. A, 10; Steven V. Roberts, "Carter Wins House Vote on Canal, But Loses on Aid Grant to Turkey," *New York Times,* 22 June 1979, sec. A, 1, 8; A. O. Sulzberger, Jr., "House Vote Defeats a Bill to Carry Out Panama Canal Pact," *New York Times,* 21 September 1979, sec. A, 1, 5; A. O. Sulzberger, Jr., "House Enacts Bill to Carry Out Terms of Panama Treaty," *New York Times,* 27 September 1979, sec. A, 1, 8. Also see "Panama Leader Killed in Crash in Bad Weather," *New York Times,* 2 August 1981, sec. A, 1.

2. George Moffett, III, for instance, argues that Carter's failure to "educate" the public on Panama "was the product of a variety of circumstances over which the administration had no control and which effectively doomed the public relations campaign to futility." Moffett's list of excuses for the administration's failure emphasizes, above all, the ignorance and emotionalism of the public. He ultimately blames the campaign's failure on "barriers to communication" erected by the public: "the inability to hear, the unwillingness to hear, the disposition to draw different conclusions from the same evidence, the phenomenon of selective hearing, the absence of prior conditioning." Never considering the possibility that the protreaty case did not *warrant* belief, Moffett concludes that the "treaty campaign became an object lesson in the limits of public education." See Moffett, *The Limits of Victory,* 127–37.

3. See Crawford, *Thunder on the Right,* 8, 272–89.

4. In his memoirs, Carter wrote that the treaty debate "left deep and serious political wounds that have never healed; and, I am convinced, a large number of members of Congress were later defeated for reelection because

they voted for the Panama treaties." See Carter, *Keeping Faith*, 184. See Viguerie's assessment of the contributions of the Panama campaign to the New Right's growth and electoral success in Viguerie, *The New Right*, 65–77.

     5. Committee on the Judiciary, *Panama Canal Treaties*, 2:3671.

     6. Committee on the Judiciary, *Panama Canal Treaties*, 2:3670.

BIBLIOGRAPHY

ARTICLES

Abramson, Rudy. "Conservatives Against the Canal Treaties Planning a Multi-Media Blitz for January." *Los Angeles Times*, 7 November 1977, sec. 1, 5.
"After Carter's Panama Victory." *U.S. News and World Report*, 1 May 1978, 25–27.
Baker, George W., Jr. "The Wilson Administration and Panama, 1913–1931." *Journal of Inter-American Studies* 8 (April 1966): 279–93.
Baldwin, Hanson W. "The Panama Canal: Sovereignty and Security." *AEI Defense Review*, August 1977, 12–34.
Benson, Lee. "An Approach to the Scientific Study of Past Public Opinion." *Public Opinion Quarterly* 31 (1967–68): 522–67.
"A Bid for Votes on Panama." *Business Week*, 12 September 1977, 41.
Bigelow, Poultney. "Our Mismanagement in Panama." *Independent*, 4 January 1906, 9–21.
———. "Panama: The Human Side." *Cosmopolitan Magazine*, September 1906, 455–62.
Bishop, Joseph B. "Panama's Bridge of Water." *Scribner's Magazine*, July 1913, 7–20.
———. "Sanitation on the Isthmus." *Scribner's Magazine*, February 1913, 234–51.
Bode, Ken. "Carter and the Canal." *New Republic*, 14 January 1978, 8–10.
———. "The Hero of Panama." *New Republic*, 21 January 1978, 10–15.
Boeth, Richard; Lindsay, John J.; Clift, Eleanor; Whitmore, Jane; and Moreau, Ron. "Victory on the Canal." *Newsweek*, 1 May 1978, 23–25.
Boeth, Richard; Lindsay, John J.; DeFrank, Thomas M.; and Moreau, Ron. "Canal Showdown." *Newsweek*, 24 April 1978, 26–29.
Boeth, Richard; Sniffen, Michael J.; Doyle, James; and Sciolino, Elaine. "The New Activists." *Newsweek*, 7 November 1977, 41.
Bohning, Don. "U.S. Chamber Backs Negotiations for New Panama Canal Treaty." *ARA-PAF Press Clips*, 19 November 1975, 1–2.
Buckley, William F., Jr. "And Finally on Panama." *National Review*, 12 November 1976, 1252–53.

263

Bibliography

———. "The Panama Canal and General Torrijos." *National Review,* 26 November 1976, 1306.

———. "Panama—Si." *National Review,* 30 September 1977, 1132–33.

Buckley, William F., Jr., and Reagan, Ronald. "On Voting Yes or No on the Panama Canal Treaties." Excerpts of a debate aired on the Public Broadcasting System, 13 January 1978. *National Review,* 17 February 1978, 210–17.

Buell, R. L. "Panama and the United States." *Foreign Policy Reports,* 20 January 1932, 409–26.

"Carter's Panama Triumph—What It Cost." *U.S. News and World Report,* 27 March 1978, 27–28.

"Carter Wins on Panama." *Time,* 27 March 1978, 8–11.

"Catholic Bishops Call for a New Panama Treaty." *Washington Post,* 11 November 1976, sec. A, 3.

"Ceding the Canal—Slowly." *Time,* 22 August 1977, 8–13.

"Clarification Please." *Newsweek,* 17 October 1977, 61–62.

Clymer, Adam. "TV Campaign Begun Against Panama Canal Treaty." *New York Times,* 31 October 1977, sec. 1, 20.

Crichfield, George W. "The Panama Canal from a Contractor's Standpoint." *North American Review,* January 1905, 74–87.

Deming, Angus; Hubbard, Henry W.; Sullivan, Scott; and DeFrank, Thomas M. "Carter, Congress and the Canal." *Newsweek,* 4 July 1977, 49.

Deming, Angus; Sullivan, Scott; DeFrank, Thomas M.; Hubbard, Henry W.; Moreau, Ron. "The Canal: Time to Go?" *Newsweek,* 22 August 1977, 28–32.

Deming, Angus; Sullivan, Scott; Whitmore, Jane; and Lindsay, John J. "A Panama Production." *Newsweek,* 19 September 1977, 46–48.

Destler, I. M. "Treaty Troubles: Versailles in Reverse." *Foreign Policy,* Winter 1978–79, 45–65.

DeYoung, Karen. "State Dept. Is 'Selling' Canal Treaties." *Washington Post,* 26 February 1978, sec. A, 1.

"Drug Debate: A Bust." *Time,* 6 March 1978, 22.

Flood, Daniel J. "The Challenge to Congress over the Panama Canal." Transcript of broadcast no. 1151. *Manion Forum,* 31 October 1976, 1–4.

Fraker, Susan, and Lindsay, John J. "Courting Zorinsky." *Newsweek,* 27 March 1978, 45.

Goethals, George W. "The Panama Canal." *National Geographic,* February 1911, 148–211.

Goshko, John M. "Conservatives Set TV Film Opposing Panama Treaties." *Washington Post,* 28 October 1977, sec. A, 2.

"Gospel Disk Jockey Aids Carter in Bid for Panama Canal Treaties." *New York Times,* 18 November 1977, sec. A, 17.

"The Great Canal Debate." *Public Opinion,* March-April 1978, 33–34.

Grey, Elmer. "The Panama-Pacific International Exposition of 1915." *Scribner's Magazine,* July 1913, 44–57.

Hager, Barry M. "White House Pushing for Approval of Treaties." *Congres-*

sional Quarterly, 21 January 1978, 137.

"Halftime Confidence on Panama." *Time*, 3 April 1978, 22.

"Hold Everything Till Panama's Through." *Economist*, 10 September 1977, 51–52.

Holt, Don, and Moreau, Ron. "The Other Lobbyist." *Newsweek*, 13 February 1978, 20.

"How the Treaty Was Saved." *Time*, 1 May 1978, 12–15.

Hudson, Richard. "Storm Over the Canal." *New York Times Magazine*, 16 May 1976, 18–22.

Ivins, Molly. "Treaty Foes, Led by Reagan, Crusade in Denver." *New York Times*, 20 January 1978, sec. A, 3.

Kalke, David J. "Panamanian Purpose and the U.S. Presence." *Christian Century*, 24 December 1975, 1185–86.

Karnow, Stanley. "The Politics of Bluster and Ballyhoo." *Saturday Review*, 24 July 1976, 13.

"Keeping the Canal Pacts Afloat." *Time*, 24 October 1977, 35–38.

LaFeber, Walter. "Covering the Canal, or, How the Press Missed the Boat." *More*, June 1978, 26–31.

Langley, Lester D. "U.S.-Panamanian Relations since 1941." *Journal of Inter-American Studies* 12 (July 1970): 339–66.

Lanouette, William J. "The Panama Canal Treaties—Playing in Peoria and in the Senate." *National Journal*, 8 October 1977, 1556–62.

"Last Test of a Battered Treaty." *Time*, 24 April 1978, 22.

Lernoux, Penny. "U.S. Imperialists, Old and New." *Nation*, 3 April 1976, 391–96.

"Let It Go." *Economist*, 17 April 1976, 15.

Linowitz, Sol M., and Helms, Jesse. "Should Senate OK Panama Treaties?" *U.S. News and World Report*, 12 December 1977, 33–34.

Lowther, William. "Teddy Roosevelt Must Be Turning in His Grave." *McLeans*, 23 January 1978, 41–42.

Lucier, James. "Another Vietnam?" *National Review*, 12 September 1975, 989–90.

Maechling, Charles, Jr. "The Panama Canal: A Fresh Start." *Orbis* 20 (Winter 1977): 1007–23.

Mahan, Alfred T. "Fortify the Panama Canal." *North American Review*, March 1911, 331–39.

———. "The Panama Canal and Sea Power in the Pacific." *Century Magazine*, June 1911, 240–48.

———. "The United States Looking Outward." *Atlantic Monthly*, December 1890, 816–24.

Markham, Charles. "The Making of the Panama Canal." *Blackwood's Magazine*, August 1912, 263–74.

Maxfield, David M. "Panama Canal: Groups Favoring Treaties Fight to Offset Opponents' Massive Lobbying Effort." *Congressional Quarterly*, 21 January 1978, 135–37.

May, Ernest R. "An American Tradition in Foreign Policy: The Role of Public

Opinion." In *Theory and Practice in American Politics,* edited by William H. Nelson. 1964. Reprint. Chicago: Univ. of Chicago Press, Phoenix Books, 1967.

Mayer, Martin. "The Man from Xerox Multiplies His Roles." *New York Times Magazine,* 24 April 1976, 44.

Michaelson, Wes. "U.S. Imperial Instincts in Panama." *Sojourners,* November 1977, 8–9.

"The NCC and Carter." *Christian Century,* 23 November 1977, 1084.

"New Deals for the Big Ditch." *Time,* 25 July 1977, 28.

"Now for the Hard Part." *Time,* 19 September 1977, 19–21.

Oberdorfer, Don. "Panama Plans Intense Publicity Effort to Push New Treaty." *Washington Post,* 24 March 1977, sec. A, 12.

"Opening the Great Canal Debate." *Time,* 20 February 1978, 19.

"Panama: A Doomed Treaty?" *U.S. News and World Report,* 19 September 1977, 18–23.

"Panama Canal Fight: Senators Feel the Heat." *U.S. News and World Report,* 13 February 1978, 37–38.

"The Panama Canal Treaties." *Crisis,* December 1977, 457.

"The Panama Canal: Round One." *Newsweek,* 20 February 1978, 30.

"Panama Canal: What Happens Next?" *Nation's Business,* October 1977, 56–61.

"Panama's Flexibility Assures OK of Canal Pacts." *Capital Times* (Madison, Wis.), 19 January 1978, 6.

"Panama Leader Killed in Crash in Bad Weather." *New York Times,* 2 August 1981, sec. A, 1.

"Panamanian Students Burn U.S. Vehicle, Deface Embassy." *Daily Progress* (Charlottesville, Va.), 19 January 1984, sec. A, 7.

"Panama Theatrics." *Time,* 26 April 1976, 16.

Peters, Joan. "Panama's Genial Despot." *Harper's,* April 1978, 61–70.

Peterson, Bill. "Notables Unite in Endorsing Canal Treaties." *Washington Post,* 16 October 1977, sec. A, 9.

Prewett, Virginia. "The Panama Canal: Past and Present in Perspective." *Sea Power,* August 1976, 23–31.

"Profile: Efforts of Major Conservative Groups Opposing Ratification of the Panama Canal Treaties." *Democratic Congressional Campaign Committee Report,* February 1978, 1–4.

"Reagan on the Canal." *Newsweek,* 19 September 1977, 50.

Reagan, Ronald. "The Canal as Opportunity: A New Relationship with Latin America." *Orbis* 21 (Fall 1977): 547–63.

Riding, Alan. "Is America Giving Away the Panama Canal?" *Saturday Review,* 24 July 1976, 6–14.

Rippy, J. Fred. "United States and Panama: The High Cost of Appeasement." *Inter-American Economic Affairs* 17 (Spring 1964): 87–94.

Roberts, Steven V. "Administration Wins Crucial Vote in the House on Panama Canal Bill." *New York Times,* 21 June 1979, sec. A, 10.

———. "Carter Wins House Vote on Canal, But Loses on Aid Grant to Turkey." *New York Times,* 22 June 1979, sec. A, 1, 8.

———. "Panama Treaties at Stake in Bitter Propaganda War." *New York Times,* 20 January 1978, sec. A, 3.

Roosevelt, Theodore. "The Influence of Sea Power upon History." *Atlantic Monthly,* October 1890, 563–67.

———. "The Monroe Doctrine and the Panama Canal." *Outlook,* 6 December 1913, 745–54.

"Roper: High Audience for Canal Debates." *CPB Report* (Corporation for Public Broadcasting), 19 June 1978, 3.

Rosenfeld, Stephen S. "The Panama Negotiations: A Close-Run Thing." *Foreign Affairs,* October 1975, 1–13.

Roshco, Bernard. "The Polls: Polling on Panama—Si; Don't Know; Hell No!" *Public Opinion Quarterly* 42 (Winter 1978): 551–62.

Ryan, Paul. "Canal Diplomacy and United States Interests." *U.S. Naval Institute Proceedings* 103 (January 1977): 44–53.

Safire, William. "Panama Townhouse." *New York Times,* 2 January 1978, sec. 1, 21.

"Should the U.S. Retain Present Jurisdiction over the Panama Canal and Canal Zone?" *Congressional Digest,* April 1976, 108–27.

Showalter, William J. "The Panama Canal." *National Geographic,* February 1912, 195–205.

Shrum, Robert. "The Narrow Passage of the Canal Treaty." *New Times,* 15 May 1978, 6–7.

Sidey, Hugh. "Does Congress Need a Nanny?" *Time,* 27 March 1978, 13.

"Squaring Off on the Canal." *Time,* 30 January 1978, 31.

Steel, Ronald. "Rough Passage." *New York Review of Books,* 23 March 1978, 10–14.

Steele, Richard, and Bruno, Hal. "Stand Up and Be Counted." *Newsweek,* 12 September 1977, 26–27.

Steele, Richard; DeFrank, Thomas M.; and Cliff, Eleanor. "Heading for a Win?" *Newsweek,* 13 February 1978, 18–20.

Stimson, Henry L. "The Defense of the Panama Canal." *Scribner's Magazine,* July 1913, 1–6.

"Storm Over the Canal." *Time,* 29 August 1977, 28.

Strother, Robert S. "The Panama Canal Question: An Alternative to U.S. Defeatism." *National Review,* 12 September 1975, 986–89.

Sulzberger, A. O., Jr. "House Enacts Bill to Carry Out Terms of Panama Treaty." *New York Times,* 27 September 1979, sec. A, 1, 8.

———. "House Vote Defeats a Bill to Carry Out Panama Canal Pact." *New York Times,* 21 September 1979, sec. A, 1, 5.

Taft, William Howard. "The Panama Canal: Why the Lock-System Was Chosen." *Century Magazine,* December 1906, 300–313.

Talbot, Hayden. "What Shall We Do with It? The Next Vital Question about the Panama Canal Answered by the Canal's Builder, Colonel Goethals: An Interview." *Outlook,* 8 July 1911, 531–36.

Bibliography

Thimmesch, N. "Panama: More Than Just a Ditch." *New York*, 23 January 1978, 6–8.

Ungar, S. J. "Soft-Selling the Treaties." *Atlantic*, December 1977, 16.

Wall, James M. "Are the Panama Canal Treaties Just?" *Christian Century*, 15 February 1978, 147–48.

————. "Church Support for Canal Treaties." *Christian Century*, 2 November 1977, 995–96.

Warner, Edwin. "Mythologizing the Panama Canal." *Time*, 17 April 1978, 27.

Willey, Fay, and Sullivan, Scott. "A Deal on the Canal." *Newsweek*, 15 August 1977, 29–30.

Willoughby, William F. "Catholic Bishops Vote Request for Lenient Treaty with Panama." *Washington Star*, 11 November 1976, sec. A, 4.

"The Wooing of Senator Zorinsky." *Time*, 27 March 1978, 12–13.

BOOKS AND PAMPHLETS

Abbot, Willis J. *Panama and the Canal in Picture and Prose: A Complete Story of Panama, As Well As the History, Purpose and Promise of Its World-Famous Canal—the Most Gigantic Engineering Undertaking Since the Dawn of Time.* New York: Syndicate, 1913.

Adams, Brooks. *The Law of Civilization and Decay: An Essay on History.* 1896. Reprint. New York: Alfred A. Knopf, 1943.

Adams, Charles F. *The Panama Canal Zone: An Epochal Event in Sanitation.* Boston: Massachusetts Historical Society, 1911.

Almond Gabriel A. *The American People and Foreign Policy.* 1950. Reprint. New York: Praeger, 1967.

Avery, Ralph E. *The Greatest Engineering Feat in the World at Panama: The Authentic and Complete Story of the Building and Operation of the Great Waterway—the Eighth Wonder of the World.* Rev. ed. New York: Leslie-Judge, 1915.

Bailey, Thomas A. *A Diplomatic History of the American People.* New York: F. S. Crofts, 1940.

Bakenhus, Reuben E.; Knapp, Harry S.; and Johnson, Emory R. *The Panama Canal: Comprising Its History and Construction, and Its Relation to the Navy, International Law and Commerce.* New York: John Wiley and Sons, 1915.

Barker, Samuel H. *The Panama Canal and Restoration of American Merchant Marine.* Washington: GPO, 1912.

Barrett, John. *Panama Canal: What It Is; What It Means.* Washington: Pan American Union, 1913.

Beale, Howard K. *Theodore Roosevelt and the Rise of America to World Power.* 1956. Reprint. New York: Collier Books, 1967.

Bennett, Ira E., ed. *History of the Panama Canal: Its Construction and Builders.* Washington: Historical Publishing, 1915.

Bennett, W. Lance. *Public Opinion in American Politics*. New York: Harcourt Brace Jovanovich, 1980.

Berkhofer, Robert F., Jr. *A Behavioral Approach to Historical Analysis*. New York: Free Press, 1969.

Bishop, Farnham. *Panama Past and Present*. New York: Century, 1913.

Bishop, Joseph B. *The Panama Gateway*. New York: Charles Scribner's Sons, 1913.

————. *Theodore Roosevelt and His Time Shown in His Own Letters*. 2 Vols. New York: Charles Scribner's Sons, 1920.

[Bishop, Joseph B.], comp. *Official Handbook of the Panama Canal*. 3d ed. Ancon, C.Z.: [I.C.C. Press], 1913.

Bishop, Joseph B., and Peary, Robert E. *Uncle Sam's Panama Canal and World History: Its Achievement an Honor to the United States and a Blessing to the World*. New York: World Syndicate, 1913.

Bitzer, Lloyd, and Reuter, Theodore. *Carter vs. Ford: The Counterfeit Debates of 1976*. Madison: Univ. of Wisconsin Press, 1980.

Blum, John M. *The Republican Roosevelt*. Rev. ed. New York: Atheneum, 1968.

Blumenthal, Sidney. *The Permanent Campaign*. Rev. ed. New York: Touchstone, 1982.

Bullard, Arthur [Albert Edwards]. *Panama: The Canal, the Country, and the People*. New York: MacMillan, 1911.

Bunau-Varilla, Philippe. *Panama: The Creation, Destruction, and Resurrection*. New York: McBride, Nast, 1914.

Busey, James L. *Political Aspects of the Panama Canal: The Problem of Location*. Tucson: Univ. of Arizona Press, 1974.

Campbell, Angus; Converse, Philip E.; Miller, Warren E.; and Stokes, Donald E. *The American Voter*. New York: John Wiley and Sons, 1960.

Carter, Jimmy. *A Government as Good as Its People*. New York: Simon and Schuster, 1977.

————. *Keeping Faith: Memoirs of a President*. New York: Bantam Books, 1982.

Center for Strategic Studies, Georgetown University. *Panama: Canal Issues and Treaty Talks*. Washington: Georgetown University, 1967.

Cohen, Bernard C. *The Public's Impact on Foreign Policy*. Boston: Little, Brown, 1973.

Collins, John O. *The Panama Guide*. Mt. Hope, C.Z.: I.C.C. Press, 1912.

Commission on United States–Latin American Relations. *The Americas in a Changing World: A Report of the Commission on United States–Latin American Relations*. New York: Quadrangle, 1975.

————. *The United States and Latin America: Next Steps. A Second Report of the Commission on United States–Latin American Relations*. New York: Center for Inter-American Relations, 1976.

Committee of Americans for the Canal Treaties. *COACT: The Bi-Partisan Citizens' Committee of Americans for the Canal Treaties*. Washington: Committee of Americans for the Canal Treaties, [1977].

Crane, Philip. *Surrender in Panama: The Case Against the Treaty*. New York: Dale Books, 1978.

Bibliography

Council of the Americas, Work Group on Panama. *United States, Panama, and the Panama Canal: A Guide to the Issues.* Washington: Council of the Americas, 1976.

Crawford, Alan. *Thunder on the Right: The "New Right" and the Politics of Resentment.* New York: Pantheon Books, 1980.

Cullom, Shelby Moore. *Fifty Years of Public Service.* Chicago: A. C. McClurg, 1911.

DuBois, Jules. *Danger Over Panama.* Indianapolis: Bobbs-Merrill, 1964.

DuVal, Miles P., Jr. *And the Mountains Will Move: The Story of the Building of the Panama Canal.* Stanford: Stanford Univ. Press, 1947.

————. *Cadiz to Cathay: The Story of the Long Diplomatic Struggle for the Panama Canal.* Rev. ed. Stanford: Stanford Univ. Press, 1947.

Ealy, Lawrence O. *Yanqui Politics and the Isthmian Canal.* University Park: Pennsylvania State Univ. Press, 1971.

Ecumenical Program for Inter-American Communication and Action. *Panama: Sovereignty for a Land Divided: A People's Primer by the EPICA Task Force.* Washington: EPICA Task Force, 1976.

————. *Treaty for Us, Treaty for Them: Two Analyses of the Panama Canal Treaties.* Washington: EPICA Task Force, 1977.

Edelman, Murray. *Political Language: Words that Succeed and Policies that Fail.* New York: Academic Press, 1977.

————. *Politics as Symbolic Action: Mass Arousal and Quiescence.* Chicago: Markham, 1971.

Eisenhower, Milton S. *The Wine is Bitter: The United States and Latin America.* Garden City, N.Y.: Doubleday, 1963.

Elliot, Jonathan, ed. *The Debates in the Several State Conventions on the Adoption of the Federal Constitution.* Rev. ed. 5 vols. 1836. Reprint. New York: Burt Franklin Reprints, 1974.

Fiske, John. *American Political Ideas Viewed from the Standpoint of Universal History.* New York: Harper and Brothers, 1885.

Forbes-Lindsay, Charles H. *Panama and the Canal Today: An Historical Account of the Canal Project . . . and the First Comprehensive Account of Its Physical Features and Natural Resources.* Rev. ed. Boston: L. C. Page, 1912.

————. *Panama: The Isthmus and the Canal.* Philadelphia: J. C. Winston, 1906.

————. *The Story of Panama and the Canal: A Complete History . . . and a Detailed Description of the American Enterprise.* N.p., [1913].

Franck, Harry A. *Zone Policeman 88: A Close Range Study of the Canal and Its Workers.* New York: Century, 1913.

Franck, Thomas M., and Weisband, Edward. *Word Politics: Verbal Strategy among the Superpowers.* New York: Oxford Univ. Press, 1972.

Fraser, John F. *Panama and What It Means.* London: Cassell, 1913.

Gause, Frank A., and Carr, Charles C. *The Story of Panama: The New Route to India.* 1912. Reprint. New York: Arno Press, 1970.

Gil, Federico G. *Latin American–United States Relations.* New York: Harcourt Brace Jovanovich, 1971.

Goethals, George W. *The Isthmian Canal*. Washington: GPO, 1909.
————, ed. *The Panama Canal: An Engineering Treatise*. 2 vols. New York: McGraw-Hill, 1916.
Goldman, Eric F. *The Tragedy of Lyndon Johnson*. New York: Alfred A. Knopf, 1969.
Gorgas, William C. *Sanitation in Panama*. New York: D. Appleton, 1915.
Haskin, Frederic J. *The Panama Canal*. Garden City, N.Y.: Doubleday, Page, 1913.
Hoyt, Edwin C. *National Policy and International Law: Case Studies From American Canal Policy*. Denver: Social Science Foundation and Graduate School of International Relations, University of Denver, 1967.
Jacobs, Walter D. *The Panama Canal: Its Role in Hemispheric Security*. New York: American Emergency Committee on the Panama Canal, 1968.
Jessup, Philip C. *Elihu Root*. 2 vols. New York: Dodd, Mead, 1938.
Johnson, Willis F. *Four Centuries of the Panama Canal*. New York: Henry Holt, 1906.
Jorden, William J. *Panama Odyssey*. Austin: Univ. of Texas Press, 1984.
Kitchel, Denison. *The Truth about the Panama Canal*. New Rochelle, N.Y.: Arlington House, 1978.
Kolko, Gabriel. *The Roots of American Foreign Policy: An Analysis of Power and Purpose*. Boston: Beacon Press, 1969.
Kolko, Joyce, and Kolko, Gabriel. *The Limits of Power: The World and United States Foreign Policy, 1945–1954*. New York: Harper and Row, 1972.
LaFeber, Walter. *The New Empire: An Interpretation of American Expansion, 1860–1898*. Ithaca, N.Y.: Cornell Univ. Press, 1963.
————. *The Panama Canal: The Crisis in Historical Perspective*. Rev. ed. New York: Oxford Univ. Press, 1979.
Link, Arthur S., and Catton, William B. *The Era of the Cold War, 1946–1973*. Vol. I of *American Epoch: A History of the United States since 1900*. 4th ed. New York: Alfred A. Knopf, 1974.
Liss, Sheldon B. *The Canal: Aspects of United States–Panamanian Relations*. Notre Dame, Ind.: Univ. of Notre Dame Press, 1967.
Lucas, Stephen E. *Portents of Rebellion: Rhetoric and Revolution in Philadelphia, 1765–1776*. Philadelphia: Temple Univ. Press, 1976.
McCain, William D. *The United States and the Republic of Panama*. Durham, N.C.: Duke Univ. Press, 1937.
McCullough, David. *The Path between the Seas: The Creation of the Panama Canal, 1870–1914*. New York: Simon and Schuster, 1977.
McGarret, John W. *The Key to the Panama Canal Treaty Issue*. Self-published, 1978.
McIntyre, Thomas J. *The Fear Brokers: Peddling the Hate Politics of the New Right*. Boston: Beacon Press, 1979.
Mack, Gerstle. *The Land Divided: A History of the Panama Canal and Other Isthmian Canal Projects*. New York: Alfred A. Knopf, 1944.
Mahan, Alfred T. *The Influence of Sea Power upon History, 1660–1783*. 1890. Re-

print. New York: Hill and Wang, 1957.

———. *The Interest of America in Sea Power, Present and Future*. Boston: Little, Brown, 1898.

———. *Mahan on Naval Warfare: Selections From the Writings of Rear Admiral Alfred T. Mahan*. Edited by Allan Westcott. Boston: Little, Brown, 1941.

Marshall, Logan. *The Story of the Panama Canal: The Wonderful Account of the Gigantic Undertaking Commenced by the French, and Brought to Triumphant Completion by the United States*. N.p., [1913].

Mason, Charles F. *Sanitation in the Panama Canal Zone*. Mt. Hope, C.Z.: Panama Canal Press, 1916.

May, Ernest R. *"Lessons" of the Past: The Use and Misuse of History in American Foreign Policy*. New York: Oxford Univ. Press, 1973.

Merli, Frank J., and Wilson, Theodore A., eds. *Makers of American Diplomacy: From Theodore Roosevelt to Henry Kissinger*. New York: Charles Scribner's Sons, 1974.

Merry, William L. *The Nicaragua Canal: The Gateway Between the Oceans*. San Francisco: Commercial Publishing, 1895.

Millis, Walter. *Arms and Men: A Study of American Military History*. New York: Mentor Books, 1956.

Mills, John S. *The Panama Canal: A History and Description of the Enterprise*. London: Thomas Nelson and Sons, 1913.

Miner, Dwight C. *The Fight for the Panama Route: The Story of the Spooner Act and the Hay-Herran Treaty*. New York: Columbia Univ. Press, 1940.

Moffett, George D., III. *The Limits of Victory: The Ratification of the Panama Canal Treaties*. Ithaca, N.Y.: Cornell Univ. Press, 1985.

Mowry, George E. *The Era of Theodore Roosevelt and the Birth of Modern America, 1900–1912*. Rev. ed. New York: Harper Torchbooks, 1962.

Nesbitt, Wallace. *The Panama Canal and Its Treaty Obligations*. N.p., 1912.

Nida, William L. *The Story of Panama and the Canal*. Chicago: Hall and McCreary, 1913.

Nie, Norman H.; Verba, Sidney; and Petrocik, John R. *The Changing American Voter*. Cambridge: Harvard Univ. Press, 1976.

Norman, Albert. *The Panama Canal Treaties of 1977: A Political Evaluation*. Northfield, Vt.: Self-published, 1978.

Parrish, Samuel L. *The Hay-Pauncefote Treaty and the Panama Canal*. N.p., 1913.

Payne, Donald G. [Ian Cameron]. *The Impossible Dream: The Building of the Panama Canal*. New York: William Morrow, 1972.

Pennell, Joseph. *Joseph Pennell's Pictures of the Panama Canal: Reproductions of a Series of Lithographs Made by Him on the Isthmus of Panama, January–March 1912, Together with Impressions and Notes by the Artist*. 1912. Reprint. Philadelphia: J.B. Lippincott, 1913.

Pepperman, W. Leon. *Who Built the Panama Canal?* New York: E. P. Dutton, 1915.

Phillips, Howard, ed. *The New Right at Harvard*. Vienna, Va.: Conservative Caucus, 1983.

Pomper, Gerald. *Voters' Choice: Varieties of American Electoral Behavior.* New York: Harper and Row, 1975.

Pringle, Henry F. *Theodore Roosevelt: A Biography.* New York: Harcourt, Brace, 1931.

———. *Theodore Roosevelt: A Biography.* Rev. ed. New York: Harvest Books, 1956.

Roll, Charles W., and Cantril, Albert. *Polls: Their Use and Misuse in Politics.* Rev. ed. Cabin John, Md.: Seven Locks Press, 1980.

Roosevelt, Theodore. *Addresses and Presidential Messages of Theodore Roosevelt, 1902–1904.* New York: G. P. Putnam's Sons, 1904.

———. *American Ideals and Other Essays, Social and Political.* Rev. ed. New York: Knickerbocker Press, 1903.

———. *An Autobiography.* 1913. Reprint. New York: Charles Scribner's Sons, 1924.

———. *Presidential Addresses and State Papers of Theodore Roosevelt.* 4 vols. New York: P. F. Collier and Son, n.d. Reprint. New York: Kraus Reprint, 1970.

———. *The Strenuous Life: Essays and Addresses.* New York: Century, 1902.

———. *The Works of Theodore Roosevelt.* Memorial Edition. Edited by Joseph B. Bishop. 24 vols. New York: Charles Scribner's Sons, 1923–1926.

———. *The Writings of Theodore Roosevelt.* Edited by William H. Harbaugh. Indianapolis: Bobbs-Merrill, 1967.

Ryan, Paul B. *The Panama Canal Controversy: U.S. Diplomacy and Defense Interests.* Stanford: Hoover Institution Press, 1977.

Sabato, Larry J. *The Rise of Political Consultants: New Ways of Winning Elections.* New York: Basic Books, 1981.

Scott, William R. *The Americans in Panama.* 1912. Reprint. New York: Statler, 1912.

Shonts, Theodore. *Speech . . . Before the American Hardware Manufacturers' Association . . . , Washington, D.C. . . . November 9, 1905.* Washington: GPO, 1905.

———. *Speech . . . Before the Commercial Club, Cincinnati, Ohio, . . . January 20, 1906.* Washington: GPO, 1906.

———. *Speech . . . Before the Knife-and-Fork Club, Kansas City, . . . January 24, 1907.* Washington: GPO, 1907.

Society of the Chagres. *Society of the Chagres 1911 Year Book.* Mt. Hope, C.Z.: I.C.C. Press, 1911.

Stevens, Walter B. *A Trip to Panama: The Narrative of a Tour . . . by the Commercial Clubs of Boston, Chicago, Cincinnati, and St. Louis, February 18th–March 14th, 1907.* St. Louis: Lesani-Gould, 1907.

Stimson, Henry L. *Some Problems of the Panama Canal.* Washington: GPO, 1911.

Thayer, William R. *Life and Letters of John Hay.* 2 vols. Boston: Houghton Mifflin, 1915.

———. *Theodore Roosevelt: An Intimate Biography.* Boston: Houghton Mifflin, 1919.

Bibliography

Thomas, Addison C. *Roosevelt Among the People: Being an Account of the Fourteen Thousand Mile Journey From Ocean to Ocean of Theodore Roosevelt . . . Together With the Public Speeches Made by Him During the Journey.* Chicago: L. W. Walter, 1910.

Trumbell, Frank. *The Panama Canal: Some Impressions and Comments.* New York: Self-published, 1913.

Viguerie, Richard A. *The New Right: We're Ready to Lead.* Falls Church, Va.: The Viguerie Co., 1981.

Weir, Hugh C. *The Conquest of the Isthmus: The Men Who Are Building the Panama Canal—Their Daily Lives, Perils, and Adventures.* New York: G. P. Putnam's Sons, 1909.

Weisburg, Herbert F., and Bowen, Bruce D. *An Introduction to Survey Research and Data Analysis.* San Francisco: W. H. Freeman, 1977.

Wilde, Margaret D., ed. *The Panama Canal and Social Justice.* Washington: Office of International Justice and Peace, United States Catholic Conference, 1976.

GOVERNMENT DOCUMENTS

Bunker, Ellsworth. "Panama and the United States: Toward a New Relationship." Address before the Rainer Club, Seattle, 22 May 1975. U.S. Department of State. News Release. Washington: Department of State, 1975.

———. "Panama Canal Treaties: A Negotiator's Perspective." Address before the Des Moines Chamber of Commerce and Rotary Club, 26 January 1978. U.S. Department of State. Speech. Washington: Department of State, 1978.

Eisenhower, Dwight D. *Public Papers of the Presidents of the United States: Dwight D. Eisenhower, 1956–59.* Washington: GPO, 1958–1960.

Johnson, Lyndon B. *Public Papers of the Presidents of the United States: Lyndon B. Johnson, 1963–64.* Vol. 1. Washington: GPO, 1965.

Kennedy, John F. *Public Papers of the Presidents of the United States: John F. Kennedy, 1962.* Washington: GPO, 1963.

Richardson, James D., ed. *A Compilation of the Messages and Papers of the Presidents.* 11 vols. Washington: GPO, 1914.

Roosevelt, Theodore. *Special Message of the President of the United States Concerning the Panama Canal.* 59th Cong., 2d sess., 1906. S. Doc. 144.

U.S. Congress. *Congressional Record.* Washington, 1903, 1904, 1955, 1958, 1959, 1960.

———. House. Committee on Foreign Affairs. *Congress and Foreign Policy—1978.* 96th Cong., 1st sess., 1979. Committee Print.

———. *The Story of Panama: Hearings on the Rainey Resolution. . . .* 62d Cong., 2d sess., 1912.

————. Senate. *The Panama Canal and Our Relations with Colombia: Papers Relating to the Acquisition of the Canal Zone.* . . . 63d Cong., 2d sess., 1914. S. Doc. 471.

————. Committee on Foreign Relations. *Background Documents Relating to the Panama Canal.* 95th Cong., 1st sess., 1977. Committee Print.

————. *A Chronology of Events Relating to the Panama Canal.* 95th Cong., 1st sess., 1977. Committee Print.

————. *Executive Sessions of the Senate Foreign Relations Committee.* Historical Series. 84th Cong., 1st sess., 1955. Vol. 7. Washington: GPO, 1978.

————. *Panama Canal Treaties: Hearings . . . on . . . the Panama Canal Treaty and the Treaty Concerning the Permanent Neutrality and Operation of the Panama Canal, Signed . . . on September 7, 1977.* 95th Cong., 1st and 2d sess., 1977–1978.

————. *Panama Canal Treaties: Report . . . on the Treaty Concerning the Permanent Neutrality and Operation of the Panama Canal and the Panama Canal Treaty, Signed . . . on September 7, 1977.* 95th Cong., 2d sess., 1978. Exec. Rept. 95–12.

————. *The Panama Treaty: Hearings on Executive F.* 84th Cong., 1st sess., 1955.

————. *Senate Debate on the Panama Canal Treaties: A Compendium of Major Statements, Documents, Record Votes and Relevant Events.* 96th Cong., 1st sess., 1979. Committee Print.

————. Committee on Interoceanic Canals. *Hearings . . . on the Senate Resolution Providing for an Investigation of Matters Relating to the Panama Canal.* 59th Cong., 2d sess., 1907. S. Doc. 401.

————. Committee on the Judiciary. Subcommittee on Separation of Powers. *Panama Canal Treaties [United States Senate Debate], 1977–78.* 95th Cong., 2d sess., 1978. Committee Print.

————. *The Proposed Panama Canal Treaties: A Digest of Information.* 95th Cong., 2d sess., 1978. Committee Print.

U.S. Department of State. *Bulletin.* Washington, 1952–1953, 1956, 1958–1960, 1962, 1964, 1965, 1968, 1970, 1975, 1977–1978.

————. *Documents Associated with the Panama Canal Treaties.* Selected Documents. No. 6B. Washington: Department of State, 1977.

————. *Papers Relating to the Foreign Relations of the United States, 1904.* Washington: GPO, 1905.

————. *Panama Canal Treaties Information.* Washington: Department of State, 1977.

UNPUBLISHED SOURCES

American Conservative Union. "There Is No Panama Canal; There Is an American Canal in Panama." Transcript of half-hour television program. Files of Democratic Congressional Campaign Committee, Washington, D.C.

Bibliography

American Council for World Freedom. Statement on membership, activities, goals, and projects. N.p., n.d. Files of Congressional Research Service, Library of Congress, Washington, D.C.

Burkholder, Steven N. "Some Persons and Groups Lobbying For and Against the Panama Canal Treaties." Washington, n.d. Files of Congressional Research Service, Library of Congress, Washington, D.C.

CBS News. "The Gospel According to Whom?" *Sixty Minutes*. 23 January 1983. Transcript provided for the writer by CBS News.

Christian Church (Disciples of Christ). Department of Latin America of the Division of Overseas Ministries and the Departments of Christian Education and Church in Society of the Division of Homeland Ministries. "The Panama Canal Treaties." Indianapolis, n.d.

———. General Assembly. "Resolution No. 7756 Concerning New Treaties with the Republic of Panama." Adopted at the Kansas City, Missouri, Assembly, 21–26 October 1977.

Council of the Americas. "Council of the Americas Announces Support for the Panama Canal Treaties." Letter from Otto J. Reich, Director of Washington, D.C., Operations, to the membership. Washington, n.d. Files of Congressional Research Service, Library of Congress, Washington, D.C.

———. Letter from Henry R. Geyelin, President, to U.S. senators. Washington, January 1977. Files of Congressional Research Service, Library of Congress, Washington, D.C.

———. Letter from Otto J. Reich, Director of Washington, D.C., Operations, to Barry Sklar, Congressional Research Service. Washington, 2 February 1977. Files of Congressional Research Service, Library of Congress, Washington, D.C.

———. "President's Letter: The Panama Canal Treaty." New York, 22 February 1978. Files of Congressional Research Service, Library of Congress, Washington, D.C.

Dozer, Donald M. Letter to "Citizens of the United States." Santa Barbara, Calif., 15 March 1976. Files of Congressional Research Service, Library of Congress, Washington, D.C.

———. "Panama Canal in Danger." Paper distributed by the Emergency Committee to Save the U.S. Canal Zone. Santa Barbara, Calif., 1976. Files of Congressional Research Service, Library of Congress, Washington, D.C.

Ecumenical Program for Inter-American Communication and Action. Publicity flyer for *Panama: Sovereignty for a Land Divided*. Washington, n.d. Provided for the writer by EPICA.

———. Publicity flyer for *Treaty for Us, Treaty for Them*. Washington, n.d. Provided for the writer by EPICA.

National Public Radio. "Estimated Audience for Broadcasts of Panama Canal Treaties Debate." Washington, 1978. Provided for the writer by NPR.

Reagan, Ronald. Address recorded from *The Panama Canal: An Opposition*

View. A CBS News Special Report. 8 February 1978.

Richard, Alfred C. "The Panama Canal in American National Consciousness, 1870–1922." Ph.D. dissertation, Boston University, 1969.

Smith, Ted J., III, and Hogan, J. Michael. "Opinion Polls and the Panama Canal Treaties of 1977: A Critical Analysis." Paper presented to the annual meeting of the American Association for Public Opinion Research, McAfee, N.J., 1985.

United States Committee for Panamanian Sovereignty. Letter from E. Bradford Burns and Sheldon Liss to specialists in Latin American studies. Philadelphia, 1976. Files of Congressional Research Service, Library of Congress, Washington, D.C.

———. "Principles of Unity." Philadelphia, n.d. Files of Congressional Research Service, Library of Congress, Washington, D.C.

Washington Office on Latin America. "Action Memo on the New Canal Treaty." Washington, n.d. Files of Congressional Research Service, Library of Congress, Washington, D.C.

———. "Special Update on Panama." Washington, n.d. Files of Congressional Research Service, Library of Congress, Washington, D.C.

———. Memorandum distributed to members of Congress. Washington, n.d. Files of Congressional Research Service, Library of Congress, Washington, D.C.

INDEX

Index

Index

Index